ASIA PACIFIC SECURITY OUTLOOK 2004

The cosponsors of this project wish to thank

Asia Pacific Agenda Project

ASIA PACIFIC SECURITY OUTLOOK

2004

edited by
Charles E. Morrison

cosponsored by

 ASEAN Institutes for Strategic and International Studies

 East-West Center

 Japan Center for International Exchange

AN APAP PROJECT

Tokyo • Japan Center for International Exchange • *New York*

The surnames of the authors and other persons mentioned in this book are
positioned according to country practice.

Copyediting by Pamela J. Noda.
Cover design by Kennedy & Preiss Graphic Design, Honolulu, Hawaii.
Typographic design by Becky Davis, EDS Inc., Editorial & Design Services, Tokyo.
Typesetting and production by EDS Inc.

Printed in Japan.
ISBN 4-88907-070-2

Distributed outside Japan by Brookings Institution Press (1775 Massachusetts
Avenue, N.W., Washington, D.C. 20036-2188 U.S.A.) and Kinokuniya
Company Ltd. (5-38-1 Sakuragaoka, Setagaya-ku, Tokyo 156-8691).

Japan Center for International Exchange
9-7 Minami Azabu 4-chome, Minato-ku, Tokyo 106-0047 Japan
URL: http://www.jcie.or.jp

Japan Center for International Exchange, Inc. (JCIE/USA)
274 Madison Avenue, Suite 1102, New York, N.Y. 10016 U.S.A.
URL: http://www.jcie.org

Contents

Foreword   7
Regional Overview   9

SUBREGIONAL THEMES

1 Northeast Asia: The Korean Peninsula Nuclear Crisis   23
2 Southeast Asia: The Terrorist Threat   34
3 South Asia: New Promise and Old Problems   44

COUNTRY CHAPTERS

4 Australia   57
5 Brunei Darussalam   66
6 Canada   71
7 China   80
8 European Union   89
9 Indonesia   99
10 Japan   108
11 Republic of Korea   118
12 Malaysia   125
13 Mongolia   134
14 New Zealand   140
15 Papua New Guinea   147
16 Philippines   153
17 Russia   159
18 Singapore   168
19 Thailand   176
20 United States   183
21 Vietnam   192

List of Abbreviations   199
The APSO Project Team   203
Index   205

Foreword

This year's *Asia Pacific Security Outlook* (APSO) presents the first change in the basic format since the project began in 1997. The cover design has been changed, but more substantively, we have also altered the format slightly. In seven previous *Outlooks* we have placed country perspectives side by side with a brief overview to cover general trends and tie together issues not adequately covered from a country perspective. This year we are including two topical chapters to cover the North Korean crisis and terrorism in Southeast Asia. We have also included a general South Asian paper rather than a separate country perspective from India. This change reflects the salience of different issues in each of the subregions and the difficulty of capturing their dynamics in either country chapters or a general overview.

Aside from these changes, the *Outlook 2004* continues our tradition of providing country perspectives based in virtually all cases on background papers by analysts from the country concerned. These perspectives cover three basic topical areas: the changing security perception, defense doctrine and issues, and contributions to regional and global security. The purpose of the exercise remains the same—to increase understanding of each other's perspectives among security analysts in the region and to elucidate key issues that affect future regional security and stability.

The *Outlook* presents perspectives from countries that are members of the 23-member ASEAN Regional Forum (ARF). The background papers are written by members of academic and research institutions, not governments. Moreover, they are further edited before appearing in the *Outlook*. The chapters are intended to present mainstream views and identify areas of policy debate in the governments and societies of each country. They are not governmental statements and may not necessarily represent government views.

Charles E. Morrison, Yamamoto Tadashi, and Jusuf Wanandi remain the directors of the *Asia Pacific Security Outlook*. We are grateful to the authors of the signed chapters—Ralph A. Cossa, Rohan Gunaratna, and

7

Dipankar Banerjee—as well as to the authors of the background papers. Their names are listed at the back of the volume. We are particularly grateful to Richard Baker of the East-West Center, who contributed a country paper on the United States, was a co-author of the overview chapter, and assumed the lion's share of the editing work for this volume. Ito Hyōma of the Japan Center for International Exchange (JCIE) handled administrative aspects of the project, provided coordination among members of the team, and organized the APSO workshop in Tokyo in November 2003. He was ably assisted by Lucy van der Wall. Pamela J. Noda of JCIE again oversaw the copyediting and publishing process.

The sponsoring institutions are grateful for the continuing financial support of the Asia Pacific Agenda Project, which is designed to promote policy-oriented dialogue among nongovernmental analysts in the Asia Pacific region.

CHARLES E. MORRISON
PRESIDENT
EAST-WEST CENTER

JUSUF WANANDI
FOUNDING MEMBER
ASEAN INSTITUTES FOR
STRATEGIC AND INTERNATIONAL STUDIES

YAMAMOTO TADASHI
PRESIDENT
JAPAN CENTER FOR INTERNATIONAL EXCHANGE

Regional Overview

The 2003 *Asia Pacific Security Outlook* (APSO) reported that the overall outlook for the region was "bleaker" even though large power relationships in Asia and the Pacific were as healthy as they had ever been. It appeared to us that crises in Iraq and North Korea, both casting long shadows on the outlook and creating anxieties in the region, would come to a head in the early part of 2003. This turned out to be true for Iraq, but regional repercussions were less than many had feared. There were no large demonstrations or threats to social stability in the Muslim countries of the region. The Muslim governments by and large were able to walk the fine line of being critical of aspects of the U.S. policy without alienating the United States. This was partly because they were committed to fighting terrorism at home and cooperating on intelligence, thus contributing to the war on terrorism in their own way. Japan and South Korea also performed careful balancing acts, with leaders of both countries promising to contribute troops for the reconstruction phase in Iraq—when they would be more wanted and needed—after the conventional fighting had ceased. However, the Iraq war reinforced negative stereotypes around the region of a United States that is interventionist and unilateralist (the questionnaire of our analyst team indicated strong agreement with the statement that "U.S. policy is unilateral").

As described below, and in chapter 1 by Ralph A. Cossa, contrary to our expectations the North Korean crisis did not come to a head and remains very much on the agenda in 2004. The United States sought a multilateral approach to this problem rather than bilateral negotiations. Although only two rounds of talks took place in 2003—a meeting with the United States and North Korea hosted by China in April, and Six-Party Talks (including China, Japan, Russia, South and North Korea, and the United States) in August—the combination of continued

Chinese diplomatic initiatives, the absence of provocations, and the U.S. absorption with Iraq helped contain tensions. Despite ever-increasing economic problems in the North, it is widely expected that the resolution of the North Korean nuclear weapons program will be a drawn-out affair.

Although neither the Iraq war nor the North Korean weapons program produced a genuine crisis atmosphere in Asia and the Pacific during the past year, anxiety about security remains high or is increasing in much of the region, particularly at the personal level. Terrorism is one factor in this. Throughout the region, and indeed the world, there are visible signs of societies in fear of terrorists, such as increased security at airports, embassies, and public buildings and also in some cities, in hotels and even shopping malls. But in most places in most countries, death from a terrorist act is still regarded a very remote possibility. A more immediate source of personal insecurity in 2003 came from the outbreak of severe acute respiratory syndrome (SARS) in March through May. Although fewer than 1,000 people worldwide lost their lives to SARS, far less than to ordinary influenza, the novelty and initial deadliness of SARS, the mysterious manner in which it seemed to spread, and the lack of medicines to treat it created widespread fear sometimes verging on panic. At the beginning of 2004, it seemed unlikely that SARS would reappear with any force, but an outbreak of avian flu, with some associated human deaths in Southeast Asia, illustrates the point that virtually each year now brings a new medical threat. Some of the diseases involved, like HIV/AIDS (which is on the rise in many developing countries of Asia and the Pacific), remain long-term challenges.

Another noteworthy development is that heightened awareness of threats to states and individuals has led to a contrary, offsetting phenomenon: cooperation among the governments of the region has never been better. Because terrorism is widely perceived as a direct threat to the state system, established governments have strong incentives to work together to combat terrorism. Infectious diseases such as SARS also put an extraordinary premium on international cooperation since the epidemic cannot be contained in any one country without the help of other countries. States that are uncooperative come under great pressure. Thus, increasingly, states have come to see a common stake in addressing many global issues, with terrorism and infectious diseases at the top of the list.

Other factors have helped drive greater cooperation among governments. One is the growing importance of regional production networks (interconnected groups of factories and processors) leading to higher levels of investment and trade. Interdependence creates new sources of stress, but it also increases the costs to societies and thus to their governments of political tensions. Second, on balance, domestic politics have probably reinforced cooperation. Most leaders do not want to be criticized for a failure to maintain stable relationships with other key countries. The existence of a regular mechanism for meetings among Asia Pacific leaders, the Asia-Pacific Economic Cooperation (APEC) forum, has also played a role.

A New Watch List

Within the region covered by APSO—East and Southeast Asia with contributions from countries outside this region with significant regional security interests—the first APSO team identified four watch list areas: large power relations, the Korean peninsula, territorial disputes, and potential arms races. Later additions were economic problems after the Asian economic crisis (1998), instability in Indonesia with the fall of the Suharto government (1999), and terrorism (2002). The generic categories within which these issues fall—geopolitics, flashpoints, economics, domestic political change—continue to be major themes in the security environment in the region and as such must continue to be "watched." We also are providing again this year a table summarizing defense spending and armed forces in the Asia Pacific region (see table 1).

Current priority issues, however, as they are presented by governments, analytical communities, and the media, are somewhat different. Some of the watch list issues, including territorial conflicts and arms races, have faded from the active scene, although they could reemerge as issues of analytical or policy concern. Accordingly, with this APSO overview, we are offering a somewhat modified watch list of issues that are difficult to capture fully in single country chapters—Sino-American relations, the Korean crisis, terrorism in Southeast Asia, and South Asian international relations. We have provided special, individual contributions on two issues that are of highest priority in their respective subregions: the North Korean crisis, engaging virtually all the

Table 1. Asia Pacific Defense Spending and Armed Forces

Country	Defense Spending (2002)[a]			GDP (2002)		Armed Forces (2003)[b]				Population (2003)	
	US$ m.	% GDP	Rank	US$ m.	Rank	Number	Rank	% Pop.	Rank	in 1,000s	Rank
United States	348,500	3.4	9	10,400,000	1	1,427,000	3	0.49	9	289,696	4
Europe (EU/NATO)[c]	171,008	1.9	17	8,868,000	2	1,473,580	2	0.41	12	356,330	3
China	51,000	3.9	6	1,300,000	4	2,250,000	1	0.17	18	1,299,278	1
Russia[d]	50,800	4.8	5	1,069,000	5	960,600	6	0.66	7	146,300	6
Japan	39,500	1.0	21	4,000,000	3	239,900	12	0.19	17	127,647	7
India	13,800	2.7	11	505,000	7	1,325,000	4	0.13	21	1,040,245	2
South Korea	13,300	2.8	10	476,000	8	686,000	7	1.44	4	47,479	11
Australia	8,000	2.0	16	401,000	9	53,650	18	0.32	13	19,476	16
Taiwan	7,900	2.7	12	295,000	10	290,000	11	1.30	5	22,260	14
Canada	6,800	1.1	20	604,000	6	66,600	17	0.21	16	29,236	12
Indonesia	6,600	3.7	7	177,000	11	302,000	10	0.14	19	218,509	5
North Korea	5,000	25.0	1	20,000	18	1,082,000	5	4.89	1	22,145	15
Singapore	4,600	5.2	3	88,000	14	72,500	16	1.69	3	4,292	19
Malaysia	3,400	3.6	8	94,000	13	104,000	15	0.46	11	22,533	13
Vietnam	2,400	7.1	2	34,000	17	484,000	8	0.60	8	80,048	8
Thailand	1,800	1.5	18	121,000	12	314,200	9	0.49	10	64,123	10
Philippines	1,600	2.1	15	77,000	15	106,000	14	0.14	20	78,415	9
New Zealand	667	1.2	19	56,000	16	8,610	19	0.22	15	3,844	20
Brunei	267	5.2	4	5,100	19	7,000	21	2.05	2	341	22
Cambodia	92	2.5	13	3,700	20	125,000	13	0.89	6	14,007	17
Mongolia	25	2.3	14	1,100	22	8,600	20	0.32	14	2,674	21
Papua New Guinea	14	1.0	22	2,800	21	3,100	22	0.06	22	4,992	18

SOURCE: Based on data from *The Military Balance 2003/2004*. London: International Institute of Strategic Studies (IISS), 2003.

[a] Defense spending figures are IISS estimates of total defense spending (not official budgets).

[b] Figures are for active duty regular armed forces.

[c] Europe figures are for the 12 members of the European Union that are also members of the North Atlantic Treaty Organization: Belgium, Denmark, France, Germany, Greece, Italy, Luxembourg, the Netherlands, Norway, Portugal, Spain, and the United Kingdom.

[d] Defense spending and GDP estimates for Russia are based on purchasing power parity (Russia's official 2002 defense budget was US$8.4 billion at US$1 = 31.3 rubles, which was 2.4 percent of Russia's GDP expressed in rubles).

Northeast Asian countries, and the threat of terrorism in Southeast Asia.

Finally, the APSO is based upon the ASEAN Regional Forum and therefore does not cover South Asia as part of its basic footprint. However, the dynamics of South Asia have become so integral to East and Southeast Asian security, as explained below, that it is logical to monitor this neighboring region in a more comprehensive fashion than brought out in our previous single-country chapter on India. Hence, we have added a separate contribution on the subcontinent.

SINO-AMERICAN RELATIONS   Of all the bilateral large power relations in the region, in the post–cold war era the relationship between Beijing and Washington has had the most critical systemic implications for regional security as well as a special degree of volatility. While common interests have certainly grown, they still are relatively thin compared to the U.S.-Japan relationship. Important positive factors include trade and investment relations and complementary interests in regional stability and fighting terrorism. Two other factors stress the relationship: a sense of geopolitical competition, which permeates the publics as well as the two countries' military and analytical communities, and Taiwan.

China faces many difficult problems as it modernizes, including resource and environmental constraints, growing income gaps, the need to remake its financial system, and the inevitable issue of political reform. Assuming that China meets these challenges and continues its modernization path, China's "rise" will clearly reshape the geopolitical equation in the region. The worst scenario associated with this rise is a possible new cold war or bipolar competition, forcing smaller states to choose sides. In another, still largely negative scenario for smaller states, China and the United States might reach some "condominium" arrangement, dividing the region into loose nonhostile spheres of influence. A third and clearly more desirable scenario is that both China and the United States will find their interests accommodated within the existing international system and that the forces driving smooth adjustment and cooperation will continue to strengthen. There is considerable evidence that such a process is occurring.

Some in both the United States and China, basing their conclusion on traditional geopolitical logic, believe that confrontation is inevitable and that their countries need to be preparing for this era. However, the governments of both countries are taking a different approach, seizing the opening provided by the heightened terrorist threat and the North

Korean problem to work for a significant, positive change in the tone and nature of their relationship.

Taiwan remains the most critical potential flashpoint in Sino-American relations. The island is claimed as an integral part of China by Beijing, which also reserves the right to use force to reunify its country should this be necessary. The United States is committed to protect the people of Taiwan against an unprovoked determination of their future by force, even though the United States recognizes that both Beijing and Taipei acknowledge that there is one China. This situation makes China and the United States potential adversaries over Taiwan, but clearly neither wants Taiwan to disrupt their evolving relationship.

For this reason, Washington and Beijing found themselves in a quandary at the end of 2003, when Taiwan President Chen Shui-bian announced that he would hold a "defensive" referendum on the mainland's missiles at the time of Taiwan's presidential election on March 20, 2004. Chen and his Democratic Progressive Party also promised to change Taiwan's constitution to make the island a "normal" country. Beijing denounced these steps as a push toward independence, and Washington signaled its reservations, including sending an envoy on a secret mission to ask Chen to desist. Chen did not, and in December 2003 U.S. President George W. Bush, in the context of a visit by China's Premier Wen Jiabao, underscored the "one China" premise of American policy and criticized Chen for appearing to seek to alter the status quo unilaterally.

Analysts in Beijing, Washington, and elsewhere seem united in believing the referendum and proposed constitutional reforms were a political strategy by Chen to restore his base of support among Taiwan's independence-minded voters prior to the elections. They differ as to how seriously he would pursue his campaign promises if reelected, but even if he did not, it seems likely that a Chen victory would delay further positive developments in cross-Strait relations. In contrast to two previous Taiwan elections where strong-armed Chinese tactics had backfired, China's new leaders seem anxious not to overreact. They have urged Washington to pressure Chen, similar to Washington's requests for Beijing to pressure Kim Jong Il to end his nuclear weapons programs. Thus Beijing and Washington seem to be seeking maximum benefit from each other's reputed influence in Pyongyang and Taipei, respectively. However, neither China nor the United States may have the level of influence or the political will to use its influence that the other believes it should.

THE KOREAN CRISIS   Despite some small movement, the Korean situation remained essentially stalemated through 2003 and the prospects for an early breakthrough in 2004 seem bleak. North Korea says that it is willing to freeze its plutonium reprocessing program in exchange for benefits from the United States, including aid and trade relations. It denies having a second uranium enrichment program. The United States insists that it is not going to give in to North Korean blackmail and pay twice for a freeze in the North's weapons programs. It demands that North Korea agree to a complete, verifiable, and irreversible end for all its nuclear weapons programs and to rejoining the Nonproliferation Treaty.

As outlined by Cossa, the basic parameters of an agreement meeting the articulated needs of both parties can be identified. Both sides, however, are suspicious of the real intentions of the other. A significant body of opinion in Washington believes that the North Korean government is not just bargaining for aid, but wants the status and protection it associates with nuclear weapons. In Pyongyang it is believed that the basic U.S. strategy is not to contain nuclear weapons but to terminate the Kim Jong Il regime. Nevertheless, under Chinese pressure, both sides are reexamining their positions and trying to repackage them to make them more attractive. A breakthrough may occur as a result of negotiations, but in an election year in the United States and with North Korea perhaps no worse off economically than in the previous year, it is also possible that the standoff will continue with little overt provocation and continued, periodic negotiations. The absence of movement, however, may eventually rekindle a crisis, as Washington will have a strong incentive to escalate economic pressure and seek international inspections of North Korean ships and cargo movements.

TERRORISM IN SOUTHEAST ASIA   Despite the moderate forms of Islam in the region and in its secular Muslim majority states of Indonesia and Malaysia, Southeast Asia has always had small extremist groups using terror in the name of Islam. Their targets were local. In Muslim majority countries, these groups sought to establish Islamic states, and in Muslim minority countries such as the Philippines and Thailand they emphasized separation or autonomy as a mode to protect their ethnic or religious community. Sometimes also bandit groups with little demonstrable interest in religious issues, such as the southern Philippines' Abu Sayyaf Group, used religion for recruitment and justification of their activities.

As Rohan Gunaratna shows in chapter 2, terrorism took on a new dimension in the 1990s and particularly after the September 11, 2001, attacks in the United States. In the 1990s, links were forged between local extremists and al Qaeda, which took an interest in Southeast Asia almost from its founding and infiltrated Southeast Asian Islamic and separatist groups using connections built during the anti-Soviet resistance in Afghanistan. Al Qaeda also provided resources and training, and brought new strategies, tactics, and a vision of universal jihad. After September 11, some Southeast Asian groups, notably Jemaah Islamiah (JI), turned their sights on spectacular displays aimed at foreigners. JI also introduced suicide tactics.

So far all attacks by Southeast Asian terrorists have taken place within Southeast Asia, and many of the victims have been Southeast Asian nationals. Southeast Asian governments have responded with various degrees of haste and urgency. Because of domestic sensitivities or fear of harming their tourist industries, Indonesia and Thailand initially downplayed the terrorism problem. At the beginning of 2004, however, there is significantly more cooperation among the Southeast Asian governments and between them and outside governments, including the United States and Australia. Counterterrorism training and intelligence centers are being established in the region.

As Gunaratna points out, however, cooperation still has a long way to go and terrorism is a long-term challenge. Terrorists are adapting their tactics and have many soft targets. Although many JI terrorists have been arrested and some networks disrupted, Moro Islamic Liberation Front (MILF) camps hidden in Mindanao jungles still provide safe training facilities. Governments do not yet have the intelligence or capabilities to root out all the terrorist networks. Moreover, policies and their proper implementation are needed to reduce the pool of alienated youth and young adults from whom the terrorist networks mainly recruit. These are very complex policy challenges, the success or failure of which will be felt decades into the future.

SOUTH ASIAN INTERNATIONAL RELATIONS   We add South Asia to the watch list because of its increasing connection to East and Southeast Asia. In the past, South Asia was more acted upon by other regions than it was affecting them. For example, India's nuclear program was motivated in part by a perceived need for a deterrent against China. This is beginning to change. One factor is South Asia's own capabilities. Stimulated by the loosening of previously stifling regulations,

India's economy is now moving rapidly. It has grown above 5 percent annually for several years and expects 7 percent or more growth in 2004. India is also becoming increasingly competitive, not simply in computer software but in such areas as automobiles. South Asia's competitive nuclear programs in India and Pakistan also have proliferation implications outside South Asia. These include not just potential emulation, but also the transfer of nuclear technology as from Pakistan to North Korea. Finally, South Asia, particularly Pakistan and (previously) Afghanistan, has been home to al Qaeda and associated terrorist networks and has been a source of techniques such as modern forms of suicide bombing, first used in the 1980s by the Tamil rebels in Sri Lanka.

As detailed by Dipankar Banerjee in chapter 3, South Asia has complex security problems. These include the ethnic-based Tamil insurgency in Sri Lanka (where a promising peace-building effort is stalled) and an ideology-based Maoist insurgency in Nepal. As debilitating as these are for the nations concerned, they are largely confined to the domestic sphere. Other issues, however, and particularly the future of Indo-Pakistani relations and the nation-building process in Afghanistan, have more significant extra–South Asian implications.

Competition between India and Pakistan over Kashmir involves territory but is more fundamentally about the identity of the two successor states of British India: a Muslim-majority state like Kashmir underscores India's secular nature, while Pakistan asserts that as a state set up to be a home for the Muslim majority areas (the "K" in Pakistan stands for Kashmir), Kashmir should properly be part of Pakistan and would be if India had permitted a referendum on its future. In late 2003 and early 2004, after two years of tensions, the outlook for cooperation between the two countries has brightened as new bilateral talks begin. The path toward reconciliation appears highly dependent on the two individual leaders—Atal Bihari Vajpayee in India and General Pervez Musharraf in Pakistan. The 79-year-old Vajpayee, who initiated the current effort, is reported to have health problems. Musharraf survived two assassination attempts in December 2003 and faces extremist as well as significant parliamentary opposition to his peace moves, including his dropping of the demand for a Kashmir referendum. However, the broader climate may be right for reconciliation to continue. In both countries there is weariness with conflict and growing awareness of its economic costs. These include not just the losses to the two countries from restricted trade and travel, but also the inability to move ahead with promising regional cooperation efforts such as a proposed South Asia free trade agreement. A successful settlement could literally open a new chapter in the history and extra-regional relations of the subcontinent.

In Afghanistan, the 2001 U.S. intervention disrupted al Qaeda bases and removed the regime that protected them. In the longer run, keeping a terrorist-free Afghanistan will depend on success in building a modern nation capable of establishing a legitimate rule of law over the entire country and of fulfilling its international obligations. Ethnic rivalries, warlords, and increased Taliban resistance during the past year have complicated nation building. The International Security Assistance Force of multinational peacekeepers led by the North Atlantic Treaty Organisation (NATO) is currently deployed only in the capital city, Kabul, while the development of an Afghan National Army, loyal to the central government, is a slow process. Foreign assistance is relatively low on a per capita basis (compared to Bosnia and Kosovo, for example), and disbursement has been slow. In a significant development at the beginning of 2004, a traditional assembly (*loya jirga*) of 502 delegates reached a compromise on a national constitution after a difficult debate. The new constitution provides for a strong presidential system, while purporting to protect minority interests. However, many of the underlying tensions and conditions that have kept Afghanistan fractured continue, outside attention and aid is quite limited, and internal security is so poor that it is hard to envisage how a free and fair election can take place in June 2004 as now scheduled.

CONCLUSION

As typically pointed out in the overviews to APSO, the security order in Asia and the Pacific remains quite fragile, particularly at its domestic roots. However, despite increased personal security concerns, the most important trend may be the increased cooperation among governments. As evidenced in previous editions of APSO, this is a longer-term phenomenon that began as a result of the primacy of internal priorities, particularly economic development, but which has accelerated with the war on terrorism. This trend is particularly striking when viewed against the backdrop of the region a quarter century ago when Sino-Japanese and Sino-American ties were first normalized. At that time, China's external relations with the region were very limited, there were virtually no Asia Pacific–wide regional organizations, and at least limited international wars (as between China and Vietnam in 1979) were regarded as a real prospect.

Today, China's foreign trade is a remarkable 50 percent of its gross domestic product and it is deeply entwined in regional and global production networks. There is relatively little fear of international war (with the possible exception of the Korean peninsula). The leaders of Asia and the Pacific meet annually at APEC, and there are dense networks of other cooperative arrangements. But as the heightened sense of personal insecurity attests, globalization has brought forward new challenges for intergovernmental cooperation. Although interdependence is sometimes thought to have undermined the role of governments, in reality it has made them more important than ever before. This is because order building in an independent world requires much more elaborate sets of international rules and effective domestic enforcement. Trade, terrorism, SARS, and in another way the North Korean crisis are all generating yet more multilateral consultations, more explicit rules for the sharing of information and addressing common challenges, and heightened expectations of national obligations and accountability to the international community. In international society as it exists today, governments are the authoritative units for establishing and enforcing rules. Thus the longer-term trend toward greater intergovernmental cooperation in the region is responsive to the key contemporary security challenges. But whether the governments are as aware of the challenges or as capable and willing to cooperate as they need to be is still uncertain.

SUBREGIONAL THEMES

1 Northeast Asia:
The Korean Peninsula Nuclear Crisis

RALPH A. COSSA

The ongoing crisis on the Korean peninsula, caused by the apparent pursuit of nuclear weapons on the part of North Korea, represents a serious challenge not only to the United States and South Korea, but also to regional stability and to the national security interests of all of Korea's Northeast Asian neighbors.

The "diplomatic breakthrough" of 2003—in the form of Pyongyang's presumed willingness "in principle" to continue to participate in the Six-Party Talks to discuss the nuclear weapons crisis—provides cause for cautious optimism. But it remains to be proven if North Korea's professed commitment to a nuclear weapons–free peninsula is genuine. In the meantime, how Washington handles (or fails to handle) this crisis will have serious implications for its relations with Seoul, Tokyo, Beijing, Moscow, and, potentially, Taipei.

There is an ominous terrorist dimension to this crisis as well, given substantial evidence that organizations like al Qaeda would pay dearly to obtain the plutonium and highly enriched uranium that North Korea claims to have extracted from its spent fuel rods at the Yongbyon reprocessing facility. North Korea's suspected nuclear weapons program, if confirmed and left unchecked, will also test the fabric, if not the foundation, of the global nonproliferation regime.

Ralph A. Cossa is president of the Pacific Forum CSIS, a Honolulu-based nonprofit research institute affiliated with the Center for Strategic and International Studies in Washington, D.C., and senior editor of Comparative Connections, *a quarterly electronic journal.*

How We Got to Where We Are

The crisis began as a consequence of a deliberate action by Pyongyang: a decision to circumvent the 1994 Geneva U.S.-North Korea Agreed Framework by pursuing a uranium enrichment program. The fact that Pyongyang's nuclear aspirations predate the Bush administration indicates that more recent events, while perhaps causing an acceleration of the North's clandestine nuclear activities, were not the primary stimulants. The root cause is North Korea's nuclear weapons aspirations.

The event that triggered the crisis was U.S Assistant Secretary of State James Kelly's visit to Pyongyang in early October 2002. The Bush administration states that it was prepared to pursue a "bold approach" in its dealings with Pyongyang, but it insisted that North Korea first honor its previous commitments. According to Kelly, Pyongyang responded to his allegations of cheating on its nuclear promises by defiantly acknowledging that it had a uranium enrichment program. Later it claimed to merely have said it was "entitled" to have a nuclear weapons program.

Once the details of the Kelly meeting emerged from the U.S. side, Pyongyang escalated the crisis by expelling International Atomic Energy Agency (IAEA) inspectors and removing IAEA monitoring devices and seals from its nuclear facilities at Yongbyon while announcing plans to restart its frozen nuclear reactor. When Washington refused to be "blackmailed" into bilateral negotiations, the North announced in early January 2003 its withdrawal from the nuclear Nonproliferation Treaty (NPT). It subsequently threatened to withdraw from the 1953 Armistice, while warning of "World War Three" if the UN Security Council (UNSC) or the United States attempted to coerce the North into curtailing its suspected nuclear weapons program.

Making matters worse, North Korea reactivated its nuclear facilities at Yongbyon and claimed to be reprocessing its spent fuel rods. There is some question as to how much reprocessing has actually occurred, but if North Korean pronouncements prove true this would be a dangerous escalation and a clear violation of the 1992 Joint Agreement on the Denuclearization of the Korean Peninsula (which Pyongyang declared to be "nullified" after announcing that it had begun reprocessing). It also makes the nuclear crisis an antiterrorism as well as a nonproliferation issue, given terrorist aspirations for a "dirty bomb" or worse, and North Korea's demonstrated willingness to sell weapons to any buyer willing to pay the price.

TRILATERAL COOPERATION SETS THE STAGE
FOR A MULTILATERAL APPROACH

Although the Bush administration stressed that it was taking a different (and tougher) approach toward North Korea than its predecessor, one Clinton-era initiative that has survived and continues to play a crucial coordinating role in the nuclear crisis is the Trilateral Coordination and Oversight Group (TCOG), involving the United States and its two Northeast Asia treaty allies, South Korea and Japan. From the beginning, the TCOG has been successful in papering over many of the differences among the three partners, allowing Washington, Seoul, and Tokyo generally to speak with one voice, at least at the broad policy level, on the North Korea nuclear issue.

This was immediately evident when U.S. President George W. Bush, then–South Korean President Kim Dae Jung, and Japanese Prime Minister Koizumi Jun'ichirō met along the sidelines of the October 2002 Asia-Pacific Economic Cooperation (APEC) Economic Leaders' Meeting in Los Cabos, Mexico, and issued a joint statement calling on North Korea to dismantle its nuclear weapons program "in a prompt and verifiable manner." This spirit of cooperation was reinforced at the January 6–7, 2003, TCOG meeting in Washington when all three parties once again called on North Korea to take "prompt and verifiable action to completely dismantle its nuclear weapons program and come into full compliance with its international nuclear commitments." The joint pronouncement also included several Bush administration olive branches toward Pyongyang, first by stating, in writing, that the United States "has no intention of invading North Korea" and then by stating that the United States "is willing to talk to North Korea about how it will meet its obligations to the international community." Washington also called for multilateral dialogue to address the nuclear situation (but with the promise of bilateral U.S.-North Korea consultations within this larger multilateral context). It is reasonable to conclude that quiet and effective South Korean and especially Japanese diplomacy helped change Washington's earlier, less flexible approach.

The North Korean response was to completely reject a multilateral approach and to announce its immediate withdrawal from the NPT. Ironically, this hard-line, openly confrontational approach by North Korea made the U.S. offer of multilateral dialogue more appealing to the other concerned parties (including China). This helped set the stage for the April "mini-lateral" meeting in Beijing among the United States,

North Korea, and China—labeled by Washington as "talks about talks"
—during which each side was able to express its views and to put its
opening proposals on the table. As expected, there was not much progress at the meeting, although there was considerable controversy over
reported off-the-record comments made by the North Korean representative privately to his American counterpart that the North did indeed have nuclear weapons and that it was prepared to further develop,
produce, test, and/or export these weapons depending on Washington's
responsiveness to Pyongyang's demands.

Following this meeting, Washington held firm in its demand for a
broader multilateral gathering, insisting that the presence of South Korea and Japan at future talks was "essential." The May 2003 summit
meetings between Bush and new South Korean President Roh Moo
Hyun (in Washington on May 14) and Koizumi (in Crawford, Texas, on
May 23) reinforced this point. The two summits also closed many (but
not all) of the remaining policy and perception gaps between Washington and its two key allies in dealing with North Korea. In both meetings, Bush and his Asian counterparts reiterated that they "would not
tolerate" nuclear weapons in North Korea, while demanding a "complete, verifiable, and irreversible" elimination of North Korea's nuclear
weapons program.

The mutual recognition during both summits that South Korea and
Japan were "essential" for a successful and comprehensive settlement
also put Pyongyang on notice that there would be no separate bilateral
deal with Washington. The firm position taken by all three parties, and
the belated support for this position first by Beijing and then by Moscow, resulted, finally, in Pyongyang's agreement to Six-Party Talks.

SIX-PARTY TALKS, ROUND ONE:
LITTLE PROGRESS EXPECTED OR ACHIEVED

The North went into the first round of Six-Party Talks on August
27–29, 2003, in Beijing, demanding a "fundamental switchover" in
Washington's attitude, insisting that the Bush administration conclude
"a legally binding nonaggression treaty and establish diplomatic relations." For its part, Pyonyang would "declare its will to scrap its nuclear program." Monitoring and inspection could only come later, after
the treaty was signed and diplomatic relations established. Before, during, and since the talks, Washington steadfastly rejected the bilateral

nonaggression pact proposal for a variety of reasons, not least of which is because it cut Seoul out of the peninsula peace-making process, a long-time North Korean objective that all previous South Korean and U.S. governments have consistently rejected.

Washington reportedly showed some added flexibility at the Beijing talks, indicating that a "phased approach" might be considered once North Korean compliance had been assured. In the days leading up to the talks, Washington had also hinted that some type of multilateral security assurances might be provided in lieu of a bilateral pact. Kelly reportedly also assured Pyongyang that the United States had no intention of threatening North Korea, no intention of invading and attacking North Korea, and no intention of working for regime change in North Korea. Unfortunately, while the other five continued to talk about multilateral approaches to addressing North Korea's security concerns, Pyongyang declared that any collective security guarantee would be "meaningless."

SIX-PARTY TALKS: ROUND TWO?

The first round of talks ended on a negative note, when the North Korean representative announced that the North was "no longer interested" in multilateral dialogue. However, subsequent Chinese diplomatic efforts—and economic incentives—apparently convinced Pyongyang finally to agree "in principle" to resume negotiations. North Korea also announced that it was willing "to consider" Bush's offer of written assurances, albeit in a multilateral context, that the United States would not attack North Korea if it gave up its nuclear ambitions.

As 2004 began, it was still too soon to be overly optimistic even that the next round of talks would occur, much less that substantive progress would be made. What seems certain is that the road ahead will be a long and difficult one, presenting challenges as well as opportunities, for Washington and its Northeast Asian partners.

SOUTH KOREA REMAINS THE KEY

South Korea clearly has the most at stake and has insisted upon and largely been given a prominent role in dealing with this crisis. As noted, the TCOG process has been used effectively, with almost monthly meetings taking place at the assistant secretary level to ensure that the U.S., South Korean, and Japanese positions are in tune. But Washington and Seoul are still not fully in harmony. The South Korean government, like its electorate, seems evenly divided on how best to deal with North Korea, and the Roh administration is both politically weak and preoccupied with domestic issues. While it is inaccurate to say that Roh ran for president on an anti-U.S. platform, he clearly capitalized upon growing anti-American sentiments during the campaign.

After his election, Roh reasserted the primacy of the U.S.-South Korea security alliance—especially during his summit meeting with Bush in Washington—but his core supporters have since accused him of "selling out" and have somewhat limited his flexibility in dealing both with Washington and with Pyongyang. Roh has his own version of his predecessor's "Sunshine Policy," called the policy for peace and prosperity on the peninsula. But relations with the North do not enjoy the pride of place they had during the Kim Dae Jung administration, and both a reinvigorated opposition (which controls the National Assembly) and North Korea's surly behavior have made it impossible for Roh to enthusiastically pursue a policy of continued engagement with the North. A further factor has been the scandal over revelations that Kim Dae Jung paid US$500 million for his meeting with Kim Jong Il.

Nonetheless, South Korea remains much more tolerant and forgiving of Pyongyang and much more eager to "reward bad behavior" (a Washington hard-line phrase) than does the United States. While Roh has stated repeatedly that he "will not tolerate" nuclear weapons in the North and has threatened to end all economic assistance if North Korea pursues such weapons, his credibility on this point can be questioned. It is not clear what would constitute sufficient proof to trigger a cut-off of assistance by South Korea. While Washington and Seoul have also made great strides in agreeing on a way forward—both seek a diplomatic solution which takes North Korea's security concerns into account—there does not appear to be any common agreement on what to do if, at the end of the day, North Korea simply fails to cooperate or deliberately makes matters worse. If this should happen it would add to already existing strains in U.S.-South Korea relations and create domestic political nightmares for at least one, if not both, political leaders.

Talks about (long-overdue) U.S. force realignment and repositioning on the Korean peninsula have also added to alliance tensions.

More contentious was the decision to relocate forces currently spread throughout the country into several hubs south of Seoul. While this move is at least three to five years away, many Korean critics claim that this is preparation for a preemptive attack on the North (once U.S. forces are moved out of harm's way). The perception that the United States seems more concerned about the North Korean threat than do South Korean government officials literally living within the shadow of North Korea's long-range artillery adds an additional dimension to the challenging task of maintaining the 50-year-old alliance.

TOKYO: IN LOCK STEP WITH WASHINGTON

If the North Korean nuclear crisis has divided Washington and Seoul, it has had the opposite effect on Washington's relations with Tokyo. Tokyo has consistently taken a hard line on dealing with the North, not just because Japan sits within range of North Korea's growing missile force (which many fear could be fitted with nuclear, chemical, or biological warheads), but also because of the emotionally charged issue of the Japanese abductees to North Korea. The North Korean nuclear issue has allowed Koizumi to support Washington's missile defense program and has also increased security awareness in Japan to the extent that many are now more willing to see Japan take a more active role in regional security affairs, much to Washington's (and Koizumi's personal) satisfaction. More often than not, Japan and the United states have collaborated at the TCOG to strengthen Seoul's resolve.

Koizumi's openly stated desire to keep Washington engaged and flexible in its dealings over Korea provided much of the incentive behind his largely unpopular decision to send the Self-Defense Forces (SDF) to assist in the rebuilding of Iraq, despite the unsettled conditions and the possibility that SDF personnel could be killed. Thus far, Koizumi has been able to weather this political storm, although many observers anticipate that a serious political crisis will ensue if Japanese forces in Iraq sustain casualties. In the meantime, Koizumi's solid support for Bush's North Korea and Iraq policies has resulted in what both sides cheerfully acknowledge are the best bilateral relations in years, perhaps ever, between the two long-standing allies. The improved security relationship has also helped to paper over continuing differences over the pace and extent of Japan's economic reforms and other economic and trade issues.

CHINA: THE HONEST BROKER?

After initial reluctance to become more actively engaged, China has now jumped into the diplomatic fray and is currently playing the role of honest broker between Washington and Pyongyang both by arranging and hosting the Six-Party Talks and by otherwise serving as an intermediary. Beijing's involvement has likely been motivated by both the fact that North Korean actions threaten Chinese interests (as well as regional stability) and a desire by China's new leadership to play a more active role in regional geopolitics. China's leadership in helping to deal with this crisis and its endorsement of the multilateral approach favored by Washington have helped to improve relations between Washington and Beijing to the extent that officials in both countries are also proudly proclaiming relations to be "the best ever." Cooperation in the post-September 11 war on terrorism has given a major impetus to the overall improvement, but mutual concerns and overlapping near-term interests vis-à-vis North Korea have brought the two potential adversaries closer than most would have predicted. Cooperation on North Korea has also served to temper Washington's disappointment with Chinese objections to many aspects of Washington's war on terrorism, especially as regards Iraq.

The one thing that has risen faster than the level of Sino-U.S. cooperation regarding North Korea, however, has been the level of expectation in Washington regarding what China should be able to convince or compel North Korea to do. This may cause future disappointment if China fails to deliver or appears to be tilting more toward its "close as lips to teeth" allies in Pyongyang than toward its new-found "partner in diplomacy" in Washington. The current close cooperation could rapidly dissolve if North Korea takes actions (such as a nuclear test) that would impel Washington to demand a tougher approach and call for UN Security Council sanctions. In short, how the nuclear crisis plays out on the peninsula can either solidify or undermine the current close working relationship between Beijing and Washington; neither outcome is assured at this point.

RUSSIA: BETTER IN THAN OUT

From the start, Russia has seen itself as an important actor on the peninsula, an opinion initially shared by few others. The addition of

Russia to what was originally envisioned as a five-way dialogue was at Pyongyang's request, as North Korea sought another potentially friendly (or at least less hostile) face at the table. It also reflected Kim Jong Il's apparent growing annoyance at pressure from Beijing. Kim reportedly asked Russia to host (instead of China), but Moscow parried this obvious attempt to play Moscow and Beijing against one another. While the other four showed varying levels of enthusiasm, none objected to Russian participation. Moscow could prove helpful, and could have opposed an approach from which it felt excluded.

Taiwan: Always the Wild Card

Taiwan has been closely (and nervously) watching as the nuclear crisis has evolved, with its nervousness centered primarily on the growing closeness between Washington and Beijing. For those who see Washington's respective relationships with China and Taiwan as part of a zero-sum game, close Sino-U.S. collaboration vis-à-vis North Korea is a potential threat to Taipei's "special relationship" with Washington. Many in Taipei express fear that in exchange for China's help in neutralizing the North Korean nuclear threat, Washington will either stand back or even somehow contribute to Beijing's absorption of Taiwan. Taiwan's anxiety becomes cause for greater concern if—reflecting zero-sum game thinking—President Chen Shui-bian begins (or is seen as beginning) to take active steps to undermine Sino-U.S. relations.

The First Nuclear Domino?

For the longer term, there is the real and growing concern that if North Korea is allowed to pursue a nuclear weapons program without penalty, this could represent the first in a number of Northeast Asian nuclear dominos, with Japan, South Korea, and/or Taiwan rapidly following suit. Japan, however, might not be tempted to go nuclear as long as it remains confident in the American nuclear umbrella. Whether Seoul would feel compelled to do so—or might come to assume that it will inherit this capability upon reunification—is more subject to question. Of greater concern is Taiwan's response. Some in Taipei are already arguing for an "offensive option" in response to the growing Chinese missile threat. In the 1970s the United States had to intercede to halt embryonic nuclear programs both in South Korea and Taiwan; Washington's leverage over the current governments (and its ability to detect clandestine activities in both) has arguably diminished, even as their incentive for nuclear weapons seems to be growing.

FUTURE PROSPECTS:
NEITHER HOPEFUL NOR HOPELESS

In short, the nuclear crisis on the Korean peninsula can have serious implications for regional security on and beyond the peninsula, depending on how successfully the current standoff is handled. A successful outcome will depend in large part on the ability of the other five participants of the Six-Party Talks to speak with Pyongyang with one voice in expressing common concerns and offering potential solutions. While there is little cause for near-term optimism, the long-term prospects are not necessarily hopeless.

There are several points on which all six parties already agree. First is that a war on the peninsula serves no one's interests. Pyongyang must realize that the outcome of any major confrontation (nuclear or not) would be the destruction of the North Korean state. Nor does Washington seek a military solution, given its preoccupation elsewhere and the high human costs of any military option. Costs are even more central for Seoul. While few people or governments would shed tears if Kim Jong Il himself were to fall, the uncertainty and costs involved in bringing about regime change in North Korea, at least at present, seem far higher than the presumed benefits. Beijing and Moscow see the utility of a North Korean buffer state remaining, though not necessarily under Kim's rule. As a result, all seem prepared to live with an outcome that leaves the current North Korean regime in place. Finally, all six (North Korea included) reportedly agreed in Beijing to seek a nuclear weapons–free peninsula.

Washington, Seoul, Tokyo, Beijing, and Moscow would insist, with one voice and at a minimum, that North Korea fully, verifiably, and irreversibly freeze its nuclear weapons programs as a precondition to further negotiations. This would include a return of IAEA inspectors and the placing of spent fuel canisters (and any extracted plutonium) back under observation. In return, the other members would guarantee no military strikes against North Korea's facilities or its leadership as long as negotiations continue in good faith and the North likewise refrains from aggressive behavior. Washington, in close consultation with Seoul and Tokyo, and with Moscow and Beijing's concurrence, would lay out a clear roadmap of what it is prepared to offer, and when, in return for North Korea's verifiable cooperative actions.

Negotiations, however, may not succeed. Pyongyang may have decided that it needs nuclear weapons for its survival and may be unwilling to accept Washington's demands for a complete, verifiable, and irreversible end to its weapons program. Or the dialogue partners in the Six-Party Talks may not be sufficiently unified to be persuasive. In this event, the United States at some point is likely to request other measures, such as inspections of North Korean cargoes, a step that can be effective only with the cooperation of China and Russia. Thus at the start of 2004, the Korean crisis remains one of the most volatile and unpredictable issues facing Northeast Asia and the wider region.

2 Southeast Asia: The Terrorist Threat

ROHAN GUNARATNA

In Southeast Asia, terrorism—the politically motivated targeting of civilians—has traditionally been the byproduct of internal armed conflicts. With the steadfast penetration of Islamist political and violent groups in Southeast Asia by al Qaeda throughout the 1990s, terrorism in the region has assumed a new dimension since September 11, 2001. In addition to influencing the groups fighting to create Islamic states to target their opposing governments, al Qaeda has provided them with ideological and operational training to attack the United States, its allies, and its friends. Furthermore, al Qaeda has infiltrated Jemaah Islamiah (JI), an Islamist group that traditionally fought to create an Islamic state in Indonesia, to wage a pan-Islamist campaign within and outside the region.

Government response to the threat posed by terrorism has been uneven. Some governments such as Singapore and Malaysia have been decisive; others such as Indonesia and Thailand have vacillated. The Philippines, a third category, has lacked the resources to combat terrorism effectively. To reduce the immediate threat of terrorism in the region, governments have no option but to strengthen their domestic and regional security, intelligence, and law enforcement capabilities. Counteracting terrorism over the longer term will involve two additional elements: cooperation with the international community to break

Rohan Gunaratna is head of terrorism research at the Institute of Defense and Strategic Studies, Singapore, and honorary fellow at the International Policy Institute for Counter Terrorism, Israel. He designed the UN database on al Qaeda, the Taliban, and its associates and is the author of Inside Al Qaeda: Global Network of Terror *(2003).*

international networks such as al Qaeda that have global reach, and co-opting national and regional Muslim leaders and their parties in order to build social norms and ethics that resist politically motivated violence.

THE CONTEXT

Historically, the tactic of terrorism has been practiced in Southeast Asia by groups driven by left- and right-wing, ethno-nationalist, and politico-religious ideologies. Nonetheless, the groups that are of the deepest concern both within and outside the region today are the violent Islamist groups, especially those groups with ideological and operational links to al Qaeda.

Al Qaeda's successful attack on America's most iconic landmarks transformed this relatively small group into the flagship of international terrorism and the vanguard and model for violent Islamist groups throughout the world. To survive the U.S.-led global hunt after September 11, al Qaeda came to rely increasingly on associated Islamist groups, many of whose members it had trained in Afghanistan during the 1990s, to actually conduct the fight. In contrast to the old al Qaeda, a single entity with an estimated 4,000 members in October 2001, the post–September 11 al Qaeda is a conglomerate of organizations involving three dozen associated Islamist groups.

In Southeast Asia, JI and several other groups are continuing al Qaeda's mission. The Bali bombings by JI in October 2002, the world's worst terrorist attack since September 11, made clear the magnitude and the scale of the threat in Southeast Asia. As the determination of Southeast Asian groups to target regional governments and Western interests has not diminished, the region is likely to witness more attacks in 2004.

Al Qaeda and its associated groups threaten military, diplomatic, and civilian targets; use conventional and unconventional weapons; and are capable of operating in the air, on land, and at sea. Therefore, a wide range of security measures and countermeasures are necessary to protect both populations and infrastructure.

BACKGROUND

Southeast Asian Muslims are widely regarded as more tolerant and moderate than their Middle Eastern counterparts. Having lived under the shadow of large Buddhist, Hindu, Christian, and other non-Muslim communities, Southeast Asian Muslims interact well with non-Muslims. However, small radical elements have long existed in almost all Muslim communities in Southeast Asia, and there are historic and other grievances on the part of segments of the Islamic communities, both in Muslim majority and minority countries, against local governments, which in most cases are secular. Over recent years, feelings of resentment have been exacerbated by a series of external influences, particularly what was seen as the one-sided anti-Islamic U.S. policy toward the Palestinian issue and the recent U.S. military actions in Afghanistan and Iraq. Where local governments have supported the United States, resentment and pressures are also focused on these governments and leaders. Anger with the United States is now a major element unifying Muslim sentiment, facilitating recruitment and incitement by radical elements, and keeping the situation fluid and dynamic.

Virtually from its founding in March 1988, al Qaeda imparted ideological, financial, training, and operational support to a variety of Southeast Asian groups. One of the earliest contacts in the region occurred in 1988, when Mohammad Jamal Khalifa, the brother-in-law of Osama bin Laden, established the Manila branch of the International Islamic Relief Organization, a respectable Saudi charity providing assistance to Islamist groups in the region. Groups contacted and supported by al Qaeda included the Moro Islamic Liberation Front (MILF) and the Abu Sayyaf Group (ASG) in the Philippines; Lashkar Jundullah in Indonesia; Kumpulan Militan Malaysia (KMM); Jemmah Salafiyah (JS) in Thailand; Arakan Rohingya National Organization (ARNO) and Rohingya Solidarity Organization (RSO) in Myanmar and Bangladesh; and JI, a regional group with a presence throughout the region extending as far as Australia.

Al Qaeda worked with some success to persuade groups fighting local or subregional struggles to adopt its mission of a universal jihad as well as its strategy and tactics. For example, before his arrest in Bintan, Indonesia, in February 2003, the Singaporean JI chief, Mas Selamat Kastari, was planning to hijack and crash an Aeroflot aircraft from Bangkok, Thailand, into the Changi International Airport, Singapore. Kastari told his interrogators that the choice of a Russian aircraft was to teach Moscow a lesson for what it was doing to Muslim brothers in Chechnya. Similarly, Bali was a mass fatality attack, an al Qaeda hallmark. The JW Marriott Hotel Jakarta bombing in 2003 was also intended to be a mass fatality. Furthermore, the Bali and Marriott attacks were suicide bombings, a tactic hitherto alien to Southeast Asian groups.

Al Qaeda provided the Southeast Asian groups with financiers, operatives, and organizers of attacks. Riduan Isamuddin, alias Hambali, the operational leader of JI and organizer of the Bali bombings arrested in Thailand in August 2003, was also a regional al Qaeda leader. Al Qaeda also provided trainers—both combat tacticians and explosives experts. Within the MILF Camp Abu Bakar complex, the Kuwaiti trainer Omar Al Farooq established Camp Vietnam, to train Southeast Asian groups in guerrilla warfare and terrorism. Farooq, who subsequently married the daughter of a Darul Islam activist, moved to Indonesia to continue al Qaeda activities in that country. Farooq's visit and stay were arranged by Abu Zubeidah, the director of external support activities of al Qaeda. (Abu Zubaidah and Farooq were arrested by the Pakistani and Indonesian security and intelligence services in 2002.)

Al Qaeda also provided an organizational framework for the operation of disparate Islamist groups worldwide. In February 1998, Osama bin Laden created an umbrella group, the World Islamic Front for Jihad Against Jews and Crusaders, to unite al Qaeda's Middle Eastern, African, Caucasian, and Asian groups and give them a common agenda. Similarly, in 1999 al Qaeda created a regional umbrella group in Southeast Asia, Rabitat-ul-Mujahidin (Legion of the Fighters of God), with the same purpose. Some Southeast Asian groups such as the two wings of the Free Aceh Movement (GAM, or Gerakan Aceh Merdeka), an ethno-nationalist Muslim group in Indonesia, resisted attempts to enroll and influence them. Nonetheless, other groups such as the MILF joined the Rabitat-ul Mujahidin and worked closely with JI financially, technologically, and militarily.

But perhaps al Qaeda's most enduring impact on Southeast Asian groups has been to instill in them a sense of duty to fight not only nearby enemies but also the distant enemy—the United States. The United States was actively targeted in Southeast Asia as early as 1994, when Ramzi Ahmed Yousef, the February 1993 World Trade Center bomber, and al Qaeda leader Khalid Sheikh Mohammad (one of the September 11 masterminds) used Manila as the base of an unsuccessful effort to destroy 12 U.S. airliners over the Pacific. The United States was also a major target of the activities of the Singapore al Qaeda cell uncovered in December 2001.

The Evolving Threat

With worldwide arrests, al Qaeda and its associated groups are rapidly evolving to survive. Al Qaeda is adapting its operational and support networks, including its modus operandi: fund raising strategies (from charities and businesses to individual donors), communication means (satellite and mobile phones to email and human couriers), and even targeting practices (from hard to soft targets). Therefore, flexibility and agility is key for frontline law enforcement and intelligence services engaged in fighting terrorism.

Al Qaeda has proven adept in shifting its bases of operation to respond to changing circumstances. With the hardening of targets in North America, Europe, Australia, and New Zealand, al Qaeda and its associate groups have focused on targets in lawless zones of Asia, Africa, and the Middle East. When al Qaeda–JI leaders deemed that U.S. and Israeli targets in Manila were too chancy, they shifted the targets to Singapore. When the Singapore operation was disrupted, they focused on Indonesia, Taiwan, South Korea, Cambodia, and Thailand. Because many Southeast Asian countries suffer from porous borders, ready availability of firearms and explosives, lack of law and order, and corruption—in addition to local histories of conflict including grievances on the part of Muslim communities—the region remains conducive for the operation of local, regional, and extra-regional Islamist groups. Long after al Qaeda itself has faded due to sustained attrition, its overarching ideology of a universal jihad and its tactics are likely to influence the thinking and behavior of groups in Southeast Asia.

In Southeast Asia, there have been three generations of distinct but interlocking *mujahidin* (Islamic fighters) involved in terrorist networks. The experience in Afghanistan was pivotal for the first two generations. A few hundred Southeast Asians who fought in the anti-Soviet multinational Afghan jihad (December 1979–February 1989) returned to the region and joined several Islamist groups, including the core of JI. Throughout the 1990s, al Qaeda and Taliban training camps in Afghanistan trained 70,000–120,000 Muslim youths to fight in the Philippines (Mindanao), Indonesia (Maluku and Poso), Myanmar, China (Xingjiang), Kashmir, Bosnia, Kosovo, Chechnya, Dagestan, Nagorno-Karabakh, Algeria, Egypt, Jordan, Yemen, and in other regional conflicts. After September 11, to compensate for the loss of the base in Afghanistan, smaller and more mobile military training camps that are difficult to detect from the air were established in regional conflict zones of Asia, Africa, Latin America, and the Caucasus. Since September 11, Islamist camps active at various times in Southeast Asia have included Hodeibia, Palestine, and Vietnam in Mindanao, Philippines; Poso, Sulawesi, and Balikpapan in Kalimanthan, Indonesia; and Rohingya camps on the Myanmar-Bangladesh border. These camps are likely to produce the third generation of *mujahidin*.

THE CURRENT THREAT

Despite severe damage to the organization, al Qaeda is still playing a significant role in setting the agenda. Al Qaeda organizers are providing strategic and tactical direction to groups in Asia, the Middle East, the Caucasus, and the Horn of Africa. Al Qaeda also retains the ability to coordinate attacks, as indicated by the "wave attacks" of October 2002—the French oil supertanker *Limburg*, U.S. personnel in Kuwait, and the Bali bombings—and May 2003—Riyadh, two attacks in Chechnya, 21 gas stations in Karachi, and Casablanca.

In Southeast Asia, the MILF is now the principal source for al Qaeda's associates, especially to JI. Despite an active U.S. presence aimed at combating the ASG, the MILF works clandestinely with JI and al Qaeda. With the exception of the Philippines, however, the post–September 11 environment in Southeast Asia is not conducive to conducting large-scale training in the region. With increased cooperation between regional police and intelligence agencies, it is more difficult for JI to conduct cross-border training. As a result, training activities have become more clandestine. Instead of using open outdoor areas, much training takes place inside homes, with the emphasis shifted more to ideological than physical training.

Nevertheless, as long as JI can recruit and can use MILF facilities for training, it will be able to replenish its human losses and material wastage and will retain the capability to mount terrorist operations. JI infrastructure—especially propaganda, fund raising, and recruitment—is still intact in Mindanao, Indonesia, and southern Thailand. As JI is not a proscribed group in Indonesia, the authorities are constrained from dismantling its nonmilitary infrastructures. In the Philippines, within the limited resources of that country, the government has done its best to target JI and other terrorist groups. Despite denials by Thailand, that country remains a safe haven for a number of foreign terrorist groups including JI.

The threat posed by JI is not only to Western targets but also to domestic targets. In June 2003, the Philippine authorities disrupted multiple attacks in Manila by arresting the MILF Special Operations Group leader Muklis Yunos and an Egyptian counterpart. They were planning to attack the Presidential Palace with a tanker truck filled with a mixture of ammonium nitrate, sawdust, and gasoline; to attack the U.S. Embassy; and to ram an explosives-laden speed boat into a U.S. ship docked in the Manila area. Other targets included the Pandacan oil depot using a rocket-propelled grenade triggered by a mobile phone as a remote switch; the Manila International Airport by ramming an explosives-laden vehicle into the terminal; and a major commercial shipping line plying Philippine waters by remotely detonating a car bomb inside the ship's hold.

The co-option and integration of al Qaeda and JI elements into the infrastructure of local groups also complicate regional conflict resolution efforts. Most significantly, ongoing peace talks between the MILF and the government of the Philippines have gravely suffered as a result of the MILF-JI linkages.

The Response

Southeast Asian governments face an urgent need to prevent attacks against domestic as well as Western targets on their soil. A complicating factor in many cases is that governments that support the West in the fight against terrorism earn the wrath of domestic as well as foreign Islamist groups. Nonetheless, most governments in the "South" have no option but to cooperate with the resource-rich and technologically advanced West to fight terrorist groups. Until governments worldwide, including in Southeast Asia, develop a common strategy and cooperative structures to fight terrorism at domestic, regional, and global levels, terrorism will remain a significant threat.

Due primarily to varying domestic compulsions, the response of Southeast Asian governments to the threat of global, networked terrorism in the region has been uneven. The detection of the JI network in Singapore in December 2001, based on information from Afghanistan, led to the uncovering of the links between al Qaeda and local groups. The governments of Singapore and Malaysia, faced with direct evidence of JI presence and activities, responded quickly and energetically to the threat, arresting and detaining dozens of suspected JI members. The government of the Philippines, which for years has been dealing with home-grown terrorism in the southern Mindinao region, also quickly identified and reacted to the widened threat. However, Indonesia, until the Bali bombings in October 2002, and Thailand, until the disruption of further JI bombing plans in June 2003, publicly denied the existence of terrorist networks on their soil.

The nature of the threat is constantly changing as terrorist groups rapidly adapt to security measures and countermeasures. Before September 11, al Qaeda focused only on conducting spectacular attacks. Although al Qaeda and its associate groups are no longer able to mount coordinated multiple suicide attacks of the scale of September 11 inside the United States, they are still capable of mounting small and medium-scale attacks such as those in Bali, Riyadh, or Casablanca in the global south. This situation has several key implications for Southeast Asian governments. First, there is a need for increased and sustained vigilance (including intelligence gathering and expansion of human sources) to detect threats. Second, there must be an unprecedented level of international and domestic law enforcement, security, and intelligence cooperation. Finally, however, the hunt against al Qaeda must be maintained on all fronts, to deny the group time, space, and resources to plan, prepare, and mount further theatrical or spectacular attacks. To weaken terrorist groups and their support bases, Southeast Asian governments need to place relevant threat information in the public domain to keep the public alert; sustain sharing of information with foreign governments; and aggressively hunt terrorist cells in the region.

To meet current and emerging threats, Southeast Asian governments —with input from the United States, Australia, Europe, and Japan— have been slowly but steadily strengthening their intelligence and strike capabilities and developing the doctrines and force structures to meet the challenge of Islamist terrorism. Elements of cooperation and coordination include harmonizing legislation, rendition, common databases, exchange of personnel, sharing of experience, transfer of expertise, joint training, and combined operations.

However, reflecting a continuing lack of trust among the member countries of the Association of Southeast Asian Nations (ASEAN), most practical counterterrorism efforts are still unilateral, and cooperation is most frequently bilateral or at best trilateral. One particular shortcoming is a lack of judicial cooperation on counterterrorism matters.

Given the nature of the post–September 11 operational environment, the terrorism threat in Southeast Asia cannot be addressed only by domestic governments working unilaterally. The terrorist networks are transnational, so an effective response must be at three levels—domestic, regional, and global. A coordinated approach is essential. Because al Qaeda is the unifying link, targeting al Qaeda is paramount. Debriefings of Khalid Sheikh Mohammed, his successor Tawfiq bin Attash, and Hambali revealed that the second wave of strikes against the United States targeting the West coast, especially California, was to be mounted from Southeast Asia. To deny al Qaeda access to Southeast Asia, it is imperative to target the linkages between al Qaeda and its Southeast Asian associates.

CONCLUSION

With al Qaeda evolving from a group into a movement of groups, the terrorist threat in Southeast Asia will persist in the long term. Today, al Qaeda is an organization of organizations with a global reach and therefore no one single country can fight and destroy it. As there is no standard textbook for fighting al Qaeda or its associated groups, each government must learn from its own successes and failures.

Despite unprecedented security measures and countermeasures, al Qaeda and its associated groups in Southeast Asia remain a formidable threat to domestic and international security. The ideology of al Qaeda determines its staying power as well as the strength of its associate groups. Until al Qaeda is destroyed, Southeast Asian groups linked to al Qaeda will draw ideological and tactical inspiration from it.

Progress is being made; since September 11, more than 100 attacks have been aborted or disrupted. But at the same time, as the Bali, Casablanca, Djerba, Chechnya, Mindanao, and Karachi bombings have demonstrated, the threat has moved beyond al Qaeda. Al Qaeda's regional associates have proved beyond doubt that they are as lethal as their parent group, and the robust Islamist milieu is facilitating their activities. Despite the arrest of 4,000 al Qaeda members and associated members in 102 countries, the network has been able to replenish its rank and file and continue the fight. Based on recent history, terrorist groups tend to enjoy a life span of over a decade, so the fight against the al Qaeda brand of terrorism will be long and hard.

Al Qaeda's associates and off-shoots have learned and will increasingly use al Qaeda tactics and technologies such as hijacking and crashing aircraft, contact poisons, anti-aircraft weapons, and so on. As the

East Africa bombings in August 1998, the attack on the USS *Cole* in October 2000, September 11, and the Bali bombings demonstrated, suicide terrorism will remain a weapon in the arsenal of these groups—perhaps even their most effective tool. They are likely to develop a range of other technologies, tactics, and techniques to inflict mass fatalities on their enemies.

To reduce the immediate threat, it is essential for Southeast Asian law enforcement and intelligence agencies to build counterterrorist structures and train personnel to target the terrorist support and operational infrastructures on their soil. Yet treating terrorism purely from the security perspective does not adequately address the threat and could actually exacerbate it. In addition to cooperation on military, security, and intelligence arenas, the "silent front" of diplomacy and economic reforms is also critical. As the response to terrorism to date has been largely military, both at a global and a regional level, the immediate (one-year to two-year) threat has been reduced but not eliminated, and the medium- to long-term threat has not diminished.

To manage this situation and contain the dangers, it is also imperative for Southeast Asian governments to work closely with Islamic community leaders and community institutions. Al Qaeda ideology appeals to a cross section of society—the group recruits from the rich, poor, educated, and less educated. Therefore, governments need to enlist the support of the whole range of educational and religious institutions as well as community and other influential leaders in the public and private sectors to build norms ethics that reject the use, misuse, and abuse of religion for political purposes.

It is particularly critical for governments of countries with Muslim minorities to learn to effectively work with their Muslim communities so as to deter, contain, and ultimately marginalize the radical Islamist elements. By providing Muslims with more power and authority in the government structures, governments can strengthen the Muslim elite's willingness and ability to lead and manage the community.

Reducing the long-term threat will depend on effective responses and policies in all these areas on the part of Southeast Asian governments. But U.S. policies and actions will also play an important part in the success or failure of restraining terrorism in Southeast Asia. The U.S. role remains critical because of its power, its prominence in the world, and its ability (and willingness) to undertake adventures such as in Iraq that stimulate and enable the radical Islamists to make greater inroads into the Muslim communities.

3 South Asia:
New Promise and Old Problems

DIPANKAR BANERJEE

The year 2004 looks more promising for South Asia than the previous year, although longer-term projections are more cautious for some countries. The most positive development, coming at the very end of 2003 and spilling over into the first days of 2004, is a sudden thaw in relations between India and Pakistan. Nevertheless, the region is a major theater in the global war on terrorism, and this problem remains the principal concern in all capitals. Internal law and order, simmering insurgencies, and terrorism pose continuing serious challenges in most states. There is basic domestic political stability and predictability in Bangladesh, Bhutan, India, and Maldives, while the internal situation in Nepal, Pakistan, and Sri Lanka is more uncertain.

Economically, the outlook in South Asia is increasingly encouraging. All South Asian states except Nepal have achieved high gross domestic product growth. India's growth rate is predicted to be above 7 percent in 2004, with others averaging between 5 percent and 6 percent. Regional currencies have strengthened against the U.S. dollar, and the major countries have larger foreign exchange reserves than ever before. All regional stock exchanges have shown dramatic growth in line with global trends, with the Mumbai exchange in India growing faster in 2003 than any in Asia except that in Bangkok.

Maj. Gen. (Ret.) Dipankar Banerjee is the director of the Institute of Peace and Conflict Studies, New Delhi; the former executive director of the Regional Centre for Strategic Studies in Colombo (1999–2002); and a 2002–2003 Jennings Randolph Fellow at the U.S. Institute of Peace, Washington, D.C.

Thus South Asia enters 2004 with a combination of new prospects for improved security in the region and old, nagging, unsolved problems.

THE SECURITY ENVIRONMENT

REGIONAL   Several developments at the end of 2003 and the first days of 2004 bode well for regional security in South Asia in 2004 and beyond. The most important of these took place at the summit meeting of the South Asian Association for Regional Cooperation (SAARC) in the first week of January 2004.

The development with the greatest potential to transform the regional security outlook in 2004 and beyond was a breakthrough in India-Pakistan relations on the sidelines of the SAARC meeting. Indian Prime Minister Atal Bihari Vajpayee and Pakistan President Pervez Musharraf agreed to undertake a comprehensive and composite dialogue to address all outstanding issues between the two countries, including the lynchpin issue of Jammu and Kashmir. This agreement was the culmination of a carefully developed and orchestrated series of steps and lower-level confidential discussions during 2003. The process began with initiatives by Vajpayee in April, leading to measures announced by Pakistan in November that included a ceasefire along the Line of Control in Jammu and Kashmir. This is the most positive development in bilateral relations between the two countries in years, and though it is only the beginning of a process, this development holds out the promise that outstanding issues can be resolved. A genuine change in India-Pakistan relations would impact the security situation and interstate relations throughout South Asia and would boost South Asia's image and position in the broader international community.

A further outcome of the SAARC summit with potential future importance was the signing of a regional free trade agreement. After years of talk and temporizing, the signing of this agreement represented a breakthrough in economic cooperation. Though the agreement will come into force only after ratification in two years and is to be implemented over a period of seven to ten years with a number of options for negative lists for each country, it is still a major achievement. If pursued sincerely it will significantly enhance regional economic cooperation.

Though on a smaller scale, another noteworthy positive security development in 2003 was military action by Bhutan launched on December 15 against insurgents and terrorists from three outlawed organizations in adjoining India. The insurgents had been sheltering in the jungles of southern Bhutan, where they had established about 60 training camps and from which they had carried out numerous subversive acts in India. When protracted talks failed to persuade the groups to withdraw, the Royal Bhutan Army struck, clearing all camps and killing or capturing the terrorists. This action appears to have broken the back of these insurgencies and has set an example of active regional cooperation to eradicate cross-border terrorism. Myanmar has now expressed its willingness to crack down on terrorists within its borders, and India is pressing Bangladesh to do the same.

INTERNAL   The 23-party coalition government in India led by Vajpayee's Bharatiya Janata Party (BJP, or Indian People's Party) is riding high on a "feel good" factor brought about by economic growth. With the best monsoon in a decade, economic indicators are at an all-time high and growth prospects are bright. Foreign currency reserves have topped a record US$100 billion. Elections were held in four important provinces in the heart of India in October 2003, and contrary to poll predictions the BJP won resoundingly in three. Buoyed by this success, Vajpayee is likely to bring forward national parliamentary elections, now scheduled for October 2004, to April–May. As 2004 began, most projections saw the BJP increasing its seat total.

India has long been and remains a target and victim of terrorism, and the government is firmly committed to countering this scourge. Most dramatically, the entire border in the west, from Gujarat to Jammu and Kashmir, is affected. Terrorist tactics have come to include *fedayeen* (suicide) attacks, particularly in Jammu and Kashmir. The eastern part of the country continues to experience a variety of ethnic insurgencies. Communist-inspired Maoist movements are resurgent in central India. In one attack in October 2003, the car of the popular chief minister of Andhra Pradesh, Chandrababu Naidu, was targeted, though he escaped with injuries. Areas in India south of Nepal may well see a spillover of the communist insurgency in that kingdom. Given the vulnerability of the area of India adjoining Nepal, with its low level of development and widespread social inequity, the violence could easily spread unless it is addressed comprehensively.

The situation in Pakistan improved in important ways over the course of 2003. An elected government came to power at the end of 2002 after three years of military rule, although the army under President General Musharraf still calls the shots. The Legal Framework

Order (LFO) enacted by Musharraf before he handed over power to the civil government formalizes a permanent role and powers for the military in governance. The president has the power to dismiss parliament. The army dominates the National Security Council (NSC), created under the LFO to oversee security policy and monitor the democratic process. However, elections have thrown up an alliance of Islamic parties as an emerging political force. The alliance holds the majority in one of four provinces, where it has imposed Sharia' law as in Afghanistan under the Taliban. There was strong opposition to the LFO in parliament and in particular to Musharraf's retaining the positions of chief of the army as well as president; this opposition had paralyzed the assembly. Under a compromise reached at the end of 2003 that was essentially favorable to Musharraf, he will continue as president for his full term and relinquish his army position only by the end of 2004.

Internal security in Pakistan remains unstable, with the divide between Shia and Sunni Muslims producing sectarian conflict across the country. The western border with Afghanistan witnessed periodic cross-border artillery shelling between the Pakistani army and Afghan militias. Remnants of al Qaeda operate astride the border, with Osama bin Laden suspected to be hiding in the area. Anti-U.S. sentiment is high in much of the country, particularly in the northwest. Musharraf was the target of two assassination attempts in Rawalpindi in December 2003, in at least one of which there seems to have been inside involvement. Should a future assassination attempt succeed, there may well be some turmoil in the country, though it seems more likely that a military general would replace Musharraf than that the parliament would recover the lost political space.

Pakistan's economy is performing relatively well. It grew 5.1 percent in 2002–2003 and is projected to grow at over 5 percent in 2003–2004. The manufacturing and agricultural sectors have emerged as the main engines of growth. Reflecting the new post–September 11 closeness in U.S.-Pakistan relations, U.S. aid has totaled US$1.5 billion, and the International Monetary Fund and the World Bank have provided even larger amounts with U.S. backing. Foreign currency reserves totaled US$12 billion at the start of 2004, the highest ever in the country's history. However, continuing fundamental and structural weaknesses, including the absence of foreign investment, may hamper future growth.

Bangladesh is one of only two Islamic states with a functioning democracy (the other being Turkey), though this has not led to stability or to particularly good governance. The leading political parties are constantly at loggerheads. The opposition Bangladesh Awami League boycotted parliament for most of 2003 and frequently attempted to paralyze the administration. The ruling Bangladesh National Party is pro-Islamic, which leads to some tensions with India. The internal law and order situation deteriorated during 2003 to such an extent that the army had to be called out twice, in April and again in August. This situation is unlikely to improve as long as the basic confrontation between pro-Islamic groups and secular forces continues. However, and somewhat surprisingly, Bangladesh's economy has not been badly affected by the political turmoil, and is estimated to have grown 5.7 percent in 2003. Nevertheless, macro-economic prospects are not favorable and the economy remains fragile. A continuing very high level of corruption discourages new foreign investment, depressing prospects for future growth.

Sri Lanka had a basically good year in 2003, but the future remains uncertain. There has been peace in the country and all-round economic growth for more than two years. The GDP has been growing at 5.5 percent, even though a high level of external debt continues to cause concern.

The major problem plaguing Sri Lanka's outlook is that the peace process with the Liberation Tigers of Tamil Eelam (LTTE), launched with promising momentum and relief on all sides in 2002, has stalled because of disagreements over interim administration and power-sharing arrangements. Donor assistance totaling a massive US$4.5 billion pledged at a meeting in Tokyo in June 2003 remains largely unimplemented. On October 31, 2003, the LTTE announced its position on the devolution of powers, asking for an interim self-governing authority for the northeast. This position was close to a demand for independence, but it was also the first time that the LTTE had spelled out its political position and said it was willing to negotiate on the subject.

Negotiations then suffered a major setback on November 4, when President Kumaratunga assumed direct control over the key ministries of defense, interior, and mass communications and prorogued the parliament, even as Prime Minister Ranil Wickramasingne was in the United States on an official visit. While constitutionally Sri Lanka's executive president is fully entitled to take these steps, Kumaratunga's action broke the southern (non-LTTE) consensus regarding the peace process, which had been initiated and was being conducted by the prime minister. As 2004 began, political stalemate in the south was continuing with no solution in sight. The Norwegian facilitators (who had played a key intermediary role in the drawn-out negotiations) have withdrawn, declaring that they will return only when the political impasse in Colombo is resolved. This appears possible only through new elections and a new political mandate. The year 2004 will see the next steps in this critical area for Sri Lanka's stability and future.

Nepal's troubles seem to be never ending, and its immediate outlook for internal security is the least favorable in the region. Beginning with regicide in mid-2001, Nepal has entered a period of political instability and intense insurgency mounted by a Maoist guerrilla movement. A peace process and then a cease-fire in January 2003 led to some respite and hope, but in September the Maoists withdrew from the cease-fire and resumed violence. The three major domestic players—the king, the Maoists, and the political parties—seem unable to agree on anything. With continuing uncertainty and violence, the country's economy has deteriorated rapidly. Future prospects, at least for the near term, are gloomy.

By contrast with Nepal, the neighboring Himalayan kingdom of Bhutan has had a long period of calm and stability. The kingdom is transitioning from an absolute monarchy to a constitutional democracy, guided by the king in a remarkably peaceful manner. Bhutan has carefully maintained an excellent relationship with India, has enjoyed enormous aid and support from Delhi over the years, and has developed a self-sustaining economy based on tourism and the sale of hydropower to India. Bhutan's economy has demonstrated sustained growth, currently at over 7 percent per year.

EXTERNAL RELATIONS   India has been expanding and consolidating its international relationships. Indo-U.S. relations particularly are undergoing a qualitative transformation, moving toward a strategic relationship based on shared interests and goals.

A major breakthrough in India's relations with China was achieved in 2003 with Vajpayee's visit to Beijing in June. A new formulation on Tibet was presented as a compromise by Delhi. China accepted Sikkim's merger with India through the mechanism of agreeing to establish a border trade post at the China-India border in Sikkim. Both sides agreed to double trade by 2005 and explore new areas of economic cooperation and investment. It was agreed to raise the level of border talks to the political level, with the first round being held in Delhi in October.

Vajpayee attended the Bali summit in September between India and the Association of Southeast Asian Nations (ASEAN), where the concept of developing a free trade agreement between India and the region was approved. The Bangladesh-India-Myanmar-Sri Lanka-Thailand Economic Cooperation (BIMST-EC), initiated by India in 1997, is beginning to make progress. India has cemented a three-year military agreement with Vietnam by agreeing to maintain the latter's Soviet-series aircraft in exchange for counterinsurgency training.

India extended cooperation with Afghanistan in 2003 by opening new consulates, arranging for the training of the Afghan National Army, and helping in road construction. Relations with the Central Asian republics are being given priority; a joint military exercise was conducted with Tajikistan, facilitated by the only Indian air base abroad, established in 2002 at Farkhor. Security cooperation with Tehran in 2003 included joint naval exercises in the Arabian Sea and agreement by India to help Iran maintain its Soviet naval equipment. India and Iran are also exploring the possibilities of building gas and oil pipelines from the Caspian basin, via new ports to be developed along the Iranian coast.

In Pakistan, having put a civilian government in place, Musharraf is seeking to improve Pakistan's international image. His visit to the United States in June 2003 demonstrated close relations with and support for Pakistan by the United States, with President George W. Bush according him a welcome at Camp David. The United States offered to sell weapons to Pakistan and has provided substantial antiterrorist capability, including a large number of helicopters. Although the U.S. ban on the sale of F-16 aircraft continues, Pakistan was offered an aid package of US$3 billion in five years, with half allocated for purchase of military supplies. In 2003, Musharraf also visited the United Nations, the Organization of the Islamic Conference, and China and a number of other countries. Pakistan's relations with Afghanistan remain difficult, however, with Kabul accusing Islamabad of supporting raids by the Taliban inside Afghanistan.

Bangladesh's relations with India have remained strained under the new government but there were other successes in its foreign relations. U.S. Secretary of State Colin Powell in a visit to Dhaka in June 2003 encouraged the leaders to make democracy work in the country. Musharraf visited in July, leading to agreement to enhance cooperation in several areas, including defense and trade. Dhaka also attempted to improve relations with Myanmar, enhance trade, and resolve the outstanding Rohingya refugee issue.

The Maoist insurgency in Nepal has put stresses on its relations with India, with the Nepal government concerned over support to the insurgents from the south. The water-sharing agreement over the Mahakali river treaty remains unimplemented. The United States, the United Kingdom, and India cooperate in supporting anti-insurgency operations with equipment and training. China has refrained from assistance to the Maoist groups and constantly expressed support for the Nepal government. Nepal's relations with Bhutan remain strained over the influx of people of Nepalese origin from Bhutan to eastern Nepal, where they live under refugee conditions.

DEFENSE TRENDS AND ISSUES

DEFENSE POLICIES India's defense forces have been severely stretched by having to counter terrorism, fight insurgency, defend the country's borders against cross-border terrorism, and sustain deployments at high altitude in the Himalayas. They must simultaneously prepare for and develop high-technology war-fighting capabilities. A cabinet-level review of defense capabilities completed in 2000 is beginning to bear fruit. Counterinsurgency operations are now primarily the responsibility of paramilitary forces under the Ministry of Home Affairs. Their personnel strength, at 1.3 million and growing, is now greater than the regular armed forces. The army continues to man the border in Jammu and Kashmir and remains responsible for countering cross-border terrorism from Pakistan. Other counterinsurgency and counterterrorist operations within India are increasingly under the jurisdiction of a number of paramilitary forces of varying operational effectiveness. Nuclear deterrence capabilities have been enhanced and a nuclear command authority was set up and announced in early 2003. An integrated defense staff has been established, but there is no decision yet over a chief of defense staff, without which many of the new measures will not be effective.

Pakistan's military also has been stretched through having to fight on several fronts, facing the Indian army in the east and confronting Afghan militias as well as the Taliban in the west. Many military officers now have a dual task, administering the country and manning its many entirely civilian posts. A major challenge for the security forces is to control growing sectarian clashes.

Bangladesh and China agreed in 2003 to form a joint working group on modernization of police and paramilitary forces. India has accused Bangladesh of not doing enough to root out terrorists from northeast India sheltering in Bangladesh, and even providing sanctuary and assistance. Bangladesh denies this, but the issue creates tension between the two, particularly given Bhutan's success at removing all terrorists from its southern territory. The Sri Lankan armed forces have had a badly needed respite from the intense counterinsurgency operations against the LTTE of the last two decades. The cease-fire since early 2002 has provided an opportunity to train and reorganize, but not yet to recoup equipment losses or make up strength. Over the last two years the Royal Nepalese Army has had to bear the brunt of counterinsurgency operations against the Maoists for which it was neither prepared nor fully trained. Recent U.S. military supplies, and training by both the U.S. and Indian armies, have helped reorient the Royal Nepalese Army's operational preparedness, though great inadequacies remain. Bhutan has a small army of about 7,000 soldiers mainly trained for border surveillance and local defense.

DEFENSE BUDGET   There is a steady increase in defense budgets across the region except for Sri Lanka. This is mainly to counter insurgency and terrorism and to maintain internal law and order. Only India provides anything like a proper defense budget (see table 1), which has to be presented and approved by parliament.

Table 1. India's Defense Budget in Billions of Rupees

	2000–2001	2001–2002	2002–2003	2003–2004
Army	278.78	311.00	317.11	342.00
Air Force	106.11	118.00	124.89	154.00
Navy	73.85	84.00	84.72	120.00
Research & development	33.42	31.23	32.56	36.00
Defense production	4.05	−1.00	2.35	5.00
Total	496.22	543.00	560.00	653.00

SOURCE: Indian Ministry of Defense Annual Report presented to Parliament in February 2003.
NOTE: US$1 = Rs47 at the time the budget was presented in February 2003. The exchange rate at the end of 2003 was US$1 = Rs45.

A characteristic of recent Indian defense budgets is that much of the funds remain unspent. Therefore, in 2002–2003, although the budget was much higher, the amount actually expended was only 3 percent more than that spent the previous year.

No details are published on Pakistan's defense budget, hence the figures announced in the annual budget are the best publicly available. It was claimed that the budget did not increase in 2003–2004 and remained at PKR160.3 billion (US$2.79 billion at US$1 = PKR57.38).

Bangladesh's defense budget for 2003–2004 is 39.95 billion taka (US$681.16 million at US$1 = 58.65 taka), which though high in overall government expenditure, is only 1.3 percent of its GDP. Nepal's defense expenditure has increased substantially to counter the Maoist insurgency.

MILITARY ACQUISITIONS   The year 2003 was particularly marked by military acquisitions by India. An important purchase was the long-awaited order for 66 Hawk jet trainers from the United Kingdom's BAE Systems for US$1.3 billion including training for pilots. Twenty-four aircraft will be manufactured in the United Kingdom and the rest in India. Agreement to acquire the Russian aircraft carrier *Admiral Gorshkov* seems to have been finalized, with only costs still to be negotiated. An agreement was also signed with Russia in January 2003 for the joint development of the next-generation fighter aircraft and other weapons systems. Meanwhile, the jointly produced supersonic cruise missile Brahmos with a range of 260 kilometers was successfully test flown in India and is likely to enter service in 2004. The growing military relationship with Israel was demonstrated by clearance for the supply of the Phalcon warning-and-control system to be mounted on the Russian IL-76 aircraft. A major arms deal was signed with the United States for eight Raytheon AN/TPQ-37 Firefinder counterbattery artillery radars.

SOUTH ASIA AND GLOBAL SECURITY

Despite local and regional security concerns, the states of South Asia have a long record of participation in international security forums and activities. The overall level of South Asian commitments to international peacekeeping is not expected to change in the future.

Though India and Pakistan are not signatories to the Nonproliferation Treaty or the Comprehensive Test Ban Treaty, both countries are adherents to many other international disarmament treaties. For example, India has actively engaged in the Conference on Disarmament in Geneva on the verification protocol to the Biological and Toxin Weapons Convention. Both Pakistan and India have a record of sustained participation in UN peacekeeping operations, with Pakistan presently contributing the second largest and India the third largest numbers of soldiers to these operations.

Bangladesh currently contributes the largest force to UN peacekeeping operations, which in 2003 came to 5,324 troops in ten different peacekeeping operations around the world. This included 1,276 soldiers sent to the Democratic Republic of Congo in July 2003.

Nepal has been a substantial contributor to UN peacekeeping operations in the last decade. Currently it is the fifth largest troop contributor with about 1,500 soldiers.

COUNTRY CHAPTERS

4 Australia

THE SECURITY ENVIRONMENT

Terrorism remains the main threat to Australia. Since the September
11, 2001, terrorist attacks in the United States, the Australian government of Liberal Party (conservative) leader John Howard has followed
the U.S. lead in giving highest priority to countering terrorism. There
have been no serious incidents on Australian territory, but Australia
has been identified as a target of terrorists and Australians have been
victims. The threat posed to Australian citizens and interests in the region remains quite high, and more attacks are expected to occur in the
region.

This orientation constitutes a marked shift in Australian government policy, after a period in which (as noted in *Asia Pacific Security
Outlook 2003*) the previous Australian policy of closer engagement
with its Asian neighbors, which was promoted strongly under the Labor Party governments of the 1980s–1990s, had been allowed to drift.
In the new circumstances, cooperation against terrorism is the focus of
regional policy, and very close alignment with the United States is at the
center of the government's global security policy.

Internally there have been few cases of suspected terrorism in Australia and these have mainly involved individuals linked to activities
overseas. Pressures on Muslim communities within Australia have
abated as local and state authorities have strengthened consultative
and other liaison links, and the strengths of Australia's evolving multi-
cultural society have been reaffirmed. (Broader anti-immigration sentiment, a major issue at the time of the 2001 parliamentary election, is
not now a feature in the national political debate.)

57

Externally, prospects are less clear or reassuring. The extent and intensity of terrorist activity has been documented in the trials in Indonesia of those responsible for the October 2002 bombings in Bali. Those trials were made possible through close cooperation between the Indonesian and Australian police. The trials were notably thorough and timely. But despite improved police work and a number of arrests, there is no confidence that the major terrorist network involved, Jemaah Islamiah (JI), has been broken or even fully unearthed. And even if JI were eliminated, al Qaeda may have other independent capabilities in the region.

JI is a truly transnational terrorist organization, the first of its kind in Southeast Asia, both pursuing global Islamist objectives and attempting to settle local scores. It is seen as posing threats to the secular governments of Indonesia and Malaysia in particular, invoking as it does a vision of some form of more purely Islamic governance for those countries, the southern Philippines, and southern Thailand.

Further attacks in the region are not likely to be confined to soft civilian targets such as churches, tourist venues, and public transport, which have been attacked so far. Future targets could include domestic political figures and manifestations of Western presence, such as embassies, oil installations, and other significant economic features. JI is also expected to continue to develop its links with other extremist groups in the region.

Australian perceptions of China are strongly positive. The interaction of Australia's long-standing, close alliance with the United States on the one hand (including ongoing negotiations for a bilateral free trade agreement accelerated as a result of cooperation in Iraq), and Australia's strong and growing relationship with China on the other was highlighted during the simultaneous visits of U.S. President George W. Bush and Chinese President Hu Jintao to Australia in October 2003. Australia's merchandise trade with China is expanding faster than trade with any other of Australia's major trading partners. The prospect of a strategic economic partnership, with potential described by Hu as "immense," was clearly registered with his Australian audience, and a trade and economic framework agreement was signed during the visit.

Hu firmly insisted on a "one-China" policy, which Prime Minister Howard publicly reaffirmed, while restating Australia's preference for "calm and constructive" relations between Beijing and Taipei. Howard explicitly declined to join the United States in calling on China to allow the appreciation of the Chinese renminbi. In his speech to a joint sitting of the Australian federal parliament, Bush included possible conflict over Taiwan among those issues important to the alliance, underlining the potential significance of the Taiwan issue for Australia.

Although Australians feel generally less secure than before September 11, they continue to prosper economically. With the economy having recovered from the effects of severe drought and from the immediate shock of the enhanced terrorist threat, as well as the Iraq war, the country is expected to achieve a rate of economic growth in 2004 among the highest in the Organisation for Economic Cooperation and Development. Confidence in economic performance in turn supports a readiness to engage in antiterrorist operations in distant areas.

Awareness of the terrorist threat has facilitated a change in the Australian view of small states in the Southwest Pacific. The prospect of failed or failing states providing openings for terrorist activity has led to a new readiness to advocate preventive, multilateral intervention, notably in the Solomon Islands. While Australia's leaders are more prepared to intervene than in the recent past, there is a broad consensus that Australia cannot, however, provide a blanket solution to the problems of state failure in the South Pacific or scale up its Solomon Islands package to suit the larger countries of the Southwest Pacific.

North Korea's nuclear development and proliferation risks are seen as posing serious threats to Australia's security and other interests. Several of Australia's largest economic partners are in North Asia, but Australia has long looked to the United States to take the lead among the major powers on this problem. While the United States has unquestionably superior military power to deal with North Korea, Australians clearly prefer avoidance of military force in this case, and see China as playing the key negotiating role in seeking a solution through multilateral processes.

DEFENSE POLICIES AND ISSUES

Fundamental policy as set out in the white paper of 2000 defines Australia's defense priorities as, first, the defense of Australia and its direct approaches; second, "to foster the security of Australia's immediate neighborhood"; third, to work with other powers to promote stability and cooperation in Southeast Asia; and fourth, "to contribute in appropriate ways to maintaining strategic stability in the wider Asia-Pacific region."

Australian policy sees these priorities as being pursued in close cooperation with allies, neighbors, and regional partners. An interest in working with the Indonesian government "to establish over time a new defense relationship" continues, while New Zealand remains a "valued defense partner."

The military strategy in support of Australia's defense priorities remains as stated in the white paper. This strategy basically looks to a capacity to defend the country's shores without relying on the combat forces of other countries. Australia needs to be able to control its air and sea approaches, and, although the general posture is defensive, Australian forces can seek to attack hostile forces as far from the coast as possible. Australia's military strategy also seeks to contribute to the security of Australia's nearest neighbors, not only in time of war, but also in responding to nonmilitary needs such as peacekeeping and natural disasters. Finally, its forces are expected to support Australia's wider interests by contributing to international activities intended to resolve crises beyond Australia's immediate neighborhood.

The force capability plan in the white paper provided for:
- Replacement of the F/A-18 fighters and F-111 bombers from about 2006, but leaving open the options of a greater emphasis on missiles and the possibility of using a single type of aircraft where there are currently two types;
- Acquisition of airborne early warning aircraft: four in the short term and possibly three more later;
- Major refurbishment or replacement of P3C maritime patrol aircraft;
- Upgrading of Collins-class submarines: All six will have their combat systems replaced and all other modifications needed to bring them to full potential;
- Acquisition of air warfare–capable destroyers: Eventually the navy will have three, but they will start entering service only after the ten-year span of the white paper;
- A slight increase in the size of the army, with six battalions to be kept at high readiness;
- Acquisition of helicopters: two squadrons of armed reconnaissance helicopters, as well as a further squadron of troop-lift helicopters; and

- Other measures to round out ground force capability, including a change in the role of the Reserves, upgrading armored personnel carriers, and acquiring thermal imaging, body armor, air defense mortars, and anti-armor weapons.

The government responded to the changing strategic environment with a statement entitled "Defence Update 2003," released in February. The Update noted that, with globalization, Southeast Asia and the Southwest Pacific were more exposed to world events. It cited the increased reach of terrorism and evidence that militant extremists in the region were prepared to take up the al Qaeda cause. It pointed to cases of political weakness and governance issues within the region as posing major challenges, along with issues surrounding illegal people movement, organized crime, and illegal fishing. In this less certain environment, the Update called for increased emphasis on ensuring flexibility and adaptability to meet the unexpected as much as the expected.

In the changed circumstances after September 11, the Update saw the risk of conventional attack on Australian territory as having been reduced because of the stabilizing effect of U.S. primacy and determination. New priorities for the Australian Defense Force (ADF) derive from an increased threat of transnational terrorism and the spread of weapons of mass destruction, as well as a growing need to participate in coalition operations particularly with niche capabilities. Those priorities in turn underline the need for interoperability, readiness, and sustainability. Finally, the Update saw new pressures arising from the greater likelihood of involvement in operations other than war, and the growth of nonmilitary threats such as illegal immigration, illegal fishing, and drug smuggling.

Previously endorsed force structure plans have come under increasing pressure as the threat of terrorism loomed, along with the wars in Afghanistan and Iraq. There has been stronger advocacy from the military of more expeditionary forces able to assist the United States and any other likely coalition partners at distance from Australia. As well as increased infantry, this could involve reequipping the army with heavy tanks. Such a change in strategic priorities would involve large additional expenditure.

Moreover, the achievability of the commitments to long-term defense capabilities had in any case been open to question for some time (see, for example, *Asia Pacific Security Outlook 2002* and *2003*). Even if successive governments were to hold to the program over its full term, defense spending at the end of the ten-year period would still have been only a relatively modest 1.9 percent of Australia's gross domestic product.

The combined effect of such pressures obliged the government in December to announce a broader review at cabinet level. While the cabinet review endorsed the broad policy guidance contained in the Update and reaffirmed the policy of the white paper as "sound," it in essence provided for significant change from the pre-2003 plan. The review, which is to apply to the ten years to 2013, provides for:

- Army: The aging Leopard tanks are to be replaced, though no decision has been made as to type. The army will also acquire combat identification, more capable communications and increased night vision equipment, as well as armed reconnaissance helicopters.
- Navy: More advanced missiles (SM2) will be fitted to the guided missile frigates, and three air warfare destroyers will be acquired, but only from 2013. Two aging guided missile destroyers will be withdrawn. Two amphibious vessels of 20,000 tons or more, each capable of carrying five or six helicopters, will be acquired from 2010, as well as a third sealift ship of a type yet to be defined. The existing refueling ship will be replaced by a newer but smaller ship.
- Air Force: The existing F-111 bombers will be withdrawn from 2010, with upgraded F/A-18 Hornet fighters to take over their roles. This is a few years earlier than stated in the white paper. The F/A-18 will in turn be replaced by up to 100 Joint Strike Fighters.

Some observers have noted that some elements of strike capability are likely to be weakened for some years by these decisions, relative to the position set out in the white paper.

The review has been conducted on a "budget neutral" basis, so that no additional funding has been provided. Funding will be determined annually in the budget context. Thus there is no assurance that resource levels will be sufficient to ensure that the planned capabilities will be actually achieved within the time frames indicated.

THE DEFENSE BUDGET   Pressures on the defense budget have grown with the Iraq campaign and intervention in the Solomon Islands, coming on top of continuing commitments in East Timor.

The 2003–2004 defense budget provides A$15.8 billion (US$11.85 billion at A$1.00 = US$0.75), which represents an increase of A$1.2 billion (US$0.9 billion)—or 4.7 percent in real terms—over 2003–2004. This will rise over the next few years to the A$17 billion (US$12.75

billion) planned for 2006–2007. The defense budget represents some 1.9 percent of GDP in 2003–2004. If there were no increases to planned resource levels, that percentage would decline over the next ten years as strong economic growth is expected to continue.

Moreover, some A$642 million (US$481.5 million) of previously planned expenditure for equipment has been rescheduled, because of failure to meet deadlines. Similar slippage in each of the preceding two years has led to a backlog in the achievement of the approved program.

The main measures introduced in the 2003–2004 budget have been grouped in five blocs addressing broad objectives:

- A$1.1 billion (US$0.825 billion) over five years for increased logistics designed to correct some of the long-standing shortages and to help meet the preparedness needs of the new environment. It will benefit the F/A-18 fighter aircraft, C130-J Hercules transport aircraft, Collins-class submarines, and army vehicles;
- A$645 million (US$483.75 million) for operations in support of the rehabilitation of Iraq over three years. This is designed to cover the estimated cost of the conflict phase of operations in 2003, as well as the ongoing cost of defense contributions to reconstruction;
- A$157 million (US$117.75 million) over three years to establish a Special Operations Command and to add more than 330 additional Special Forces personnel;
- A$103 million (US$77.25 million) over three years to take advantage of favorable recruiting results in the army and the air force. This measure will bring forward the planned increase in the size of the ADF to 54,000, which should be achieved by the end of the decade. Navy numbers remain a concern, though measures to encourage retention are being implemented; and
- A$71 million (US$53.25 million) over two years to provide enhanced security for defense facilities and personnel around Australia.

CONTRIBUTIONS TO GLOBAL AND REGIONAL SECURITY

Australia contributed some 2,000 personnel to the war in Iraq, including Special Forces. Public controversy and doubts paralleled those in the United Kingdom, but with less political contention, largely because the combat phase was limited in duration, and there were no Australian casualties. Although no substantial combat units remain in Iraq and

Australia did not agree to be part of the occupying force, Australia continues to contribute specialist elements for stabilization and recovery operations, and consideration has been given to providing training for the new Iraqi armed forces. A total of some A$644 million (US$483 million) has been programmed for activities associated with Iraq over three years from 2003–2004 and some A$100 million (US$75 million) has been committed to humanitarian relief and reconstruction assistance to Iraq.

Long-standing concern over the proliferation of weapons of mass destruction (WMD) is reflected in Australia's participation in the U.S.-initiated Proliferation Security Initiative (PSI) designed to deter and inhibit the international transfer of such weapons. Australia hosted the first maritime exercise under PSI.

The campaign against terrorism is a major focus for cooperation within the region. While supporting the various regional measures adopted at meetings such as the recent Asia-Pacific Economic Cooperation (APEC) summit, the Howard government has given first priority to working bilaterally with neighbors to defeat terrorism in Southeast Asia. Australia has an extensive network of bilateral agreements to strengthen practical cooperation with key regional partners, including Cambodia, Fiji, India, Indonesia, Malaysia, the Philippines, and Thailand.

The Bali bombings made clear that the region was not immune from large-scale terrorist activity. And Afghanistan demonstrated that openings created by weak governance, or state failure, could lead eventually to major terrorist attacks. Australians are increasingly aware of these weaknesses in their own neighborhood.

The potential thus offered for exploitation by terrorists, and organized crime, has led Australia to urge concerted regional efforts to assist states in the Southwest Pacific facing these challenges. One of Australia's closest neighbors, the Solomon Islands, has particularly severe problems. A renewal of internal disorder there had led to the country being characterized by Australian officials as being on the verge of becoming a failed state. In response to a request from Allan Kemakeza, prime minister of the Solomon Islands, Australia and several other countries in the region arranged for a Regional Assistance Mission to the Solomon Islands (RAMSI) including police and some 1,500 military personnel drawn from those Southwest Pacific countries able to contribute. Military elements are to be withdrawn at an early stage, though substantial police effort will continue. Australia has established a Peace and Security Fund of A$7.5 million (US$5.625 million) to address needs in postconflict societies such as the Solomon Islands. The RAMSI operation has been supported by the United Nations.

Australia has also proposed to the Pacific Islands Forum establishing a regional police training facility, and that proposal is being developed.

Australia continues to provide substantial development assistance to Papua New Guinea (PNG), and in 2003–2004 that assistance amounts to A$336 million (US$252 million), directed toward long-term economic development, improved governance, and the alleviation of underlying causes of conflict and instability. However, in 2003 Australia placed a much stronger focus on effectiveness, with the clear implication that if assistance is to continue at this level, Australian personnel will need to be more directly involved in Papua New Guinea.

Specifically, the law and order problems are to be addressed with up to 200 Australian Federal Police sent to the main trouble spots to assist PNG police. Australian officials will also be involved in selected areas of the bureaucracy, for the purpose of monitoring expenditure with the aim of reducing corruption. After some political resistance, the PNG government accepted the new measures under which Australian personnel, including police, would work on assignment within the PNG government.

Australia's support for the Peace Monitoring Group on Bougainville, which has been playing a critical part in weapons disposal following the end of civil conflict there concluded at the end of 2003. Some A$10 million (US$7.5 million) was provided for this activity in 2003.

In East Timor, Australia continues to provide some 25 percent of the United Nations Mission of Support in East Timor (UNMISET), as well as development assistance of A$42.5 million (US$31.875 million) in 2003–2004. The police component will be drawn down to some extent during 2004.

5 Brunei Darussalam

The Security Environment

Brunei Darussalam observes its twentieth year as an independent state in 2004. In January 1984, it emerged as the smallest new state in Southeast Asia, promptly joining the Association of Southeast Asian Nations (ASEAN) and the Commonwealth, emphasizing its geographical and historical links. The last two decades of Brunei's political history have not seen any dramatic changes—political, economic, or social—and there are unlikely to be major changes in the near future. Brunei continues with its established monarchical system with an appointed cabinet and a judicial and administrative system, guided by the Malay Islamic philosophy. In terms of per capita income, Brunei still registers as one of the highest in Asia, though the debate continues as to how to reduce its dependence on oil and gas, the country's single industry.

International influences continue to have some impact on the political, economic, and social map of Brunei. There is a degree of relaxation in some aspects of the media, and rudiments of a civil society are appearing, though not in any organized manner. Sultan Haji Hassanal Bolkiah, as head of state and government, has been making frequent and unannounced visits to scrutinize the workings of certain government departments and statutory organizations. Some of those visited have drawn attention to inefficiencies and have produced criticism from the public carried in the media. In his 2004 New Year speech, the sultan admonished the public services for poor quality and called for immediate attention by the civil servants. Central to his concern is the understanding that a satisfied and prospering society is the best guard against disruption of peace and stability in the country. Thus the perception in

Brunei of threats to national security, whether from external sources or from domestic origins, is specifically focused on nontraditional issues.

Creeping poverty (despite high national incomes) and youth unemployment are the targets of both short- and long-term economic programs. The existing hydrocarbon industry is capital intensive and does not absorb many of the new entrants into the labor market. To avoid social unrest, new employment-creating industries have been under consideration for the last two years. Brunei's tourism industry continues to seek ways to contribute to national economic diversification. A revamped tourism authority was proposed under a master plan a few years back but awaits institutionalization. The Brunei Economic Development Board (BEDB) was established in November 2001 to spearhead industrial development. By 2008 it hopes to attract about US$4.5 billion in new investment and create at least 6,000 new jobs. BEDB has engaged foreign consultants and investors to study the feasibility of establishing downstream industries, smelter plants, and rubber-based industries, as well as shipping facilities, not just to boost the diversification ambitions but also to absorb local labor. If feasible, the first of these activities will commence in two selected locations during 2004. However, a study by another foreign group, while acknowledging Brunei's political and social stability as plus factors, has pointed to the slow government decision-making process and the poorly developed private sector as discouraging foreign investors. The study recommended policy reforms to encourage a culture of transparency and efficiency, and the sultan's recent speeches suggest that serious consideration is being given to changes in the administrative structure and processes.

Political and economic support for the government is seen as crucial for the continued peace and unity of the state. Thus every effort is made to ensure that discontent and demands are carefully addressed, whether they originate from the landless, the unemployed, or those complaining of poor public service. However, in its religious policies, the government is strict in insisting on adherence to the established interpretation according to the Ahli Sunnah Waljamaah (a branch of the Sunni school of Islamic thought), and does not hesitate to take stern action against deviations. A number of individuals have been arrested for reviving the teachings of the Malaysia-based radical Al Arqam group that had been banned in both countries in the early 1990s. In fact, it is not just differing schools of Islam but also the internationalization of political Islam that is of concern. Thus, in addition to providing guidance at the national level, the government also monitors students studying abroad who may fall prey to various conflicting influences. In February 2003, the Internal Security Department issued a statement insisting that the country was free from any extremist or terrorist activity despite a couple of hoax threat calls to the American Embassy. Foreign media reports have included Brunei in the Jemaah Islamiah's scheme for an Islamic state in Southeast Asia, but without specific credible evidence to date of activities in Brunei toward this end. There have also been occasional foreign travel advisories against travel to Brunei, but true to its name Brunei Darussalam continues to be an "abode of peace."

Aside from concern over Islamic radicalism and the terrorist threat, Brunei's immediate external security environment is generally benign. Brunei does have some issues with its closest neighbor, Malaysia, with which Brunei shares borders on all sides. These include the century-old claim over Limbang, unresolved land borders between the two countries, and overlapping claims in the Exclusive Economic Zone (EEZ) that have both sides competing over some lucrative oil drilling areas and Louisa Reef in the South China Sea where Malaysia has already marked its claim. While these appear to be significant issues, Brunei and Malaysia are managing them through bilateral negotiations, sometimes at the highest leadership level and sometimes at the joint commission level. This shows that both states acknowledge their strong ties and are thus able to negotiate amicably without resort to third parties. It is yet to be seen if the change in leadership in Malaysia will lead to any changes in the process of dispute management.

DEFENSE POLICIES AND ISSUES

Brunei does not foresee any sudden shift in external sources of conventional threat. Thus its defense policies will likely continue along the lines of recent years. There has been no further discussion of major new policy initiatives or of a white paper that was hinted at in 2002. Defense and military matters are not a subject of public discussion or media interest within Brunei, despite the fact that the military is the largest government employer after the civil service, with more than 5,000 personnel.

While Brunei's armed forces are still small in comparison with those of neighboring states, the government has continued to concentrate on quality rather than quantity in its armed forces. The government could expand the size of the armed forces if it desired, as the recent recruitment drive indicated: 530 youths registered for enlistment, but only 178 were selected. Force modernization, specialized training, and joint exercises with other states continue. In practice, a major focus of the armed forces is internal security. In January 2003, more than half the military personnel participated in a ten-day counterinsurgency exercise to assess the effectiveness of joint operations. Another large-scale exercise in October 2003 tested preparedness against terrorist activities and conventional warfare.

For Brunei, partnership with foreign countries is an ongoing effort to strengthen its defenses. Cooperation with traditional ASEAN partners—Indonesia, Malaysia, the Philippines, and Singapore—continues with frequent exchanges of ministerial and military visits and forces exercises. The sultan also takes a personal interest in foreign militaries, as indicated during visits in 2003 to Singapore and the Philippines. The United States Navy also conducted joint exercises with Brunei's armed forces. Other bilateral ties include those with Australia and France, and most importantly the United Kingdom. In talks between the sultan and Prime Minister Tony Blair in London in January 2003, they agreed to the continued stationing of the battalion of the British Brigade of Gurkhas in Brunei for another five years. In addition, the newly established Joint Commission for Defense Cooperation will hold regular discussions on other bilateral defense matters, including training and consultation on political and security matters. The commission includes members from the Ministry of Foreign Affairs and other agencies.

Noteworthy examples in 2003 of Brunei's expanding military relationships were visits of the Indian navy and the Japanese Maritime Self-Defense Force. Of greater significance for the future was the first naval visit by China and the signing of a Brunei-China Memorandum of Understanding on Military Exchanges. Brunei and China are also strengthening ties in other fields such as agriculture and education. China has long been a source for Brunei's imports, and oil exports to China will begin soon.

CONTRIBUTIONS TO REGIONAL AND GLOBAL SECURITY

The sultan had hoped that diplomacy would prevail and the war in Iraq could be averted, but his hopes were not realized. For its part, Brunei provides generous assistance to victims in Afghanistan, Iraq, and Palestine.

Brunei will continue to play a role appropriate to its size and status within the region. As a high-income country, it is able to host major international meetings and also to participate in a variety of forums and meetings elsewhere. Even semi-official gatherings such as the 2003 meeting of the Pacific Economic Cooperation Council (PECC) are treated with official protocol and often personally inaugurated by the sultan. This activity has helped Brunei build up friendly, generous, and open relationships with friends and visitors. Continuing diplomatic contacts and regular travel by the sultan and other ministers strengthen ties with external partners.

As a firm supporter of regional cooperation and ASEAN, Brunei has participated in all the collective activities, at summit or ministerial levels. In regional security and terrorism-related issues, Brunei has acceded to the Agreement on Information Exchange and Establishment of Communication Procedures. The agreement was initially introduced by some ASEAN members in an effort to coordinate and collaborate in common approaches to deal with terrorism, money laundering, smuggling, piracy, and other transnational crime. Brunei also exchanges information and intelligence on a bilateral basis with its friends. Another regional initiative, the ASEAN Committee on Disaster Management, held its first annual meeting in the country in 2003.

However, with terrorism and other nonconventional threats like drug trafficking, smuggling of contraband, illegal immigration, and the plundering of natural resources of increasing concern, Brunei's human resources are being stretched thin. A recent report of the United Nations monitoring committee which chided member states for not doing enough to curb terrorism and the spread of al Qaeda listed Brunei as one of 25 countries "of special concern" that have yet to file reports with the United Nations on antiterrorist measures.

6 Canada

Two thousand four will be a year of transition for Canadian domestic politics and Canadian foreign and security policy. Prime Minister Jean Chrétien retired in December 2003, ending his 13-year tenure in office. On December 12, a new government was sworn in headed by Prime Minister Paul Martin, a political rival of Chrétien in the ruling Liberal Party. Martin has initiated a major program review and is expected to call a general election early in the year. As a result, major security and defense policy initiatives and budget decisions are unlikely to be made before 2005.

The priority of the Martin government will be domestic reform and the restructuring of government, but in foreign affairs the emphasis will be placed on rebuilding the Canada-U.S. relationship. This relationship had been damaged by a number of disagreements between the Chrétien government and the U.S. administration of George W. Bush, especially the refusal of Canada to support the U.S.-led war in Iraq. While the United States will be the priority in Canada's foreign relations in 2004, the Martin government will also have to make a number of foreign and security policy decisions with respect to Iraq, Afghanistan, military spending, participation in missile defense, and the ongoing effort to enhance North American security against the threat of terrorism. In Asia Pacific, the new government is expected to emphasize enhancing trade and promoting regional stability.

INTERNAL   There are no immediate direct threats to Canada's domestic stability. Quebec nationalism and the attendant threat of Quebec separatism have not disappeared, but the national unity issue has been dormant for several years and is unlikely to resurface in the near future. However, tensions between aboriginal peoples and the federal government increased in 2003. Canada's aboriginal peoples have grown increasingly frustrated with the slow pace of land claims and self-government negotiations and with their continued political and economic marginalization in the country. A proposed First Nations Governance Act (intended to modernize the 127-year-old Indian Act) met opposition from aboriginal groups extremely sensitive to the imposition of rules from Ottawa. Acts of civil disobedience and violence are possible.

Terrorism will continue to be the Canadian government's primary internal security concern. In June 2003, Canada's solicitor-general identified Islamic extremist terrorism as Canada's most important security threat. Since the passage in 2002 of the Anti-terrorism Act, 26 organizations with operations in Canada have been identified as terrorist entities. There is growing official and public concern over the threat posed by chemical and biological weapons terrorism, as well as the threat posed to civilian airliners by man-portable surface-to-air missiles. In October 2003, the diversion of an El Al flight from Toronto's international airport was attributed to intelligence indicating a possible threat from a missile.

The United States has expressed dissatisfaction with Canadian antiterrorism policies. The U.S. Department of State's 2002 report on global terrorism praised Canada-U.S. cooperation on antiterrorism, but criticized Canada's antiterrorism budget and its restrictive privacy legislation. The ongoing counterterrorism effort has resulted in the implementation of new Canadian laws and new security measures agreed to in bilateral talks with the United States in 2001–2002. Many Canadian regulations on immigration, refugee controls, and visa policy continue to be "harmonized" with those of the United States, the political price Canada has paid to ensure the relatively unfettered flow of people and goods across the Canada-U.S. border.

Martin launched a major program review in late December 2003, aimed at restructuring government departments and finding resources to fund an ambitious agenda. But major budget decisions are not expected until after a general election, which could come as early as April 2004. There has been significant turnover in senior government posts, and Martin has created a new Department of Public Safety and Emergency Preparedness, consolidating the domestic security-related units of government into a single entity similar in concept to the U.S.

Department of Homeland Security. Other changes include a new cabinet committee on Global Affairs, permanent cabinet and parliamentary committees on Canada-U.S. relations, and a new position of national security advisor to the prime minister.

EXTERNAL   Martin is expected to inject a higher level of enthusiasm and energy into Canada's foreign and security policy. While he is unlikely to move Canada away from the general foreign policy orientation it has followed for decades, some changes will be immediately evident. The first foreign policy priority of the Martin government will be to repair Canada's frayed relationship with the United States. Martin does not share most of Chrétien's instinctive concerns about closer Canada-U.S. ties, and the tone of the relationship is expected to improve considerably. Martin has supported Canada's participation in the U.S. missile defense system. More broadly, Martin has expressed a desire to elevate Canada's international stature and to increase military spending and foreign aid. While he has stressed that multilateralism through the United Nations system will continue to be Canada's preference, he has left open the possibility that Canada might act in multilateral coalitions in the absence of UN authorization. This agenda will face two significant constraints. Limited financial resources and domestic program promises will make substantial investment in foreign and security policy activity impossible, while efforts to build closer ties to the United States must be balanced against the political need to maintain a healthy distinctiveness and independence from Washington.

The Martin government inherits growing popular concern with external threats to Canadian security. While Canada faces no direct military threat to its territory, Canadians continue to be concerned about economic volatility and political instability in the world. Regional conflicts overseas, concerns about the spread of weapons of mass destruction, terrorist incidents, environmental degradation, and the spread of infectious disease all contribute to a growing sense of vulnerability. This vulnerability was highlighted by two widely publicized public health incidents in 2003. The severe acute respiratory syndrome (SARS) virus spread to Canada in early March 2003, triggering widespread public alarm although death and infection rates remained relatively modest, with 37 deaths reported by the end of the outbreak in June 2003. The World Health Organization imposed a travel ban on Toronto that was lifted after a relatively short time, but the ban caused considerable damage to the Canadian economy: The SARS outbreak was expected to cost the Canadian economy Can$2.1 billion (US$1.62 billion at Can$1 = US$0.77) in 2003. Shortly after the SARS outbreak, in late May 2003, a single cow in Alberta was found to be infected with Bovine Spongiform Encephalopathy (BSE, or mad cow disease). This led to a national crisis in Canada's beef industry and import bans on Canadian beef sales to the United States and overseas markets.

The Canadian government's concern about the future of multilateralism and international institutions has intensified due to the political circumstances surrounding the U.S.-led war in Iraq. The war in Iraq was seen as another manifestation of the Bush administration's impatience with institutions and treaties, and was viewed by most Canadians as unnecessary, potentially dangerous, or counterproductive. The Chrétien government refused to participate without authorization of the UN Security Council of the war in Iraq, and Canadian foreign policy surrounding the Iraq crisis focused on an ultimately unsuccessful effort to bridge the acrimonious gap between the United States and its allies in the United Nations. This focus on the United Nations reflected Canadian public opinion: Prior to the outbreak of war, 83 percent of Canadians opposed any war against Iraq without a UN Security Council resolution, while nearly 60 percent supported Canadian participation in a war authorized by the United Nations. After the war began, 60 percent of Canadians were opposed to U.S. military action and 40 percent were in favor. However, three weeks into the war Canadians were evenly divided, with 48 percent opposed to U.S. military action and 48 percent supportive, as sentiments shifted amid increasing nervousness over the possible political and economic repercussions of a failure to support the United States. Canada has pledged Can$150 million (US$115.5 million) to the Iraqi reconstruction effort, but the Martin government is not expected to otherwise expand Canada's role in postwar Iraq.

The Canadian government generally regards the security environment in Asia as largely stable and not posing any serious threat to Canada's security interests. However, the Asian security environment is characterized by potential flashpoints that could destabilize the region with little warning. The government has observed the crisis over North Korea with growing concern, and remains concerned that the Taiwan Strait issue, separatism in Indonesia, and continued tensions between India and Pakistan could lead to crisis or violent conflict. Instability in Afghanistan is another area of concern, given the presence of Canadian troops in the International Security Assistance Force (ISAF) as well as the larger question of stability in Central Asia. Confidence in the safety of large parts of the Asia Pacific region as a destination for tourism, business travel, or investment has begun to recover slowly from the impact of the 2002 terrorist attack in Bali, but there are still worries that much of Asia is under siege from a wide variety of social problems stemming from poverty, environmental degradation, and political repression that can easily trigger political instability and social violence. Reflecting the continuing multilateralist orientation of Canadian policy, Canada remains disappointed with the slow pace of multilateral and institutional development in the region, and regards the current regional institutions (most notably the Asia-Pacific Economic Cooperation (APEC) forum and the ASEAN Regional Forum) as ill-suited to many of the political and security challenges facing the region.

DEFENSE POLICIES AND ISSUES

Canada's defense policy remains based on the 1994 White Paper on Defence, although a lengthy list of supplementary documents has been produced in the past decade. An internal defense policy update was completed in late 2002, but the contents were not made public. Although Martin has indicated a desire to rebuild the armed forces, the anticipated general election will mean that any defense policy review or major force structure and procurement decisions will not occur until 2005. Even after a review, major changes to Canada's defense outlook cannot be expected. Canadian security is seen as dependent on international peace and security, and Canadian defense policy has emphasized engagement in multilateral operations, preferably through established multilateral institutions such as the United Nations or the North Atlantic Treaty Organisation (NATO). Canadian military doctrine has focused on the maintenance of multipurpose, combat-capable maritime, land, and air forces. The Canadian military has emphasized the ability to deploy and sustain expeditionary operations with forces that are interoperable with Canada's allies, especially the United States.

Canada's military has faced a serious funding shortfall relative to the demands placed upon it, and this shortfall has precipitated a crisis in the Canadian Forces. Although there were moderate increases to the defense budget in 2002 and 2003, bringing the defense budget to US$9.4 billion, or 1.1 percent of gross national product, the military faces multiple challenges. Many major weapons systems are rapidly aging and require replacement or major upgrades, including combat aircraft, maritime helicopters, fleet replenishment vessels, and transport aircraft. The size of the Canadian Forces has declined by 30 percent in a decade, and active regular force strength is now down to 52,950. The military continues to face considerable retention and recruitment problems, and is short of specialists in most military occupations.

Canada's army is now only 19,300 strong and can muster only 10,000 deployable soldiers. The army has announced a 10-year restructuring plan, which will emphasize light infantry capabilities, and the army is unlikely to replace its aging tanks and will instead move toward an all-wheeled force. The air force has seen the number of aircraft in its inventory fall to 350 from 725 in 1991, and this number could drop to 290 aircraft by 2006. Canada's navy has insufficient resources to staff all of its ships and announced a "pause" in June 2003, hoping to avoid foreign deployments for a year as a rest from its operational tempo of the past two years. A new emphasis on "transformation" will also create impetus for change in all three services, but resource constraints will continue to define the force structure and operational capacities of the Canadian Forces. While it is generally expected that defense spending will increase under a Martin government, the scope of that increase is uncertain given the fiscal constraints and competing commitments the new government will face.

CONTRIBUTIONS TO REGIONAL AND GLOBAL SECURITY

Since 2001, the primary regional focus of Canadian security has been North America, and this is expected to continue under the Martin government. Canada has embarked on a number of initiatives, including many in collaboration with the United States, to enhance the security of North America from terrorism and other "asymmetric threats." These initiatives include new immigration and refugee laws, a new permanent resident card for recent immigrants, the creation of a Canadian Air Transport Security Authority responsible for airline security, technology enhancements and improved staffing at border crossings, improved security for shipping and maritime containers, and a wide variety of border agreements and information-sharing arrangements. While these measures will increase Canada's security, pressure from the United States and the possibility of tightened U.S. controls on the border are the major factors behind Canada's actions. Any interruption of cross-border traffic and trade would cripple Canada's economy. While domestic critics have charged that many of the new measures compromise Canadian sovereignty, there is considerable public support for these measures.

September 11 has also raised the profile of Canada-U.S. defense cooperation in North America. Canadian territory is now more relevant to U.S. security than at any time since the early cold war period. The Canada-U.S. defense relationship is embodied in more than 80 defense treaties or agreements, and another 250 memoranda of understanding between the Canadian Department of National Defense (DND) and the U.S. Department of Defense. The North American Aerospace Defense Command (NORAD) is the cornerstone of this security relationship, and continues to provide air defense, ballistic missile early warning, valuable intelligence-gathering functions, and (after September 11) domestic airspace surveillance. In May 2003, the Canadian government announced it would open negotiations with Washington to join the U.S. missile defense program, reversing several years of reluctance to participate in this controversial program. Canada still has no plans to integrate with the new U.S. Northern Command (USNORTHCOM) announced in April 2002. However, Canada has agreed to participate in a binational planning group established to coordinate Canadian and U.S. land forces in the event of a terrorist attack in North America.

Canada's major external military engagement in Asia is now in Afghanistan. In February 2003, the government announced it would contribute 1,900 Canadian military personnel to the ISAF in Afghanistan and would maintain that commitment until February 2004. Canada had deployed Canadian troops to Afghanistan in 2002 in cooperation with U.S. and allied forces fighting Taliban and al Qaeda forces. The decision to send Canadian forces to Afghanistan was controversial, as it places very heavy demands on the already overstretched and underfunded Canadian Forces, and places Canadian soldiers in an uncertain and unstable environment. In October 2003, two Canadian soldiers were killed when their vehicle struck a land mine. The decision to deploy Canadian troops to Afghanistan was widely interpreted as an effort to compensate for the government's unwillingness to participate in the Iraq war. The ongoing commitment to Afghanistan, and the high rate of deployment demanded of Canada's shrinking military, means that Canada is unlikely to have significant military forces available for commitment to a conflict or peacekeeping contingency elsewhere in the Pacific at least through the first half of 2004.

The Canadian government has observed the crisis over North Korea with growing concern. The Chrétien government strongly condemned North Korea's withdrawal from the Nonproliferation Treaty (NPT), calling on Pyongyang to abandon its nuclear program and comply with the NPT. Canada maintains diplomatic relations with North Korea (established in February 2001). Despite building high-level connections in Pyongyang through humanitarian assistance, the government has no plans to become directly involved in the current standoff. However, the government has made clear to North Korea that relations cannot continue as planned, and several diplomatic visits have been cancelled. The government believes that the best route to diffusing the crisis is direct dialogue between Pyongyang and Washington, with assistance from China, Russia, and Japan.

In the Asia Pacific region more broadly, Canada engages in political and security dialogues and contributes to human security and peace-building efforts. Ongoing security assistance activities in the region include funds for peace-building efforts in Sri Lanka focused on poverty alleviation and skill development, mine-risk education efforts in Cambodia, assistance to East Timor with governance, land conflict resolution and demobilization, and reconstruction and peace-building support in Afghanistan. A special emphasis has been placed on strengthening the relationships with China and India, with exchanges of visits and dialogue on security issues as well as efforts to increase trade ties (and, in the case of India, development assistance). While Canada remains supportive of APEC and approves of the political and security dialogues that have taken place at recent meetings, APEC is regarded as unlikely to achieve further significant reductions in barriers to trade in the region in the near term. As a result, Canada is now looking more to bilateral trade arrangements to build economic ties in the region, and this focus is expected to continue under the Martin government.

At the global level, Canadian foreign and security policies actively pursue multilateral diplomacy and the development of international institutions to maintain international peace and security. International stability is regarded as largely indivisible from Canadian security, given Canada's dependence on trade and the reality that major conflagrations in the international system could threaten Canada directly. Canadian diplomacy has attempted to develop a voice for Canada in world affairs, to establish "counterweights" to the United States, and to influence collective decision-making in ways beneficial to Canada. Canada contributes to global security through engagement at the United Nations and contributions to UN peacekeeping and peace-building operations around the world. Canada assumed the presidency of the Multi-national Standby Force High Readiness Brigade for UN Operations (SHIRBRIG) in January 2003. In Europe, while membership in NATO remains a cornerstone of Canadian foreign and defense policy, it is expected that Canada will reduce its commitment of troops to the NATO-led Stabilization Force in Bosnia in early 2004, and will likely withdraw its commitment to Bosnia entirely by late 2004.

Although the profile of the "human security" agenda in Ottawa has declined, Canada still contributes to development and human security initiatives around the world. Canada was chosen as the chair of the Human Security Network for 2004–2005, and the government announced it would provide substantial funds to support the International Criminal Court campaign and the follow up to the "Responsibility to Protect" report. Nevertheless, ongoing concerns over continental security, a focus on Canada-U.S. relations, an overstretched military, and the paucity of development/peace-building resources suggest that Canada's profile in security affairs will be restricted largely to a continental focus and engagement in only a few major contingencies and issue areas abroad in 2004.

7 China

THE SECURITY ENVIRONMENT

INTERNAL   China's domestic security outlook for 2004 is basically
positive in terms of the economy and politics, but as demonstrated in
2003 there can be sudden, jarring challenges. The outbreak of severe
acute respiratory syndrome (SARS) in China in 2003 was a serious public health, social, economic, and national security crisis, and a great
challenge to the new leadership. More than 600 people died of SARS,
and economic growth in the second quarter of the year was the lowest
since 1996. SARS was a nontraditional security crisis, demonstrating
how real and serious is the challenge of nontraditional security problems today. The 2003 epidemic ended in June in China and in July in
the world, but it may not have disappeared forever, as indicated by iso-
lated cases identified around the Asia Pacific region at the end of 2003
and in the first days of 2004. However, as elsewhere in the region, the
Chinese people and government are better prepared now than before
to deal with a recurrence of SARS or similar public health threats.

SARS slowed China's economic growth rate for a time, but did not
change the overall picture of economic development in China. The
economy grew at 9.1 percent in 2003, the fastest growth rate since 1997
and higher than the 7 percent target set by the government. The total
gross domestic product has reached US$1.4 trillion, and per capita GDP
is US$1,090 (based on the current exchange rate). In fact, many econo-
mists argue that China has entered another boom period, and the Chinese government actually worries that the economy is growing too
fast, which would cause new problems. The government therefore has
taken some steps to cool down the heated economy, but with little

noticeable effect to date. Many experts in and outside China expect that the economic growth rate will continue at above 9 percent in 2004, if not beyond.

Politically, the leadership transition has been stable and smooth. The new leadership continues to emphasize the "Three Represents"—expanding the Chinese Communist Party's (CCP's) representation beyond the working class—as the party's guiding principle. This indicates internal political stability and continuity in leadership consensus, and is an interesting long-term trend toward broadening the base of the party in the changing circumstances in China.

The new leadership under President Hu Jintao appears able and effective. The leadership has already taken a number of initiatives in economic development, political reform, governance, media policy, and foreign relations. A new governing style is apparent, if not yet major new theories, policies, or systems. The CCP Central Committee session in September 2003 recommended that the National People's Congress change some provisions of the country's constitution at its meeting in March 2004. Therefore, a process of moderate economic, political, and legal systemic reform is under way in China.

Cross-Taiwan Strait relations remain cool and at a standstill on the political front, while warmer in economic areas. Pro-independence remarks by Taiwan's leader in the context of the ongoing Taiwan election campaign have deepened the political deadlock between the two sides. The mainland side, however, has maintained a firm but low-profile position in response to these statements. Meanwhile, economic and social ties between the two sides continue to strengthen. For example, a number of Taiwanese airline charter planes flew to Shanghai in January 2003, via a stopover in Hong Kong, becoming the first airliners from Taiwan to arrive on the mainland since 1949; direct transportation links now look inevitable in the not-too-distant future. Trade volume across the Taiwan Strait reached US$58.37 billion in 2003, up 31 percent from the previous year, and Taiwanese business invested US$8.56 billion on the mainland during the year.

EXTERNAL   The Chinese government's initial handling of the SARS outbreak caused concern and criticism from the international community, but the overall international environment remains basically positive for China.

China's relations with neighboring countries are improving. Economic ties are becoming stronger. Bilateral trade with Japan, the

Republic of Korea, and Southeast Asian nations is growing at a rapid rate. According to Chinese statistics, bilateral trade between China and Japan has reached US$100 billion annually, and the growth rate remains high. Trade with South Korea has reached US$30 billion and China has become South Korea's largest trade partner. China's trade with the member countries of the Association of Southeast Asian Nations (ASEAN) has been growing at more than 40 percent, and the Chinese government has set a target of US$100 billion by the year 2005. During a visit to China by Indian Prime Minister Atal Bihari Vajpayee in September, China and India agreed on the goal of increasing bilateral trade to US$10 billion annually by 2005. At the same time, China is continuing its security dialogue with Japan, South Korea, the ASEAN countries, and India.

China and the ASEAN countries developed new practical cooperation in dealing with the SARS crisis. Government leaders and public health ministers of China and ASEAN met in April 2003 and discussed cooperation on SARS and other cross-border issues. They reached agreement to work toward common predeparture health screening procedures for travelers, including a ministerial-level task force on the issue. They also established a fund for China-ASEAN programs to control SARS.

China's relations with major powers remain stable and appear to be constructive and positive. China's relations with the United States have been smooth since the end of the EP-3 incident in June 2001, and the two countries are actively cooperating on counterterrorism, regional security issues such as the Korean nuclear crisis, international security issues such as Iraq, and at the United Nations. The governments of the two countries look satisfied with how relations are developing. U.S. Secretary of Sate Colin Powell stated that U.S.-Chinese relations are at the best level in 30 years, since President Richard Nixon's visit to China in 1972. Chinese leaders also regard Sino-U.S. relations as having reached a period of "stability and development." However, fundamental differences between China and the United States have not disappeared. The two countries still have serious problems and potential conflicts over Taiwan, human rights, nonproliferation, trade, and the future role of China as a power in Asia and the world. Conceptions in the United States of a "China threat" and mutual strategic suspicions are still fundamental and long-term issues between the two countries.

As China's economy continues to develop, competition between the Chinese economy and other developed and developing economies is spreading. Pressure and demands from the United States, Japan, and Europe over the value of the Chinese currency is just the latest example of economic competition and friction between China and other countries.

China's relations with Russia remain politically strong but economically weak. The two countries engage fairly intensively at the leadership and governmental levels, with regular high-level visits and meetings. Their consultation and cooperation on international issues takes place within the framework of a "consultative strategic partnership." However, the two countries have been slow in strengthening their economic ties. For example, a pipeline project and cooperation on energy between the two countries have met with frustrations and their future is uncertain.

Sino-Japanese relations are still troubled by issues connected with history. Specific incidents in 2003 included the discovery in August of abandoned Japanese chemical weapons from World War II, which killed one person and sickened 42 others in the city of Qiqihar in northeast China, and the misbehavior of Japanese tourists to China. Public opinion in the two societies toward each other continues to be negative, even as economic ties are strengthening. This is a challenge to the two governments now and into the future.

China's relations with India enjoyed significant improvement in 2003, especially through the visit of Vajpayee to China in June. A Declaration on Principles for Relations and Comprehensive Cooperation signed during the visit states that neither side will use or threaten to use force against the other, and that the two governments are ready to seek a fair, responsible, and mutually acceptable solution on the border issue. Pending an ultimate solution to be reached through new high-level talks, they pledged to work together to maintain peace in the border areas and to implement existing agreements including the clarification of the Line of Actual Control.

DEFENSE POLICIES AND ISSUES

The new leadership in China has slowed the growth of defense spending. Defense expenditure in 2003 was 185.3 billion yuan (US$22.24 billion at 1 yuan = US$0.12), an increase of 9.6 percent over the previous year. This rate of increase is much smaller than the double-digit annual growth of defense spending in recent years.

The new leadership is continuing with China's defense modernization, however. President Hu has called for rapid progress in national defense and military modernization, in light of the country's economic development and scientific advancement. Hu argues that a reliable national defense capability is needed for China to ensure its reform, opening up, and modernization in a complicated and changing international situation.

The Chinese armed forces conducted a number of counterterrorism exercises in 2003. This demonstrated the increasing involvement of the Chinese military in nontraditional security areas.

PERSONNEL REDUCTION The Chinese government announced in October 2003 that another 200,000 troops would be cut from China's armed forces by 2005, reducing the overall number to 2.3 million. This follows a previous reduction of 500,000 personnel from 1996 to 2000. The decision was explained as not only in accordance with world military trends, but also out of necessity for China's economic construction. Jiang Zemin, chairman of the Central Military Commission, stated that further reducing the scale of the army will help China concentrate its limited resources on priority objectives, particularly increasing the army's information technology capability.

SPACE PROGRAM In October 2003, China launched its first manned spacecraft into orbit. A Long March II-F rocket carried a Shenzhou-V spacecraft and China's first astronaut into space, circling the earth 14 times in 22 hours and 18 minutes, and landing at a selected zone in Inner Mongolia. This makes China the third nation to conduct a manned space flight, after the former Soviet Union and the United States. China plans to continue its space program and to launch more manned spacecrafts in the future.

Also in 2003, however, in a major military tragedy, a conventional navy submarine sank due to mechanical failure, with the loss of all 70 officers and soldiers on board. This major incident was seen as demonstrating that China still has a long way to go to modernize its military hardware and management.

HONG KONG SECURITY LEGISLATION Efforts in 2003 by the government of the Hong Kong Special Administrative Region to pass the National Security Bill met serious resistance. On July 1, approximately 500,000 people in Hong Kong demonstrated against the bill.

In response, the Hong Kong government decided to defer the resumption of the second reading of the bill, and the government made substantial changes to three controversial areas. However, the central government in Beijing and the Hong Kong government under Chief Executive Tung Chee Hwa see the passing of the bill as necessary to implement the Basic Law of the Hong Kong Administrative Region of the People's Republic of China and prevent Hong Kong from being used as a place from which China's national security can be threatened. While the governments in Beijing and Hong Kong have now withdrawn the security legislation, they have not given it up, and the bill's future is uncertain.

In contrast to previous years, China has said little recently about missile defense. However, when Japan announced in December 2003 its intention to deploy a missile defense system in the near future, the Chinese foreign ministry spokesman warned Japan not to follow a road that would cause concern to other Asian countries.

CONTRIBUTIONS TO REGIONAL AND GLOBAL SECURITY

REGIONAL   *Central and South Asia.* The Shanghai Cooperation Organization (SCO) is the major institution that China has promoted for pursuing national and subregional security interests in China's west and in Central Asia. The major theme of the organization is cooperation against the "three evil forces" of terrorism, separatism, and religious extremism. In 2003, the SCO concluded its first multilateral joint military exercise against terrorism in Kazakhstan and China. In recent SCO meetings, the six member governments have talked more about economic cooperation, and the organization is expected to expand its areas of cooperation.

China also held a joint military exercise with Pakistan in 2003. Naval warships of the two countries carried out a search-and-rescue operation in the East China Sea in October, the first time Chinese naval forces had conducted joint military exercises with a foreign counterpart in a nontraditional security field.

Korea and Northeast Asia. The Chinese government has made strenuous efforts to bring the Democratic People's Republic of Korea, the United States, and other parties together to resolve the Korean nuclear issue peacefully. China sees maintaining stability and a nuclear-free Korean peninsula as being in both its own national interest and the

interests of other countries in the region and the world. Chinese officials have shuttled between Pyongyang and Washington, and Chinese
leaders have talked extensively with leaders of the United States, North
Korea, and other countries over the issue. China hosted the trilateral
talks (North Korea, the United States, and China) in Beijing in late April
2003, and the first Six-Party Talks (North Korea, the United States,
China, South Korea, Japan, and Russia) in August. China is now working to keep the six-party process going.

China has also been active in promoting subregional cooperation in
security and other fields in Northeast Asia. China, Japan, and South
Korea signed a Joint Declaration on the Promotion of Tripartite Cooperation at a meeting on the margins of the ASEAN + 3 (the above
three Northeast Asian countries) meeting in Bali in October 2003. The
three Northeast Asian governments have agreed to set up a trilateral
committee to coordinate and plan the cooperation among the three
parties and to study the possibility of establishing a free trade area
(FTA) among the three countries. The three governments also agreed
to strengthen dialogue on security issues, including countering the proliferation of weapons of mass destruction and their means of delivery.

ASEAN and Southeast Asia. In October 2003, China formally acceded to the Treaty of Amity and Cooperation (TAC) in Southeast Asia
of ASEAN, demonstrating the strengthening of political trust between
China and the Southeast Asian nations. The Chinese government says
it is ready to work closely with ASEAN to speed up negotiations and
complete the FTA between China and ASEAN countries as scheduled
by 2010. Chinese Premier Wen Jiabao in October also called for joint
efforts to break the US$100 billion trade mark by 2005. He affirmed
that China intends to implement the joint declaration on teamwork in
nontraditional security issues as well as the Declaration on the Conduct of Parties in the South China Sea signed in 2002.

At the Bali ASEAN + 3 meeting, Wen put forward a four-point proposal for regional cooperation and partnership. The four points include
(1) studying the feasibility of an East Asia Free Trade Area; (2) phasing
in multilateral currency swap arrangements and gradually implementing the ASEAN + 3 consensus on setting up an Asian bond market, then
enhancing the investment capabilities of East Asian countries; (3) promoting dialogue on regional security and cooperation in nontraditional
security areas; and (4) establishing an ASEAN + 3 public health mechanism based on the experience of countering SARS.

The Chinese government has also decided to increase the resources put into the development of the Mekong Basin under the Greater Mekong Subregion (GMS) Economic Cooperation Program initiated by the Asian Development Bank (ADB) in 1992. The six nations of Cambodia, China, Laos, Myanmar, Thailand, and Vietnam participate in this program. China has played an active role in GMS projects such as the Kunming-Bangkok road project and human resources development. Early in 2004, China will commence construction of the Laotian section of the Kunming-Bangkok Highway, providing 50 million yuan (US$6 million) in assistance and 199 million yuan (US$24 million) in interest-free loans. China is also financing a feasibility study of the missing link of the Trans-Asian Railway inside Cambodia.

GLOBAL   *Iraq.* China sent personnel to join the United Nations weapons inspection team before the Iraq war, and a Chinese chemical expert was killed in a road accident south of Baghdad in March. China neither supports nor opposes the U.S./U.K. military action in Iraq, but China supports the resolution proposed by the United States to help Iraq realize security and stability after the war and to return sovereignty to Iraq's people as quickly as possible. China also supports the United Nations playing a larger role in peace, stability, and rebuilding in Iraq. A Chinese delegation participated in the international conference on rebuilding Iraq in Spain in October and committed US$25 million in humanitarian aid. The Chinese government also hopes that Chinese companies will be able to play a role in Iraq's rebuilding.

Iran. The Chinese government supports the efforts of the International Atomic Energy Agency (IAEA) to enhance the additional protocol to the nuclear Nonproliferation Treaty (NPT). The government believes that the Iranian nuclear issue should be handled in a pragmatic and prudent manner, and that an additional protocol with Iran would be an important contribution to improving the efficiency of the international safeguards system.

International Peacekeeping. During April–December 2003, China put a 175-member engineering brigade and a 43-member medical team on 24-hour call for the United Nations Organization Mission in the Democratic Republic of the Congo (MONUC); a second team of 218 soldiers is now in Congo. Since 1990, China has taken part in more than ten UN peacekeeping operations, sending more than 650 military observers, liaison officers, advisers, or staff officers and 800 engineering officers and soldiers. In 2003, China also supported the United Nations sending troops into Liberia to stop the fighting and chaos there. In recent years, China has become generally more positive toward UN peacekeeping, and it is likely that the country will be involved still more actively in future missions.

8 European Union

THE SECURITY ENVIRONMENT

In the future, 2003 may well be viewed as a watershed year for the security outlook of the European Union (EU). The year was marked by a crisis in Europe's primary security relationship with the United States —as well as a deep split in the Union itself—over the Iraq conflict. In addition, and partially as a response to the Iraq conflict, Europe's security perimeter was extended well beyond its own periphery, and the Union has taken several steps to further develop its Common Foreign and Security Policy (CFSP) and its European Security and Defense Policy (ESDP). While these developments indicate the Union's willingness and ability to learn from crises and to adapt to change in the international environment, a longstanding and significant "expectations-capabilities gap" remains in the Union's foreign and security policy.

In 2003, the Union launched its first independent military operations. Operation Concordia in Macedonia is being followed in 2004 by a Police Mission "Proxima," and in Operation Artemis in the Democratic Republic of Congo 11 EU-member states and five non-EU countries together sent 1,400 soldiers to stabilize the security conditions and improve the humanitarian situation in the provincial capital of Bunia. In addition, the Netherlands, then chairing the Organization for Security and Co-operation in Europe (OSCE), called on the European Union to provide military security assistance to Moldova to prevent the outbreak of violence between conflicting Moldovan and Transniestrian parties while the OSCE pushes for political settlement.

EU member states are also engaged militarily beyond Europe and its periphery (which now also includes Africa), but since this engagement takes place within the North Atlantic Treaty Organisation (NATO), it is conducted in closest military and political cooperation with the United States. In early 2003, Germany and the Netherlands took over the lead of the International Security Assistance Force (ISAF) in Afghanistan. In August, the Alliance itself took over the ISAF mission, thereby extending its operational scope beyond the traditional "transatlantic area." This clearly marks a major change in Europe's security outlook, as many European NATO states had resisted earlier U.S. initiatives to "globalize NATO." In the aftermath of the split over Iraq, NATO in 2003 provided logistical support for the Polish contingent in Iraq. European NATO members, including France and Germany, have voiced support for a limited military role of the Alliance in the Iraqi stabilization effort in 2004.

It is too early, however, to conclude that the Union's "European security perimeter" has been scrapped for good. First, the German-Dutch initiative and the NATO decision to take the leading role in ISAF must be viewed in the context of the deep transatlantic divisions over the U.S.-led intervention in Iraq. Through ISAF, "old European nations," especially Germany, tried to repair their relationship with the United States. Second, with Western European defense budgets still shrinking and ten new members (eight Eastern European states plus Cyprus and Malta) joining the Union in May 2004, Europe still seems ill prepared to take on a much larger role as a "hard security provider" in international conflicts. Third but most important, in December 2003 the Union adopted its first-ever strategic policy document, the European Security Strategy (ESS). While the ESS acknowledges new security challenges such as international terrorism and the proliferation of weapons of mass destruction (WMD), it stresses that preventive multilateral diplomatic action should always have priority and that the use of force is the last resort and then should have a UN mandate.

Hence, Europe's global role as a security provider is still limited both geographically and functionally. For the Union, the Asia Pacific region continues to be a secondary security concern. Nevertheless, several of the region's conflicts have gained prominence in European security considerations. First, the conflict in the UN Security Council over the U.S.-led intervention in Iraq and the escalation of the conflict over North Korea's aspirations to acquire nuclear weapons demonstrated that Asian nations, and China in particular, play a pivotal role in addressing conflicts in multilateral forums. Secondly, as reflected in the ESS's treatment of international terrorism and the proliferation of WMD, the Union and its member states attach most importance and resources to stabilizing the security situation in the Asia Pacific region in order to prevent these risks from spreading to other regions. This does not necessarily include active engagement in conflict prevention or management, although European nations now have taken up a major (and probably long-term) commitment in Afghanistan.

Further, in the campaign against international terrorism, European authorities are actively cooperating and assisting Southeast Asian nations, in particular Indonesia. In the nonproliferation area, several European nations have joined the United States in its Proliferation Security Initiative (PSI) to counter shipments of WMD, delivery systems, and related materials. Thus, as Asian security concerns such as terrorism and WMD proliferation have a direct impact on security in Europe and its neighboring regions, Europe's engagement is bound to develop, albeit relatively slowly due to the Union's obvious deficits in terms of hard-power projection capacities in the foreseeable future.

While security issues have gained more prominence in Asian-European relations, Europe's economic involvement in the region continues to deepen. In 2003, this was reflected by the European Union's strengthened presence (the opening of permanent offices in Taiwan, Singapore, and Cambodia) and by a sustained growth of economic transactions between the regions. Trade with China increased 8.7 percent in 2002, while transatlantic trade decreased 5.2 percent. (By contrast, trade with Japan fell 9.3 percent.) Overall trade between China and the European Union almost doubled between 1998 and 2002, from US$48.9 billion to US$86.8 billion. Similarly, the European Union has become the second largest export market for the members of the Association of Southeast Asian Nations (ASEAN) (16 percent of exports) behind only the United States, and after EU enlargement the ASEAN nations will be the third biggest overall trading partner. Reflecting these growing involvements, the European Commission issued two major policy papers in 2003 exploring ways to strengthen the political, economic, and sectoral dialogue with the Asia Pacific partners. Similarly, at their fifth meeting in Dalian economic ministers from the Asia-Europe Meeting (ASEM) partners highlighted the importance of various collaborative mechanisms including the Trade Facilitation Action Plan (TFAP).

Looking to the future, it appears that European nations will continue to address security concerns at home or in the near abroad as their first security priorities. The stabilization and transformation of the former Yugoslavia into a zone of peace remains a major challenge.

In addition, in the aftermath of the Iraq intervention, the security situation in the Middle East has deteriorated considerably so that a major European commitment in that area cannot be ruled out. However, as security threats diversify and globalize and as the United States is pressing European nations to take up a bigger burden on a global scale, most immediately in Iraq, Europe's global engagement is bound to grow.

DEFENSE POLICIES AND ISSUES

In 2003, the European Union took two steps forward and one step back to deepen and widen its role as a responsible actor in international politics. First, in June the European Convention on the future of the Union (set up by the Council of the European Union at the end of 2001 to propose changes in the Union's structure) presented a draft constitution, which is being discussed by member state governments during an intergovernmental conference that was intended to be concluded in December but will continue under the Irish EU Presidency in the first half of 2004.

Reflecting both integration and division in European security affairs, the Convention's draft proposal (formally presented at the EU-Western Balkans Summit of Thessaloniki) seeks to encourage convergence and mutual solidarity, while recognizing that further integration will have to rely on actions undertaken by a coalition of the willing. The main institutional instrument to strengthen cohesion is the proposal to establish the position of EU foreign minister, which brings together the functions of the High Representative of Common Foreign and Security Policy (currently Javier Solana) and the Commissioner in charge of External Relations (currently Chris Patten). The minister would be granted new powers, such as the right of initiative in the field of CFSP, negotiating CFSP agreements as well as representing the European Union in international organizations. Overall, however, the intergovernmental character of CFSP and the much younger ESDP remains largely unchanged: Unanimity will still be the general rule and even where qualified majority voting (QMV) is applied to implement a Council decision, member states still retain the right to veto these implementing decisions "for important and stated reasons of national interest." The European Parliament's competences (oversight, control, budget) in CFSP and ESDP matters also remain weak, ESDP decisions still requiring consultation only by the Council. In the defense area, the

Convention's proposal foresees the introduction of a "solidarity clause" (instead of a collective defense commitment). This arrangement ensures that the Union can mobilize its resources against terrorist threats and assist members that have been attacked, while it also provides for member states that want to enter into more binding commitments (so-called structured cooperation) or want to reserve this function for NATO.

Secondly, in the ESS, the Union addresses new global security threats, especially the key U.S. concerns of WMD proliferation and international terrorism. The ESS stresses two key objectives: extending the zone of security on Europe's periphery, and supporting the emergence of a stable and equitable international order as well as an effective multilateral system. It also acknowledges frankly the Union's lack of military capability as a major weakness in the EU crisis portfolio. Thus, the strategy promotes a preventive, diplomatic approach emphasizing the spread of good governance, dealing with corruption and abuse of power, and establishing the rule of law as the preferred means of strengthening both domestic and international order.

As previously noted, in 2003 the Union launched for the first time an autonomous military operation (under French leadership), the interim emergency multinational force, to stabilize the situation in Bunia, Democratic Republic of Congo. As the U.S.-led intervention in Iraq reverberated in the Middle East and around the globe, the deep divisions within the Union on Iraq made clear that a unified common foreign, security, and defense policy is still far away. The Union's split over Iraq, however, did not lead to a total halt of further integration in the security realm, nor did it push member states to unite and balance against the United States. Rather, member states and the Union as a whole tried to accommodate and to further integrate the United States while pushing for more autonomous European capabilities in a few very specific areas. In both the new security strategy and the draft EU strategy against weapons of mass destruction (December 2003), the Union tried to bring its security concerns into line with recent U.S. strategic documents. At the same time, these EU documents and member states' policies stress the necessity to give priority to preventive diplomatic instruments and the United Nations as a decision-making body, a commitment underlined by the recent mission of the foreign ministers of France, the United Kingdom, and Germany to solve the conflict over the Iranian nuclear program.

After the Iraq war that began in March 2003, heads of state and government of Belgium, France, Luxembourg, and Germany met in April in Brussels for a "defense mini summit," putting forward a host of initiatives: a European Defense College (to develop and spread a European security culture), a European rapid reaction capability, a European command for strategic air transport, but most divisively a European military headquarters for planning and conducting EU military operations. Strong criticism by the United Kingdom, the United States, and other Atlanticist nations led to the shelving of the proposal for a EU headquarters separate and autonomous from NATO; but subsequently the U.K. government shifted its position on "structured cooperation" in the EU constitution (September 2003), which may well lead to some kind of, if circumscribed, European military planning and operation capacity in the future.

Developments in EU member state security policies reflect these broader trends. In May 2003, German Defense Minister Peter Struck presented the Defense Policy Guidelines that addresses new security challenges by redirecting the Bundeswehr's operational spectrum away from territorial defense at home toward crisis prevention and management abroad. While the current German government still clings to the concept of a conscript army, force planning and acquisition are now clearly focused on operational skills such as strategic airlift and reconnaissance. In the same vein, the French government is reviewing its nuclear posture with specific focus on "states of concern" and the proliferation of WMD.

As a consequence, Europe's security role in East Asia will continue to be confined and heavily influenced by developments in transatlantic affairs.

DEFENSE BUDGETS   As expected, real European defense budgets declined further in 2003 (see table 1). Fiscal deficits in France and Germany

Table 1. Defense Expenditures in the European Union (US$ billion)

Country	2002 Defense Expenditure	% of GDP (2002)	2002 Defense Budget	2003 Defense Budget
France	40.2	2.5	30.7	34.9
United Kingdom	37.3	2.3	36.6	41.3
Germany	33.3	1.5	25.1	27.4
Italy	25.6	2.0	20.2	22.3
Spain	8.7	1.2	7.8	8.5
Netherlands	7.7	1.6	6.5	6.4

SOURCE: International Institute for Strategic Studies, The Military Balance, 2003/2004.

again exceeded the limits of the European Union's Stability and Growth Pact, which already had been watered down considerably. In addition, slow economic growth in 2003 and cautious forecasts for 2004 (1.8 percent for the European Union as a whole) indicate that defense spending is likely to remain constrained for the foreseeable future.

CONTRIBUTIONS TO REGIONAL AND GLOBAL SECURITY

As noted in *Asia Pacific Security Outlook 2003*, Europe's global security role will remain geographically and functionally circumscribed and it will thus rely on the United States for regional stability in the Asia Pacific region in the foreseeable future. The European Union and its member states, including those countries joining in 2004, continue to contribute considerable forces to UN peacekeeping operations on a global scale (4,720 out of 38,287, or 12.4 percent), although most of Europe's civilian police, military observers, and troops are deployed in the Balkans region. In the war on terrorism, 20 out of 25 present and future EU member states participate actively in Operation Iraqi Freedom. In the Afghan theater, European nations provide the majority of troops (between 3,500 and 4,200) for the 5,500-strong ISAF, but of the 11,000 soldiers-strong contingent under the mandate Operation Enduring Freedom, only a minority (less than 2,000) comes from Europe. Aside from this, only France and the United Kingdom have deployed small numbers of troops in Asia Pacific.

BILATERAL RELATIONS   The European Union collectively, and some member states individually, continues to strengthen its political and security dialogue with Asia Pacific nations. The ESS report named China, Japan, and India as strategic partners that are viewed as important for the future of development in the region. In 2003, relations between China and the European Union received more attention on both sides, as reflected in the European Commission policy paper on EU-China relations, as well as China's first European policy paper issued in October 2003.

Traditionally, the EU-China dialogue has been preoccupied with economic relations and human rights issues, and China's compliance with World Trade Organization rules remains an important topic for the European Union in its relations with Beijing. However, as China's role as a permanent member of the UN Security Council is bound to grow and its role in facilitating a settlement on the Korean peninsula remains crucial, the Union's dialogue with China will probably address more global and regional security issues in the future. This trend is also reflected in the EU-China cooperation agreement for the civil global navigation satellite system Galileo reached in October 2003, which has an economic and scientific focus but also political and strategic implications.

In contrast, the EU-Japan dialogue did not figure prominently in 2003. During the 12th EU-Japan Summit meeting in Athens in May 2003, both parties agreed only that the escalation of North Korean nuclear weapons aspirations may have serious international implications and that multilateral talks (with Japanese participation) are the preferable course of action. The future of the Korean Peninsula Energy Development Organization (KEDO), which both the European Union and Japan have supported in the past, was not mentioned, indicating the dubious future of the institution.

MULTILATERAL SECURITY   Aside from its military engagement in the region, Europe's contribution to security in Asia and the Pacific hinges on its development assistance and the diplomatic activities of its member states in various institutions such as the United Nations, the ASEAN Regional Forum, ASEM, and KEDO.

The European Union has embarked on an ambitious new initiative toward the United Nations based on a September 2003 European Commission paper called "The European Union and the United Nations: The Choice for Multilateralism." This paper is intended to complement the ESS by putting into practice close cooperation between the two institutions. The initiative envisions a "front runner approach" for the Union in the negotiation and implementation of multilateral initiatives in the fields of sustainable development, poverty reduction, and international security. Looking to the future, the Union's capacities to live up to these aims should not be overestimated, but as recent public opinion data indicate, there is now considerably stronger support for common decision-making in foreign, security, and defense policy matters and there is also strong support for a bigger role for the United Nations.

In KEDO, European participation came to a halt over the year 2003 as the organization was sidelined by the escalation of conflict over North Korea's nuclear program. In November 2002, the European Union had supported the U.S. initiative to partially suspend KEDO activities, i.e., heavy-fuel oil shipments, which led to the expulsion of International Atomic Energy Agency (IAEA) inspectors in December and the announcement of North Korea's withdrawal from the Nonpoliferation Treaty (NPT) in January. During a visit to Seoul, High Representative Javier Solana expressed the Union's concern over the NPT withdrawal but advocated further multilateral talks before the UN Security Council would take up the matter. A similar view was taken when ASEM foreign ministers met in Bali in July 2003. However, in contrast to the European initiative to find a diplomatic solution for the conflict about Iran's nuclear activities in October 2003, neither the European Union nor its member states have made any attempt to seriously engage in the resolution of this conflict.

Eight European states (France, Germany, Italy, the Netherlands, Poland, Portugal, Spain, and the United Kingdom) are participating in the PSI of the Bush administration, which calls for a coordination of national arms export policies as well as close cooperation of intelligence services in order to be able to intercept sensitive export activities. While PSI is not directly aimed at North Korea, at least from the European perspective, Pyongyang's reaction has been quite negative, interpreting PSI as the beginning of a U.S.-led strangulation strategy to push for a regime change in North Korea. European officials, however, insist that PSI is not meant to hinder legitimate exports but to prevent sensitive ones. In contrast to U.S. officials who have stated that PSI may be used in combination with Article 51 of the Charter of the United Nations (concerning self-defense) to intercept ships (or aircraft) even on the high seas, European officials stress that improved national export control laws and their strict implementation have already stopped sensitive shipments, such as the shipment of aluminum tubes from Germany to North Korea (via China) that was intercepted in Egypt in April 2003 or the shipment of uranium enrichment technology from Dubai to Libya that was seized in Italy in October 2003. However, despite the cautious initial reactions, Europe will probably eventually embrace U.S. President George W. Bush's initiative to "criminalize" the transfer of WMD material, and thus, PSI may become a practical tool for enforcing nonproliferation norms in an increasing number of cases.

ECONOMIC ASSISTANCE   The European Union and its member states remain the largest providers of Official Development Assistance (ODA) and humanitarian aid in the world. In 2001, the Union contributed over half of all ODA and 47 percent of all humanitarian aid. Combined, the Union and its member countries continue to be among the most important donors of ODA and humanitarian aid to the Asia Pacific region, but financial constraints and the special commitments in Afghanistan and Iraq shifted some resources away from traditional recipients in the 2002–2003 period.

9 Indonesia

The Security Environment

As the Republic of Indonesia enters 2004, a presidential election year, it is evident that the country's security concerns will continue to be dominated by the same issues faced during the previous year. Internally, despite a relative improvement in the economic and political situation, the Indonesian government faces tremendous difficulty in overcoming three key security challenges: the threats of terrorism, protracted secessionist movements, and the return of communal violence. Externally, the war on terrorism—both at the regional and global levels—continues to place Indonesia at the center of regional and international attention. The nature of Indonesia's response to the problem of terrorism, in which the government is constrained by domestic sensitivity, is putting a strain on Indonesia's relations with the outside world, especially with the United States.

INTERNAL *Economic Performance.* Indonesia's economy in 2003 continued to stabilize with some positive signs toward the attainment of further macroeconomic stability. At the beginning of 2004, gross domestic product growth, led by consumer demand, was between 3.5 percent and 4 percent. Inflation was moderate at less than 5 percent, and high petroleum prices had pushed up exports. Indonesia's foreign reserves had increased to around US$34.7 billion. Meanwhile, the rupiah had stabilized at Rp8,200–Rp8,500 to the U.S. dollar during the year.

However, Indonesia continued to experience a net outflow of investment funds during 2003, with direct foreign investment and official capital flows remaining negative at US$7 billion and US$0.6 billion, respectively. Without significant inflow of direct foreign investment, it is not clear whether Indonesia will be able to sustain its macroeconomic improvements and achieve a higher growth rate. Moreover, despite calm reactions from the market, the decision to leave the International Monetary Fund program by 2004 will be a crucial test of Indonesia's economic resilience. Without sustained economic improvement and higher economic growth to absorb the high unemployment, the political stability achieved during 2003 may come under new pressure in the election year of 2004.

Political Stability. As the economy continued to improve, the political situation was also marked by a degree of stability. Despite the growing domestic criticism over her style of governing, the position of President Megawati Sukarnoputri was not under serious threat. Megawati's government has also done well in dealing with domestic opposition and protests against the U.S. invasion of Iraq. In addition to constitutional amendments that make it more difficult to remove the president, there was a consensus within the political elite during 2003 that the 2004 general elections should be the only mechanism for regime change. Heated contests among rival political parties in the elections of governors, regents, and mayors across the country did not lead to political instability. While national political stability has generally improved, however, the situation remains volatile.

Terrorism. The most serious security challenge facing the government remains the threat of terrorism. The devastating impacts of the terrorist attacks on Paddy's Pub and the Sari Club in Bali on October 12, 2002, were fully felt by Indonesia during 2003. Initially, there had been serious doubt, if not pessimism, in the country whether the Megawati government would be able to find the culprits and deal with the impact in a swift and firm manner. The credibility of Megawati's government was seriously undermined by the Bali bombings, plus apparent frictions within her government on how to deal with the issue. Key government officials, including Vice President Hamzah Haz, continued to be in denial mode, and many Indonesians believed that foreign agents had perpetrated the Bali bombings in order to discredit Islam. The government was faced with a difficult task of balancing the need to crack down on terrorist networks and the imperative of taking into account Muslim sensitivities.

Within weeks, the investigation by the Indonesian National Police on the Bali bombings, assisted by the Australian Federal Police (AFP), began to reveal that a national terrorist network, with strong links to the regional terrorist organization Jemaah Islamiah (JI), had established a strong presence in Indonesia. This clearly indicated the country's susceptibility to penetration by international terrorist networks and the weakness of the intelligence and immigration apparatus in the country. Criticisms by some Islamic groups, which had earlier expressed their skepticism on the ability of the police to investigate the case, have become more muted in light of credible evidence presented by the police. The challenge by radical Islamic groups has also begun to subside. After the Bali bombings, two radical Islamic groups, Laskar Jihad and the Islamic Defenders Front (FPI), dissolved themselves. However, the bombing of the JW Marriott Hotel Jakarta on August 5, 2003, and the investigation following that incident clearly revealed that, while the terrorist network in Indonesia might have been weakened, it has definitely not been eliminated. The fact that the Marriott bombing was carried out by a suicide bomber also added a new and more dangerous dimension to the nature of the terrorist threat in Indonesia.

The government finds it difficult to address the terrorist threat for four main reasons. First, because terrorists justify their acts in terms of Islam, the government needs to crack down on the terrorist network without being seen as waging a "war" against the Muslim community as a whole. Fortunately, the leaders of Indonesia's largest Muslim organizations have denounced terrorism as contrary to the precepts of Islam. Second, the terrorist network in Indonesia is part of a broader regional network of terrorists in Southeast Asia, and possibly in the world. This requires close cooperation on the part of Indonesia's authorities with others in the region and beyond, without necessarily giving the impression to the Indonesian public that the government is bowing to the American agenda. Third, there is a problem of lack of capacity and professionalism on the part of Indonesia's security and intelligence agencies. Finally, the war against terrorism in Indonesia is being conducted during a process of democratic transition in the country, which requires a careful balancing of security and liberty. Indonesia is still seen by the outside world as not having done enough, and continuing to drag its feet, in combating the threat of terrorism.

Secessionist Movements and Communal Violence. Secessionist movements, especially in Aceh and Papua, and communal violence are also continuing difficult challenges. Indonesia made little progress on these fronts in 2003, and may even have taken a step backward. The Cessation of Hostilities Agreement (CoHA), signed by the Government of Indonesia and the Free Aceh Movement (GAM, Gerakan Aceh Merdeka) in December 2002, failed to bring a peaceful resolution to the problem of separatism in Aceh province. Following the breakdown of the peace talks in Tokyo on May 17–18, 2003, the Indonesian government imposed martial law in Aceh province and launched a massive military operation against the rebels. Despite repeated claims of success by the military, however, the war in Aceh continues to drag on. By the end of the first six months of the *Operasi Terpadu*, the military claimed to have killed 1,106 rebels, arrested 1,544, forced 504 others to surrender, and seized 488 weapons (approximately 30 percent of the estimated GAM weaponry). With these results, the military believes that it has reduced GAM's strength by 55 percent.

However, during the same period, around 395 civilians were killed in the conflict and 159 others were wounded. While there has been some evidence to suggest that the military operation has managed to undermine the military infrastructure of GAM, the rebels are still capable of launching sporadic attacks and ambushes against the government troops. Moreover, the military admits that it has not made significant progress in capturing or killing leaders of GAM. The Indonesian National Military (TNI, Tentara Nasional Indonesia) has killed or captured 37 out of 140 GAM leaders, mostly minor figures. The conflict in Aceh has also increased the number of internally displaced persons in the province, with some beginning to flee to neighboring Malaysia. In November, the government extended the martial law period for another six months; the war in Aceh will continue well into 2004. Despite the possibility of a military victory, it is not yet clear how the current government's policy can resolve the Aceh problem once and for all. The military action, however, remains widely supported by the public.

The situation in Papua did not show any significant improvement during 2003. The killing of pro-independence leader Theys Hiyo Eluay in November 2001, in which some members of Indonesia's special forces (Kopassus) are implicated, increased Papuan antipathy toward Indonesia's rule in the province. The situation became still more tense after the government announced in January 2003 that the province would be split into three new provinces. There is a strong feeling among Papuans that the central government in Jakarta is trying to employ a "divide and rule" strategy. Bloody clashes between pro-government groups and opponents of the decision have produced numerous casualties. Despite complaints by Papuan students and nongovernmental organizations (NGOs), the government has continued to send more troops to the province. People in the province also fear that the relative success of military operations in Aceh will encourage the government to undertake the same approach in dealing with separatism in Papua.

While most of 2003 witnessed significant security improvements in areas previously hit by communal violence, that problem began to return toward the end of the year. A new series of attacks against Christian villages in Poso, Central Sulawesi, in October revived fears of a new round of communal violence. This time, however, the security apparatus reacted quickly and within weeks had arrested most of those involved. One disturbing fact that emerged, however, is that several detainees came from outside Sulawesi, mainly from Central Java. This raises suspicions that the JI organization was behind the attacks.

The Consolidation of the Military. The growing threat of terrorism, and the government's decision to launch a massive military operation in Aceh, provided an opportunity for the TNI to reassert its role in both internal security and politics. The inclination of the government to give the military more authority and a greater role in dealing with the threat of terrorism—by reactivating its intelligence networks across the country—was seen by pro-democracy forces as an attempt by the TNI to return to its previous role as arbiter of internal stability. Nevertheless, and contrary to fears in some NGO circles, the new antiterrorism law does not prescribe a significant role for the military in the war on terrorism.

The political position of the TNI, in fact, has improved. The imposition of martial law in Aceh and the military campaign have strengthened public support for the military, despite criticisms from human right activists. More importantly, the influence of the TNI will grow stronger as Indonesia enters the election year in 2004. In an apparent attempt to gain support from the military, almost all political parties and presidential aspirants are avoiding any criticism of the military. The popularity of some retired military generals, such as former TNI Commander General (Ret.) Wiranto, a declared candidate for president, and Coordinating Minister for Political and Security Affairs General (Ret.) Susilo Bambang Yudhoyono, has begun to increase among the public at large.

EXTERNAL *Threat Perceptions.* Indonesian threat perceptions remain shaped primarily by internal sources of instability and conflict and suspicions of involvement of foreign actors in those internal conflicts.

Indonesia's elites, both civilian and military, continue to express concern over the possible involvement of foreign countries not only in the regional rebellions such as in Aceh and Irian Jaya (Papua) but also in the spate of terrorist attacks across the country, especially the Bali bombings. Some Indonesians believe that there is an international conspiracy (especially by the West) to undermine Indonesia's stability and security through the separatist movements in Aceh and Papua and through the issue of terrorism. Many also resent the fact that the international community, especially the United States, has come to see Indonesia as a hotbed of terrorism. These sensitivities among government officials, political and community leaders, and the public at large have in turn brought about a degree of uneasiness for Indonesia in both its relationships with neighboring countries in the regional war on terrorism and in its relations with the United States.

Regional War on Terrorism. As other ASEAN member countries have pursued aggressive counterterrorism measures in the period since the September 11, 2001, terrorist attacks in the United States, Indonesia has taken a more cautious approach primarily due to domestic considerations. While Singapore, the Philippines, and Thailand have participated significantly in the American-led war on terrorism, the Indonesian government felt uneasy about such involvement, being concerned that counterterrorism measures would be perceived by the public as resulting from American pressure. This cautious attitude has put Indonesia in a different category from some of its neighbors. For example, the Indonesian public and officials have often responded angrily to statements by Singaporean officials that Indonesia has not done enough to combat the problem.

Relations with the United States. Indonesia's relations with the United States also showed strains during 2003. The problem of terrorism clearly constitutes one issue that affects bilateral relations between the two countries. While the United States clearly expected that Indonesia would take a more active role in countering terrorism, Indonesians were more concerned with, and opposed to, the U.S. approach to the problem. The U.S. invasion of Iraq drew strong criticism from both government circles and the public at large. Some in Indonesia also continue to see the American-led war on terrorism as a disguise for a war on Islam. Relationships between the United States and Indonesia have also been constrained by the problem in military-to-military relations between the two countries. In July 2003, the U.S. Congress voted again to withhold military aid, as well as an International Military Education and Training (IMET) program of US$1 million over the next two years. Congressional opposition to such assistance was especially due to what was considered a lack of cooperation from Indonesia in uncovering the perpetrators (thought to be from TNI) of the 2002 killing in Timika, Papua, of two U.S. citizens. When in July 2003 five American F-18 jet fighters were detected maneuvering over Bawean Island off East Java, this was seen by many in Indonesia as a violation of the country's sovereignty by the United States, strengthening perceptions that the United States does not respect Indonesia and putting additional strains on bilateral relations.

DEFENSE POLICIES AND ISSUES

STRATEGIC PRIORITIES   Indonesia's defense strategy and priorities did not change during 2003. Indonesia remains preoccupied with maintaining territorial integrity, combating separatist movements, and resolving internal conflicts. Megawati, when she presented the national budget before the parliament, unveiled a government plan to improve the capability of the TNI to maintain Indonesia's territorial integrity and defend its sovereignty. Indonesia's defense white paper, issued in April by the Ministry of Defense and Security, stated that the main priorities of Indonesia's defense policy and strategy are domestic. However, it is also important to note that the white paper, for the first time in an official document, recognizes the importance of nontraditional security problems as serious security threats that need to be tackled by the military.

SPENDING AND PROCUREMENT   Despite a steady increased in the defense budget, funding continues to be the major constraint. In 2003, the government allocated Rp17.18 trillion (US$1.8 billion at US$1 = Rp8,473), a slight increase from the 2002 defense budget of Rp15.4 trillion (US$1.82 billion) and still less than 1 percent of gross domestic product. The largest segment, Rp12.02 trillion (US$1.42 billion), was allocated for salaries and welfare of the troops (routine expenditure), and only Rp5.16 trillion (US$609 million) was allocated for the development of defense capability and procurements (development expenditure). Further, it is believed that the budget allocation only covers 25 percent–30 percent of actual military spending. For fiscal year 2004, the government proposes a more significant increase, to Rp13.74 trillion

(US$1.62 billion) for routine expenditure and Rp7.66 trillion (US$904 million) for development.

Despite its small defense budget, Indonesia made several important purchases in defense equipment during 2003. In April, Indonesia signed a countertrade agreement with Russia to purchase four fighters (two Sukhoi Su-27 and two Sukhoi SU-30) and two helicopters (two Mi-35) with a value of US$192.9 million. This purchase sparked controversy and debate in the parliament because it was financed through the civilian logistical agency Bulog, not the official defense budget. Nevertheless, the aircraft were delivered in early September. The army also boosted its size in 2003 when it added ten new Raider battalions (around 7,000–8,000 personnel). The navy struck a deal with South Korea to purchase a US$35 million personnel landing dock.

Force planning in 2003 also reveals a rather ambitious defense program for the years ahead. Over the next two years, the air force plans to purchase 12 more Sukhoi fighters and six helicopters, and the navy plans to purchase four corvettes from the Netherlands. The navy also plans to purchase two new submarines from South Korea, one in 2005 and the second in 2009, costing US$270 million each. All the purchases made during 2003, and the acquisition plan for the next six years, have been described as an attempt to "fill the gap" in Indonesia's defense capability.

CONTRIBUTIONS TO REGIONAL AND GLOBAL SECURITY

Indonesia's defense cooperation with its regional neighbors is increasing. The Bali bombings opened up the opportunity for Indonesia to improve its defense relations with Australia, which has expressed interest in restoring cooperation with Kopassus. In April 2003, Indonesia signed a memorandum of understanding with Brunei on military cooperation that included joint exercises and exchanges of personnel and surveys. In July, three Japanese war vessels—one training ship and two destroyers—visited Jakarta's port as part of the activities for ASEAN-Japan Exchange Year 2003. Cooperation with the United States remains limited due to the constraints put in place by the Congress. However, the George W. Bush administration has expressed its desire to restore military-to-military relations with Indonesia. In May, five American ships visited Indonesia, and more than 400 U.S. marines took part in a joint exercise of humanitarian assistance and disaster relief with the Indonesian navy.

Indonesia's contributions to international security remain limited and focused on the regional level, especially in the war against terrorism. Indonesia has signed a number of antiterrorism agreements with some regional states. The Bali bombings and the Marriott bombing have not persuaded Jakarta to publicly support the involvement of external powers in regional problems. Indonesia continues to prefer regional solutions to regional problems.

In that context, Indonesia consistently expresses the hope that the Association of Southeast Asian Nations (ASEAN) will continue to serve as the main vehicle for regional countries to cope with security challenges in the region, especially nontraditional threats such as terrorism. During the 2003 ASEAN Summit in Bali, Indonesia obtained agreement from the other ASEAN members to transform the organization into a security community by 2020. Indonesia has also called for an increase in intra-ASEAN maritime cooperation.

10 Japan

The Security Environment

Japan continues to tackle difficult challenges both at home and abroad. Internally, despite increasing signs of economic recovery, prospects for sustainable economic growth remain uncertain. It remains to be seen if Prime Minister Koizumi Jun'ichirō's structural reform will produce durable economic growth while alleviating deflation and unemployment. There are some positive developments on the political front, including the prospects for development of a two-party system conducive to policy leadership in revamping the political and bureaucratic systems where antireform forces are entrenched. Externally, Japan's foreign policy profile has been hamstrung by its continuing economic malaise, leading to further cuts to its Official Development Assistance (ODA) for four consecutive years and a perceived decline in Japan's international stature. Among the most difficult foreign policy challenges confronting Tokyo are North Korea's nuclear weapons and ballistic missile developments, its past abduction of Japanese nationals, and the issues associated with Tokyo's contributions to the coalition effort in Iraq.

INTERNAL   The election for the House of Representatives (Lower House) of the Diet on November 9, 2003, the first since Koizumi took office in April 2001, may prove to be a watershed in the history of Japanese party politics. For the first time since the end of the 1920s, Japanese party politics appears to be evolving in the direction of a two-party system in which control of government could alternate between the Liberal Democratic Party (LDP), which has been predominant through most of the postwar years, and the Democratic Party of Japan

(DPJ), which was recently augmented by a merger with the Liberal Party. In the November election, the LDP won 237 seats in the 480-seat Lower House, just failing to secure a majority in its own right, while the DPJ won 177, up 40 seats from its preelection strength of 137. The weight of the two largest parties has put other parties on the sidelines—except for New Kōmeitō, the LDP's coalition partner, which increased its seats to 34. The Japan Communist Party (JCP), the Social Democratic Party (SDP), and the New Conservative Party suffered major setbacks. After the election, the LDP assembled a majority by taking in a few conservative independents and by absorbing the New Conservative Party. Another notable feature of the 2003 election was the prominence of policy debate in the campaign, centering on "manifestoes"—detailed lists of policy promises—first published by the DPJ, and then by other parties. Overall voter turnout, however, was slightly down from the previous election.

The implications of an emerging two-party system for Japanese politics and its foreign and security policies could be profound. With both the LDP and the DPJ supporting a constitutional amendment (including a revision of Article 9 of the constitution renouncing the use of force), and the SDP and the JCP permanently weakened, the prospects for amending the constitution have increased. The Research Commission on the Constitution, established in both Diet chambers in 2000, is expected to release its final report by 2005. Arguably, the debate on constitutional amendment has entered a new phase: the issue now is how the constitution is to be revised. The near-demise of the SDP and the JCP could also lead to greater bipartisanship generally in foreign and security policy.

EXTERNAL   The alliance relationship with the United States has been the lynchpin of Japan's foreign and security policy since the end of World War II. While emphasizing multilateral coordination and collaboration in resolving international issues, Tokyo's foreign policy record in 2003 showed that when the chips are down, consideration for the alliance with the United States remains paramount. This was pointedly illustrated by Tokyo's unequivocal support for the U.S.-led preemptive attack on Iraq even without an explicit UN mandate, broader support in the international community, or strong domestic public support. Polls showed that nearly 80 percent of Japanese opposed the war on Iraq. Yet Koizumi cited the security threat from North Korea as a major reason for backing the United States. Confronted with North Korea, which is armed with ballistic missiles and possibly several nuclear weapons, Koizumi argued that Japan has no choice but to rely on U.S. military power as a deterrent to nuclear blackmail. After the success of the initial campaign in April, Tokyo sought to play an active role in forging international cooperation in the postwar reconstruction of Iraq.

At the same time, the government prepared new legislation allowing Self-Defense Forces (SDF) troops to be dispatched to Iraq. A special measures bill enacted in July 2003 permits the SDF to go to Iraq for humanitarian and security assistance. The bill was supported by the ruling coalition, but opposed by all of the opposition parties, including the DPJ and the Liberal Party. The new law, which is in effect for four years, enables the government to send SDF units to "noncombat zones" in Iraq to provide humanitarian relief for the Iraqi people and logistic support for U.S.-led coalition forces. On December 9, 2003, the Koizumi government approved a basic plan to dispatch SDF troops to Iraq. This is the first time that Japan has decided to deploy SDF personnel in a country at war. Media reports indicated that Tokyo desired to respond to Washington's request for "boots on the ground."

The plan stipulates that SDF personnel will engage in humanitarian and reconstruction assistance in "noncombat areas" in Iraq, with up to 600 Ground Self-Defense Force (GSDF) troops to be stationed in southeastern Iraq, up to eight Air Self-Defense Force (ASDF) cargo planes for airlifting relief goods between Kuwait and Iraq, and up to two amphibious ships and two destroyers to transport GSDF equipment. Critics argue that it is extremely difficult to distinguish between combat and noncombat zones in Iraq, where widespread guerrilla attacks are occurring against U.S.-led occupation forces. Under these circumstances, SDF personnel could be forced to engage in war fighting, even under "passive" rules of engagement, thus violating the war-renouncing constitution. The assassination of two Japanese diplomats in Iraq on November 29, 2003, pointed to the possibility that SDF troops might be targeted by guerrillas and insurgents. Public opinion in Japan is divided on this issue, but an increasing majority is opposed to SDF participation.

Less controversial is Tokyo's generous financial assistance to the reconstruction of Iraq. In October 2003, Tokyo pledged to provide grant assistance totaling US$1.5 billion in 2004 to help meet basic needs including power generation, education, water, sanitation, and medical assistance. Tokyo also pledged to provide yen loans of up to US$3.5 billion through 2007. In December, Koizumi pledged to waive the majority of Iraq's debt to Japan as requested by Washington (though the precise figure has not been specified).

North Korea remains the most intractable foreign policy challenge for Japan. Koizumi's historic visit to Pyongyang in 2002 and the Pyongyang Declaration have been overshadowed by North Korea's nuclear weapons development program and its refusal to resolve issues stemming from the abductions of Japanese nationals in the 1970s and 1980s. Bilateral talks on normalization have been stalled since October 2003, and the Six-Party Talks have thus far failed to yield any substantive results. With regard to Pyongyang, Tokyo maintains a policy of "dialogue and pressure." While pursuing multilateral talks, Tokyo is pressuring Pyongyang in various ways. Japanese authorities now thoroughly inspect North Korean ships that make frequent port calls in Japan, including the cargo-passenger ferry *Mangyongbong-92*. These ships reportedly have been involved in smuggling and spying activities. Japan has also joined the U.S.-led Proliferation Security Initiative (PSI) to check the trafficking in weapons of mass destruction, missiles, and related materials.

Japan's relationship with South Korea continues maturing, to the point that there now exists something akin to a quasi-alliance between the two countries. Tokyo and Seoul share interest in pursuing a peaceful resolution of the nuclear standoff with North Korea. Together, and through the Six-Party Talks and the Trilateral Coordination and Oversight Group (TCOG) process involving Japanese, U.S., and South Korean security policymakers, Tokyo and Seoul can play a role in inducing the United States to pursue a multilateral approach vis-à-vis North Korea. Nonetheless, issues arising from wartime memories remain a source of friction, as evidenced by Seoul's strong protest against Koizumi's annual visits to the Yasukuni Shrine.

Japan's political relations with China have also been strained, due to a variety of issues including Koizumi's visits to the Yasukuni Shrine. In 2003, an accident caused by mustard gas from chemical weapons left by the Japanese military at the end of Word War II killed one person and injured 43 people (for which Tokyo agreed to pay ¥300 million [US$2.8 million at US$1 = ¥107.13] in compensation). Although the new Chinese leadership comes from the postwar generation, these historical issues will remain important in the bilateral relationship. Many

Japanese view the growth of China and its growing influence in the region with concern, but many also feel that closer cooperation with China is essential in dealing with problems associated with North Korea. However, in recent years the overall Japan-China relationship has increasingly been driven by economic activities and the accelerating integration of Japan's economy into that of China. In 2002, China for the first time replaced the United States as Japan's leading source of imports.

With the member countries of the Association of Southeast Asian Nations (ASEAN) Japan seeks to establish a Comprehensive Economic Partnership. The year 2003 was designated as "ASEAN-Japan Exchange Year 2003," with a wide range of events culminating in a Japan-ASEAN commemorative summit in Tokyo on December 11–12. Koizumi and the leaders of the ten ASEAN countries signed the Tokyo Declaration for the Dynamic and Enduring Japan-ASEAN Partnership in the New Millennium, calling for deepening ties and broadening cooperation encompassing economic and development issues, political and security affairs, and social and cultural activities. Significantly and despite its initial hesitation, Tokyo announced that it would join ASEAN's Treaty of Amity and Cooperation (TAC) in Southeast Asia, following similar action by China and India at the ASEAN summit in Bali in October. In the area of free trade agreements (FTAs), Japan has been seen as lagging behind China, which has proposed an FTA with ASEAN by 2010. However, Tokyo announced that it would begin bilateral FTA talks with Malaysia, the Philippines, and Thailand. The Tokyo Declaration also sets a long-term goal of creating an East Asian Community that can build upon the ASEAN + 3 process that also includes China and South Korea.

Since Koizumi's visit to Moscow in January 2003 (see *Asia Pacific Security Outlook 2003*), there has been noted progress in cooperation between Russia and Japan in developing energy resources. Given Japan's dependence on oil-producing countries of the Middle East for nearly 90 percent of domestic consumption, Tokyo has a strategic interest in diversifying its energy sources. On the Sakhalin shelf, an international consortium including Japan and Russia has been promoting oil and liquefied natural gas projects. Japan supports one of two competing proposals for the route of a planned oil pipeline in Eastern Siberia, a route from Angarsk to Nakhodka on the Pacific coast (China has been lobbying for a route from Angarsk to the Chinese city of Daqing).

Defense Policies and Issues

DEFENSE PLANNING   For the first time since the end of World War II, a legal framework has been established for mobilizing the SDF in the event of a military emergency. On June 6, 2003, three defense bills related to security emergencies, which had been submitted to the National Diet in April 2002, were finally endorsed. Around 90 percent of the lawmakers in both chambers supported the bills, an unprecedented development in view of the fact that emergency legislation had long been taboo in postwar Japan. An agreement between the ruling coalition and the DPJ to amend the initial bills smoothed the way for enactment. The package consisted of (a) a "bill to respond to armed attacks," which states the basic principles for response to armed attacks, the respective responsibilities of the national and local governments and public organizations, and other measures required; (b) a bill amending the SDF Law to enable the SDF to seize land and other property for operations and exempt the SDF from an array of peacetime legal procedures such as those related to road traffic, medical services, and constructing facilities for their use, thus allowing for effective operations in emergency situations; and (c) a bill amending the Law on the Establishment of the Security Council of Japan to grant the council greater power to deal with an emergency. Apparently, the near-demise of the SDP made it possible for the legislation to pass in the Diet. More generally, however, the contingency legislation suggests that Japanese have become increasingly concerned about their security environment.

The contingency legislation, however, is still not complete. The government considers that additional measures are needed, including a law to protect civilians' lives and property, legislation concerning the treatment of prisoners of war, and measures to facilitate U.S. forces' operations in the case of an armed attack against Japan.

Due to recognition of Japan's lack of capability to defend itself from North Korean ballistic missile attacks (especially those by 200 No-dong missiles whose 1,300-km range reaches most of Japan), and with considerable prodding from Washington, the government has decided to build a missile defense system beginning in the year 2007. Approximately ¥100 billion (US$933.45 million) has been earmarked for this purpose in the 2004 fiscal year defense budget. According to the plan, the launch of an enemy missile would be detected by satellites, the missile's trajectory and target would be determined by computers, and then it would be destroyed in space by a missile launched by an Aegis-equipped destroyer with SM-3s (Standard Missile-3s). If the first phase of missile defense failed, PAC-3 (Patriot Advanced Capability-3) surface-to-air missiles would be launched to counter the incoming missile before it hit a target.

Critics argue that the missile defense plan is premature, pointing to technical uncertainties, ambiguous cost-effectiveness, increasing constraints on allocation of the defense budget among the three services, the SDF's inadequate command-and-control system, and regional repercussions including objections from China. The estimated costs are daunting given Japan's tight fiscal conditions. The biggest challenge is simply the very short time available for decisionmakers, both in Tokyo and Washington, since missiles launched from North Korea would take less than ten minutes to reach targets in Japan.

Another significant development in Japan's defense planning is its growing intelligence gathering capability. The main purpose is believed to be to monitor military developments in North Korea. In March 2003, Japan launched its own surveillance satellites, one equipped with an optical sensor with one-meter resolution, and the other with a synthetic-aperture radar that has resolution of one to three meters. These satellites' capabilities are considered roughly comparable to U.S. commercial satellites such as Lockheed Martin' IKONOS. It is unlikely, however, that Japan's satellites will diminish Tokyo's reliance on U.S. satellite intelligence and communications intercepts, given the superior capabilities of the United States.

In 2003, Japan Defense Agency (JDA) officials including SDF personnel conducted joint exercises with the National Police Agency to counter terrorist and subversive activities.

Due to the burdens of preparations for the Iraq-related legislation and for the dispatch of SDF personnel to Iraq, the JDA put a planned review of the 1995 National Defense Program Outline (NDPO) on the back burner.

DEFENSE SPENDING AND PERSONNEL   Japan's defense spending continues to be constrained by a combination of overall budgetary stringency and public aversion to a military force. Japan's defense budget for fiscal 2003 was ¥4,926.5 billion (US$45.99 billion), a 0.3 percent decrease from the previous year's budget. The ratio of defense spending to gross national product was projected to be 0.988 percent in 2003. Of the budget, 45.0 percent was allocated to personnel and provisions,

18.4 percent to operational maintenance (including education and training), 18.3 percent to equipment and materials, 10.5 percent to base security and support for U.S. forces in Japan, 3.1 percent to base and facilities maintenance, and 3.0 percent to research and development. In addition, the government earmarked ¥247.36 million (US$2.3 million) for expenses for the Japan-U.S. Special Action Committee on Okinawa (SACO). (These defense expenditure figures do not include spending on the coast guard or pensions, and therefore are not comparable to measures of defense effort by the North Atlantic Treaty Organisation [NATO].) Because of the high costs of domestically produced equipment as well as the needs connected with Tokyo's recent decision to introduce a costly missile defense system, there has been growing pressure for review of the ban on arms exports.

The SDF had 239,806 active duty personnel as of March 2003: 148,226 in the GSDF, 44,375 in the Maritime Self-Defense Force (MSDF), 45,483 in the ASDF, and 1,722 on the Joint Staff Council.

PROCUREMENT Japan's current defense acquisitions follow the Mid-Term Defense Program (FY2001–FY2005) compiled in 2000. To make the defense forces more effective and compact, equipment is being significantly modernized. The major targets for fiscal 2003 include the development of a new medium-range surface-to-air guided missile for the GSDF, DDG destroyers with the Aegis system for the MSDF, and the improved Patriot system for the ASDF. Observers anticipate that a new NDPO to be formulated and adopted in 2004 will see a significant shift away from conventional equipment such as tanks and artillery to a new force structure focusing on the capabilities required for defense against missile and terrorist attacks.

CONTRIBUTIONS TO REGIONAL AND GLOBAL SECURITY

ECONOMIC CONTRIBUTIONS ODA is a key instrument of Japan's foreign policy. Japan was the world's largest aid donor for about a decade until 2000. Since then, prolonged economic stagnation and tight fiscal conditions have caused Tokyo to make substantial cutbacks in ODA levels, and Japan is now the world's second largest aid donor behind the United States. In fiscal 2003, the budget plan allocated ¥857.8 billion (US$8.0 billion) for ODA, down 5.8 percent from the initial budget for the previous year.

In recent years, Japan's ODA has been increasingly used for peace-building purposes in war-torn states. In 2003, Japan took part in reconstruction efforts in Afghanistan and peace-building efforts in East Timor and Sri Lanka.

Japan's ODA Charter, which sets out the objectives, policies, and priorities of ODA, was revised in August 2003 for the first time since it was adopted in 1992. The new charter is aimed at enhancing the strategic value, flexibility, transparency, and efficiency of ODA, highlighting the increasing "peace-building" role of ODA, more strategic and proactive policy formulation and implementation, and strengthened collaboration with international organizations and nongovernmental organizations (NGOs).

SUPPORT FOR THE WAR AGAINST TERRORISM   The Anti-Terrorism Special Measures Law, which was enacted following the September 11, 2001, attacks on the United States, enabled Japan's MSDF to provide logistic support for the U.S.-led antiterrorism operations in and around Afghanistan (discussed in *Asia Pacific Security Outlook 2002*). Three MSDF supply ships have provided a total of 320,000 kiloliters of fuel for warships of ten countries, including the United States, the United Kingdom, and France, operating in the Indian Ocean. On November 1, 2003, the law was extended for another two years. All of the opposition parties voted against the extension, questioning the need for continuing refueling ships in light of a sharp decline in the amount of refueling due to the decrease in the number of U.S. warships operating in the area from an initial 40 to two.

UN PEACEKEEPING AND HUMANITARIAN ASSISTANCE   The SDF engineering battalion (680 personnel) continues to participate in the UN Mission of Support in East Timor (UNMISET). Additionally, ten SDF personnel serve UNMISET as military section headquarters staff. Since 1996, the SDF has been taking part in the UN Disengagement Observer Force (UNDOF) in the Golan Heights.

There is now a growing likelihood that the scope of Japan's peacekeeping will expand to include support for multilateral peacekeeping forces. The Advisory Group on International Cooperation for Peace, headed by Akashi Yasushi, submitted a report to Koizumi in December 2002 calling for legislation that would enable Japan to participate in logistic support activities such as medical, communications, and transport services for multilateral peacekeeping troops deployed under

UN resolutions, in addition to traditional peacekeeping missions directly commanded by the United Nations. It also called for a relaxation of the five principles that govern Japanese participation in peacekeeping operations, participation in the UN Standby Arrangements System, strengthening support for NGOs involved in international peace cooperation, active dispatch of civilian specialists and civilian police for international peace missions, and amendment of the Self-Defense Forces Law to establish international peace cooperation as "a regular duty" of the SDF so that SDF units will have a high level of readiness for such operations.

11 Republic of Korea

The Security Environment

INTERNAL   During much of its still quite new experience with democracy, the Republic of Korea has had weak presidential leadership, as its presidents—Kim Young Sam and Kim Dae Jung—began their terms with limited mandates (both had only about 40 percent of the vote in three-way races) and ended with public approval rates of below 20 percent. Early in their terms, however, both enjoyed high public approval ratings. Current president Roh Moo Hyun has had a different and even less fortunate trajectory. His victory in South Korea's 2002 presidential election was dramatic, with almost no one predicting his win until the actual votes were counted. With only one opponent at the end of the race, he had 48 percent of the vote, but he proved a more polarizing winner, never enjoying the broad support base of his predecessors during their first year in office. Roh's problems began with his own Millennium Democratic Party (MDP), inherited from Kim Dae Jung. Within a few months of his victory it split into two rival groups and Roh established his own Our Open Party (Uri Party). (The other significant political parties in the National Assembly are the conservative Grand National Party [GNP], which has the largest bloc in the Assembly, and the United Liberal Democrats [ULD]).

The governing challenges for the president reflect not just the minority status of his party in the parliament but also his tactics, which critics argue are more suited to someone in the opposition than to a president. Roh continues to advocate reforms, but his policies are criticized as idealistic and populist, heedlessly confrontational, and often heavy on process and vague on substance. Moreover, he appears to have difficulty balancing long-term needs and immediate populism, resulting in flip-flops in economic, labor, education, and security policy. A reckless style of speech further increases his vulnerability to opposition and media attacks. A former labor lawyer, his indecisive handling of several crippling strikes has alienated the business community. Finally, some of his close associates are alleged to have been involved in a slush fund scandal.

In order to break the political deadlock and strengthen his weakened hand, Roh announced in October 2003 that he would seek a referendum to test public confidence in his presidency. In a skillful political move, he associated the proposed referendum with eradicating corruption. Initially seeing the referendum as a sign of frustration and weakness, the two largest opposition parties, the GNP and MDP, first welcomed the proposed referendum. But they quickly changed their stances when opinion polls suggested that a majority of the people would support the president. Moreover, since the announcement, the GNP itself has been falling deeper into the political quagmire with a scandal over slush funds contributed by business groups, allowing Roh some breathing space.

This awkward political situation will be reshaped in some fashion by the April 2004 parliamentary elections, but as the year began there was little sense of how the election may turn out. In the meantime, the political parties remain locked in a zero-sum struggle with high stakes, and foreign and security policies seem likely to be hostage to domestic political imperatives at least through the election season. The national mood is also negatively affected by uncertain growth as the result of a heavy overhang of consumer credit card debt (earlier encouraged by the government as a way out of the economic crisis) and by the unresolved crisis over North Korea's nuclear weapons program.

EXTERNAL   There is a severe, essentially generational divide among South Koreans on the nation's relations with the United States and the Democratic People's Republic of Korea. Roh is uneasily trying to straddle this divide by firmly supporting the centrality of the alliance for Korean security while continuing to promote the South's relations with the North and moderate the harder U.S. approach to the North. His rhetoric and policies are heavily influenced by the younger generation, especially those in their 30s and 40s with activist backgrounds. These people comprise a large portion of his support base and are destined to remain a key influence so long as the president proves unable to broaden his base. Members of this group frequently display a strong anti-American and pro-North Korean ideological orientation. They see the United States as an arrogant hyper-power that is the main cause of heightened tensions on the Korean peninsula. They argue that Washington's policies of neglect at the beginning of the George W. Bush administration and later blunt pressures caused Pyongyang to develop a siege mentality, and they believe that Pyongyang's proposed non-aggression pact is necessary for peace on the Korean peninsula. They cannot understand why the United States would resist such a pact unless it is just for buying time until the U.S. elections are over, the unrest in Iraq subsides, and Washington is in a stronger position to pressure Pyongyang militarily.

On the other hand, older-generation Koreans, especially those who experienced the Korean War, remain deeply mistrustful of the North and of policies on the part of the South that would be too accommodating of the North. This generation was outraged to learn that Kim Dae Jung had essentially purchased the June 2000 summit in Pyongyang through surreptitious payments made to Pyongyang by South Korean business circles. There is no sign of convergence across this serious ideological gap.

By sending conflicting signals, North Korea continues to exploit divisions within the South and the tactical differences of emphasis between the U.S. and South Korean governments—despite the firm opposition of both governments to the North's nuclear weapons program. As of the beginning of 2004, the North Korean crisis seemed only a little closer to resolution. South Korean public and political opinion has generally appreciated China's diplomatic role in convening the Six-Party Talks, and Roh's government in many respects seems more inclined to see itself in a similar position as a compromiser between the hard-line positions in Pyongyang and Washington. It was this kind of thinking that caused Roh to speculate that South Korea might condition the sending of its troops to Iraq on a more flexible U.S. approach to North Korea.

The ultimate fear in the South is the outbreak of conflict, which would have an absolutely devastating impact on South Korean society. As the confrontation over nuclear weapons has dragged on and the United States has become more deeply involved in Iraq, there is some reduction in the fear that the United States will push for a military solution to the crisis. But, despite the existence of the Six-Party Talks and an agreed position between Seoul, Tokyo, and Washington in favor of a security guarantee for Pyongyang in exchange for a complete and verifiable end to the North's nuclear programs, Seoul worries that the crisis will eventually turn hotter unless a compromise can be found with the North. Pyongyang continues to boast of its nuclear capabilities even as it offers to refreeze its program for the right payoff. There is also a fear in Seoul that Pyongyang may be tempted to demonstrate its capabilities with an explosion of a nuclear device or a provocative missile test.

If Pyongyang crosses an American "red line," whether as a result of miscalculation or design, it seems likely that at a minimum the United States will push for UN economic sanctions, strengthen its Proliferation Security Initiative (PSI) project with partner countries, and begin inspections of North Korean shipping. The U.S. leadership might even renew threats of military solutions and regime change. Increased tensions, even short of war, would have a significant impact on the South. South Koreans worry that there could be reduced outside investment or, depending on the severity of the crisis, capital flight and economic disaster. Therefore, to most South Koreans the most urgent short-term task is to work for continuation of the Six-Party Talks. Indicative of its unwillingness to take a hard line, the South Korean government is not participating in the PSI for fear that forceful or intrusive action may be too provocative and result in further escalation of tensions on North Korea's side.

DEFENSE POLICIES AND ISSUES

REALIGNMENT OF U.S. FORCES   In 2003, the United States announced plans for a realignment of its global force structure, reducing large, fixed bases in favor of smaller forward-operating bases maintained primarily by support units. These plans include relocation of the U.S. 2nd Infantry Division away from the Demilitarized Zone (DMZ) in South Korea to areas 75 miles south of Seoul. This would make the division more mobile and enable it to respond to other emergencies in the region. A possible reduction in the number of troops in South Korea from 37,000 to 25,000 has also been reported although not formally announced.

With this decision coming at a time of high tensions in U.S.-North Korean relations, Seoul has been buzzing with speculation about other possible motives for the realignment. A prominent and quite logical one is that the United States hopes to reduce South Korean resentment of foreign forces and the number of incidents involving South Korean citizens by removing its troops from the densely populated center of Seoul. Another line of speculation, rhetorically embraced by Pyongyang and believed by some South Koreans, is that the move is intended to better prepare the United States for a military solution to the Korean crisis. Since the 1953 armistice, the United States has kept a large number of ground troops in South Korea, mostly deployed along the DMZ as deterrence against a possible attack by the North. At the present time, however, the more likely scenario for another war might not be an attack by the North, but rather a preemptive U.S. strike on North Korean nuclear facilities. According to this line of speculation, the move south would reduce North Korea's ability to retaliate by removing U.S. forces from harm's way.

South Koreans have been concerned that a sudden U.S. move could leave a security vacuum along the DMZ. A further concern is that U.S. troops stationed in South Korea for regional missions could lead to problems in South Korea's increasingly important relationship with China. Nevertheless, the United States is proceeding with the southbound repositioning of its forces away from Seoul and the borderline with North Korea. In 2003, the U.S. command announced that ten specific military missions would be transferred to South Korea, including guard duty around the truce village of Panmunjom near the DMZ. Together with the previously agreed transfer of U.S. headquarters staff and facilities from the Yongsan base in Seoul, the relocation will involve substantial investments in new facilities. The cost is estimated at between US$2 billion and US$4 billion, with some observers expecting it will be between US$3 billion and US$5 billion, in addition to the ongoing US$11 billion U.S. military improvement plan to be completed in four years.

The South Korean government faces a number of challenges associated with the U.S. plans. With the United States more focused on air- and sea-based capabilities to fulfill its defense commitment, South Korea's own defense capabilities must be strengthened and become more self-reliant. Accordingly, despite a generally tight budget, the defense budget for 2004 was increased 8 percent over the previous year, more than any other budget category, to 14.58 trillion won (US$12.18 billion at US$1 = 1,197.3 won). (For comparison, it is estimated that North Korea spent around US$5.4 billion for military purposes in the 2002 fiscal year, less than 40 percent of South Korea's spending.) However, South Korea's ratio of defense spending to gross domestic product is only 2.8

percent, far less than that of other countries facing direct military security threats from neighboring states. The Ministry of National Defense argues that spending must rise to around 3.2 percent of GDP if South Korea is to assume the burden of deterrence and defense capability that until now has been undertaken by the U.S. troops stationed on the Korean peninsula.

CONTRIBUTIONS TO REGIONAL AND GLOBAL SECURITY

The most controversial issue for South Korea's international contributions in 2003 concerned whether and to what extent South Korea should contribute troops to the pacification and reconstruction effort in Iraq. The country sent a small noncombat group of about 700 personnel in May following the main military action. The United States wanted a more significant force, reportedly at least 5,000 troops with combat capabilities. Following passage in October of the UN resolution endorsing the dominant role of the United States in Iraq, the South Korean government decided to dispatch combat troops to Iraq to help maintain security and restore stability. This decision seemed to have less to do with Iraq itself than the dynamics and imperatives of the half-century-old alliance between Seoul and Washington.

The size and timing of the deployment was hotly debated within the government as well as in public, featuring numerous street demonstrations. The Ministry of National Defense originally considered a deployment in the range of 5,000 to 10,000 light infantry troops to be sent to the vicinity of Mosul. With continued fighting in Iraq and declining public support for the proposed force, the plan was rethought. Younger members of the National Security Council reportedly supported a 3,000-member reconstruction force, whereas the Ministry of Defense and the Ministry of Foreign Affairs and Trade argued for a more robust presence. Ultimately the government promised a 3,000-member force including some combat capabilities. This would make South Korea the third largest contributing country following the United States and the United Kingdom.

The price tag for sending troops could reach US$1 billion (7,000 troops for three years at 3.8 million won per soldier per month, plus US$260 million in reconstruction aid pledged by the South Korean government). The troop deployment was welcomed by the business sector, as corporations expect it will open the door to various projects in the rehabilitation of Iraq, with estimates reaching as high as 100 trillion won. In addition, Hyundai and other South Korean enterprises hope to retrieve over US$1 billion owed to them by the Iraqi government. Securing a sufficient supply of Iraqi oil on a long-term basis is also high on the government's list of priorities.

Elsewhere and less controversially, South Korea is contributing troops to the counterterrorism operation in Afghanistan. In addition, South Korea has military observers in Georgia, India, Liberia, and Pakistan as part of UN peacekeeping operations in those countries. The government has agreed to be prepared for rapid response to UN peacekeeping requests whenever necessary. The Ministry of National Defense is also working to establish an international peacekeeping center, which will make South Korea a regional and global center for peacekeeping. One successful intervention concluded as South Korea withdrew its infantry troops from East Timor in 2003, ending a four-year deployment as a member of the UN peacekeeping force in that country. The Evergreen Unit was largely composed of infantry, plus some medical and engineering personnel. Since late 1999, South Korea has sent a total of 3,283 troops to East Timor on a six-month rotational basis in eight separate batches, in support of the UN and the Australian-led multilateral forces.

12 Malaysia

THE SECURITY ENVIRONMENT

At the start of 2004, Malaysian concerns were focused more on internal than external stability. On October 31, 2003, Mahathir bin Mohammed laid to rest speculations of "will he, won't he?" by retiring after 22 years as prime minister of Malaysia. The country's fifth prime minister, Abdullah Ahmad Badawi, was sworn in on the same day. An acknowledged and loyal deputy to Mahathir, Abdullah's principal challenge will be to prove himself a capable premier, and win a convincing victory in the next general election. To do so, he needs to heal divisions within the governing Barisan Nasional coalition and to wrestle more support for his own United Malays National Organization (UMNO) party within the Malay community from the more conservative Parti Islam SeMalaysia (PAS, or the Islamic Party of Malaysia). Abdullah has stated that he sees his task as to continue driving Malaysia's policies toward the nation's development ideals as contained in the Vision 2020 blueprint. However, like his predecessor, the new prime minister will have to be responsive to changes in the political and socioeconomic environment as these occur, to ensure the nation stays on course.

INTERNAL In his inaugural speech to parliament, Abdullah touched on a number of the "softer" aspects of development, such as youth, women, education, and the family. This signaled that more might be expected than simply a linear continuation of policies from the Mahathir era. Abdullah's signature issue is the ongoing anticorruption drive. Concerned over the high level of corruption in the country, the new prime minister, known colloquially as "Mr. Clean," is making it a personal priority to root out corrupt practices in government, both to restore its battered image and to reinstill a sense of accountability and service in the public sector.

Abdullah's most immediate priority, however, will be ensuring a resounding victory for the ruling coalition in the next general election. Speculation has been rife about the exact date of the election, which could be called early in 2004.

Political rhetoric has already ratcheted up on all sides, triggered by the launch in November 2003 by the opposition PAS of its controversial Islamic State Document. The document is based on PAS's interpretation of *Syariah* law and includes the strict *hudud* interpretation. Although it purports to protect the religious and cultural rights and freedoms of non-Muslims, it does little to allay the concerns of the general Muslim population (much less those of minorities) wary of PAS's brand of conservative Islam. The ruling UMNO dismissed the document as a political gimmick timed for the general election. PAS's opposition allies distanced themselves from the document and the Democratic Action Party (DAP) went so far as to order all its office bearers in the PAS state governments of Kelantan and Terengganu to step down in protest. PAS's declared willingness to abolish the constitutionally protected Malay special privileges at some future time is alienating many Malays who still attach great importance to this provision. It is noteworthy, however, that the document affirms PAS's commitment to the democratic parliamentary process, seeking to distance PAS as a party from the ideology of violence as an instrument of political transformation with which it has been identified due to the association of several of its members with the radical group Jemaah Islamiah (JI). In the same spirit, and demonstrating political savvy, the chief minister of Kelantan has suggested an open forum of party leaders to discuss and clarify the blueprint. A satisfactory compromise, however, does not appear likely.

Although the Malay vote was badly split during the previous general election in 1999, primarily over Mahathir's dismissal and subsequent trial and conviction of former Deputy Prime Minister Anwar Ibrahim, this division may be largely healed in the face of nervousness over the possibility of living in a PAS-ruled "Islamic state." Further, Abdullah's succession to leadership, the strong, moderate, and progressive Islamic credentials that he brings with him, and his quiet and humble but firm character might succeed in reconciling the Malay political vote in time for the general election.

Malaysian police have expressed confidence that JI activities within the country have almost been crippled, with 106 leaders and members now in detention. However, with JI still active in neighboring countries, Malaysia will remain vigilant against future threats.

Disconcertingly, 13 Malaysian students were arrested in September 2003 by Pakistani security forces along with six Indonesian students, including the younger brother of key JI and al Qaeda leader Riduan Isamuddin, alias Hambali, who himself was arrested in Thailand in August 2003. The students were returned to Malaysia and detained under the Internal Security Act on suspicion of involvement in JI activities, posing a threat to Malaysian national security. (Four were, however, released before the Eid celebrations at the end of the Muslim holy month of Ramadan.) The incident reignited concerns on the part of the Malaysian authorities that students were being lured by militant teachings in unrecognized *madrasahs* (Islamic schools) abroad, particularly in Pakistan and Yemen. The government has estimated that 93 percent of all Malaysian students attending such institutions are in Pakistan, and has said that Malaysian authorities are working in concert with their host counterparts to identify and monitor both the students and the institutions.

EXTERNAL   Malaysia's external priorities in 2004 will focus on the continuing threats of militancy and terrorism, mending relations with neighbors, as well as resolving outstanding disputes—particularly with Singapore—preferably through diplomatic negotiations.

Although Thailand and Malaysia have long worked closely on security and intelligence issues—and especially since the uncovering of JI activities in the region—that cooperation is being further enhanced in 2004 following a series of insurgent attacks in southern Thailand in the first days of the year. In addition to joint border patrols between the Thai and Malaysian militaries along the Narathiwat-Kelantan border, the two countries have also established a joint committee for border development co-chaired by their respective foreign ministers. This effort is intended to promote stability and undermine militant recruitment in the area by increasing standards of living and improving economic opportunities through development of the fishing and tourism industries. Similarly in the case of the southern Philippines (where Malaysia will facilitate peace negotiations between the Philippine government and the Moro Islamic Liberation Front [MILF] scheduled to begin in February 2004), Abdullah has offered Malaysian training assistance and technical cooperation to aid in economic development of this region.

Malaysia is also cooperating closely with Indonesia on counterterrorism, specifically seeking to capture and apprehend Azahari Hussein and Noordin Mohamed Top who are wanted on suspicion of involvement in both the October 2002 bombings in Bali and the August 2003 bombing at the JW Marriott Hotel Jakarta. Having escaped a police raid on their rented house in Bandung, the two Malaysians are believed to be on the run in West Java and to be plotting more terrorism. Police on both sides are cautiously confident that the duo will be caught soon. Shared intelligence resulting from the arrest of JI/al Qaeda leader Hambali is expected to lead to further successes in the campaign against terrorism in 2004.

Political relations with Singapore reached another low in 2003, with flare-ups over longstanding disputes over water and territory. For example, both governments aired their grievances about the water issue openly in the media and publicly exploited favorable elements in an opinion by the International Tribunal for the Law of the Sea on a Malaysian complaint regarding a land reclamation issue. However, the start of 2004 brought an encouraging development, when on a nominally courtesy visit by Abdullah to Singapore he and Singapore Prime Minister Goh Chok Tong announced their intention to resolve most disputes through talks. This may herald a welcome thaw in bilateral relations, although it is likely that the two countries will proceed cautiously with negotiations given the sticky nature of the outstanding issues.

Overlapping border claims between Brunei and Malaysia look set to be resolved more smoothly. Malaysia has reportedly proposed the establishment of a joint development area to resolve the dispute over the oil field off the coast of Sabah. The history of amicable relations between the two governments, the fact that Brunei hosts the largest contingent of Malaysians living abroad in any country (35,000), and the basic disparity in power and therefore negotiating leverage between the two are underlying factors in the markedly different tone of diplomacy between them as compared with Malaysia-Singapore relations.

A general testiness seems likely to continue in Malaysia-Australia diplomatic relations. Although the two countries enjoy an otherwise good relationship, Prime Minister John Howard bid a curt farewell to outgoing Prime Minister Mahathir at the October Asia-Pacific Economic Cooperation (APEC) forum meeting in Bangkok and remarked that he would not do anything to mend the sour ties between the two countries. Incoming Prime Minister Abdullah shrugged off this comment, but underscored that Malaysia would continue to defend its sovereignty and interests.

Mahathir's opening speech at the 10th Session of the Islamic Summit Conference in October, and in particular his remarks about Jews on which the Western media focused, caused much consternation especially in the United States. This led to a unanimous U.S. Senate resolution to condition US$1.2 million in military training assistance to Malaysia on a determination by the secretary of state of the country's support for and promotion of religious freedom for all, including for Jews. Malaysia treated the resolution as more symbolic than substantive. It seems that with the present prime minister's less abrasive style, relations with the United States will be more nuanced, although Malaysia's leadership of the Non-Aligned Movement (NAM) and the Organization of the Islamic Conference (OIC), its long-standing position on the Palestinian issue, and interest in the World Trade Organization (WTO) will result in continuing differences between the two countries.

DEFENSE POLICIES AND ISSUES

DOCTRINE Consistent with previous years, Malaysia maintains a "defensive defense" posture. This doctrine, however, is part of the wider concept of comprehensive security, which recognizes the equal significance of economic development and national unity in the face of a broad range of internal, external, traditional, and nontraditional possible security threats. As such, Malaysia's defense policy is geared toward "full spectrum capabilities," involving not only the modernization of weaponry and technology but also a revolution in military education to cope with the so-called Revolution in Military Affairs (combining weapons and information technology advances).

Cognizant of the increasingly vital role of technology in the military, the government is dedicated to transforming the Malaysian Armed Forces (MAF). Plans are being drawn up to achieve the goal of battle space digitization, under which the operations of all services will eventually be integrated into a joint operations task force.

FORCE STRUCTURE The Royal Malaysian Army comprises 85,000 soldiers, down from 100,000 in 2001. Under the 8th Malaysia Plan, the army recently acquired PT-91 main battle tanks (MBTs) from Poland, Metis-M man-portable anti-armor missile systems, MBDA's Jernas air defense system, and man-portable surface-to-air missiles such as the Russian Igla and Pakistani Anza MK-II to add to an aging arsenal inventory. The army's tank regiment of about 80 MBTs and support vehicles will be complemented by other armored fighting vehicles. The existing Infantry Brigades are to be reorganized as combined arms formations.

The Royal Malaysian Air Force (RMAF) has a strength of 15,000 personnel and nearly 200 aircraft. The force includes 78 combat aircraft, of which 17 are MiG-29N/UB tactical air-to-air fighters, eight are F/A-18D attack planes capable of full strike and interdiction missions, 14 are (R)F-5E/F, and ten are Hawk Mk108 as well as training aircraft.

The Royal Malaysian Navy (RMN) employs 14,000 personnel. Its fleet includes guided missile and other frigates, corvettes, missile gunboats, mine hunters, and other types of patrol boats and auxiliaries. It has a variety of missiles and naval helicopters.

ACQUISITIONS   There has been much speculation in the region about Malaysia's recent military acquisitions in the past few years. In fact, the RMAF had long planned its force modernization program, but the 1997 financial crisis and spillover effects precluded defense acquisitions until 2002 when the economy was back on track.

The latest round of purchases will see the delivery of 48 PT-91 tanks and 14 support vehicles in 2004, as part of a package including training on tank battle strategy and the stationing of a Polish military adviser in Malaysia. RMAF's Scorpion light tanks, used since the 1980s, will continue to be maintained. Additionally, the RMAF's 10th Brigade Paratroopers 4,500-strong Rapid Deployment Force will be equipped with Anza MK-II surface-to-air missiles by the end of 2003. The Army Air Wing will receive 11 Agusta A109M light observation helicopters as its first component under a package agreement including support equipment, training, and technical service worth around US$75 million.

In a deal worth around US$900 million, the RMAF will be outfitted with 18 Sukhoi Su-30MKM combat aircraft by 2006 to form a squadron of multirole combat aircraft (MRCA) to complement its present capabilities. In addition, Malaysia is also contemplating buying the U.S. Navy's F/A-18F Super Hornet two-seat MRCA, which would make Malaysia the first other country to have the Super Hornet and would transform the RMAF into a truly potent regional force. The RMAF is also currently evaluating airborne early warning and control

(AEW&C) aircraft and maritime patrol aircraft (MPA), key to an air defense system.

The RMN took delivery of five of the six procured Agusta Westland Super Lynx 300 multirole helicopters at the end of August 2003, with the sixth still in the United Kingdom for trials. The RMN's new 91m New Generation Patrol Vessels (NGPVs) will replace a series of vessels that are over 30 years old. The first six of a fleet of 27 NGPVs are scheduled to be built over eight years. They will follow the "fitted for but not with" concept that will see the vessels being built to accept systems and weapons to be chosen by the RMN at a future time. Also, in anticipation of the delivery of two new SSK Scorpene submarines in 2008–2009 and one ex-French navy Agosta 70 submarine for training, a new naval base is being built in eastern Malaysia to house these submarines.

Malaysia has also expressed interest in buying high-technology air defense equipment, including air surveillance radar from the Ukraine.

CONTRIBUTIONS TO REGIONAL AND GLOBAL SECURITY

REGIONAL   Malaysia participated in the adoption at the 2003 Association of Southeast Asian Nations (ASEAN) Bali summit of the Declaration of ASEAN Concord II calling for the establishment of an ASEAN Community (AC) that envisions further peace, stability, and prosperity among the ten member nations. To achieve the AC, Malaysia is committed to the creation of an ASEAN Security Community, which aims to enhance political and security cooperation; an ASEAN Economic Community, which will eventually transform ASEAN into a single market; and an ASEAN Socio-Cultural Community, which will foster closer ties among women, youth, and communities as well as promote talented writers and artists toward forming a regional identity.

Following the outbreak of the severe acute respiratory syndrome (SARS) virus in 2002–2003, Malaysia was entrusted by the ASEAN +3 health ministers' meeting on April 26, 2003, to strengthen the capacity of ASEAN's network of laboratories for surveillance and early warning systems. The government has approved RM20 million (US$5.2 million at RM1 = US$0.26) for the establishment of a Centre for Disease Control in the country's Bio-Valley and RM50 million (US$13 million) for establishment of a high-security Enhanced Level-3 (eventually to be upgraded to Level-4) bio-security facility to contain the world's most dangerous organisms and viruses at the National Public Health laboratory, scheduled for completion in June 2005. An existing Level-3 bio-containment laboratory at the Institute for Medical Research will also be upgraded to Enhanced Level-3, and eventually to Level-4.

Former Malaysian diplomat and UN Special Envoy Tan Sri Razali Ismail is actively involved in the effort to achieve political reform in Myanmar. In talks with the ruling junta in 2003, he pressed the military government to release pro-democracy leader Aung San Suu Kyi and to move the national reconciliation process along. Although the junta has not made any promises on either, Razali is optimistic and will remain engaged in the slow-moving process.

In East Timor, a Malaysian general took over as commander of the UN peacekeeping forces and will likely remain in charge until the UN Mission of Support in East Timor (UNMISET), which includes about 3,800 peacekeepers, is terminated on May 20, 2004.

As part of the Ministerial Forum of the East Asian Seas Congress 2003, Malaysia will adopt the Sustainable Development Strategy for the Seas of East Asia, to enhance cooperation in resolving management problems of the common seas shared by East Asia's 12 coastal countries involved in the process.

Malaysia continues to be committed to the Five Power Defense Arrangements (FPDA) military exercises (with Australia, New Zealand, Singapore, and the United Kingdom) and has even suggested that future activities should reach the level of war games and higher-level command functions in a command-post exercise format to "enhance the interoperability of [our] forces." Malaysian Defense Minister Najib Tun Razak has also expressed hope that the FPDA, established when the United Kingdom pulled out of its colonial-era bases three decades ago, would remain relevant but with various changes to it, including the setting up of a permanent joint headquarters.

Finally, the Malaysia-based Southeast Asia Regional Centre for Counter-Terrorism held a five-day meeting on money laundering and terrorist financing in August 2003 as one of its first initiatives since its launch a month earlier. The meeting involved some 60 law enforcement and banking officials from Southeast Asia, the United States, and Australia. The center will conduct a series of similar workshops, meetings, and training sessions as part of the regional effort against terrorism.

GLOBAL   In 2003, Malaysia demonstrated its resolve to fight terrorism by acceding to two relevant UN conventions—the 1963 Tokyo Convention on Offences and Certain Other Acts Committed on Board

Aircraft, and the 1970 Hague Convention for the Suppression of Unlawful Seizure of Aircraft. Amendments to the domestic Penal Code are being tabled to give effect to the accession. The country is already party to five other UN conventions on terrorism.

Malaysia's global presence was boosted when it took over the chair of the NAM in February 2003 and hosted the 10th OIC summit in October. The Kuala Lumpur Declaration of the 13th NAM summit centered on the continuing revitalization of the movement. The implications of this, for practical purposes, are enormous. Malaysia, along with the other two members of the leadership Troika, will press the transformation of the NAM into a credible collective voice on the world stage, proving its enduring relevance in the post–cold war era.

The country faces another daunting task as chair of the OIC, representing 1.3 billion Muslims totaling nearly one-third of the world's population. At the summit, a resolution was passed strongly recommending the eradication of polio in Islamic states. Recognizing this, Malaysia's chairmanship, and the fact that Malaysia has been declared polio-free since 2000, the World Health Organization has asked the country to help six other Islamic countries—Afghanistan, Egypt, Nigeria, Niger, Pakistan, and Somalia—to eradicate the disease by 2005. The challenge within the OIC at large, however, goes beyond assisting member states in disease eradication. For Malaysia, as chair, it will be to unite a deeply divisive Muslim world, with a high propensity to lash out in blind anger and heated rhetoric, and caution it to act strategically in a decided, coordinated fashion. This transformation will not happen quickly, but Malaysia hopes to prove itself a Muslim model of moderation and development, and to lead by example.

13 Mongolia

THE SECURITY ENVIRONMENT

Mongolian perceptions of the security environment remain essentially unchanged, despite turmoil in other parts of the world. Enjoying good relations with both neighboring countries—the Russian Federation and the People's Republic of China—Mongolians feel militarily secure at least as long as these neighbors are internally orderly and externally committed to good relations based on secure boundaries. Threat perceptions thus focus more on socioeconomic issues. Economic security remains a strong but elusive aspiration. The fear is that Mongolia may be disadvantaged and eternally left behind in a globalized, market-oriented economy. In this respect some Mongolians do fear the economic policies of their neighbors, which could leave them dependent. The major foreign policy step of 2003 was the government's quick decision, supported by a national political consensus, to join the U.S.-led coalition in Iraq. This move may herald a shift from a largely isolationist, neutral international stance to a more activist approach, enhancing Mongolia's international visibility.

INTERNAL   There will be a general election for the nation's 76-member unicameral legislative body, the State Great Hural (Parliament) in 2004, the fifth such election since the democratic revolution of 1990. Consequently, partisan maneuvering will dominate national politics during this period, but political turbulence notwithstanding there are no serious challenges to internal security.

There is general acknowledgment in Mongolia that although the economic policies of the ruling Mongolian People's Revolutionary Party

(MPRP) government have produced growth, performance remains well below the aspirations of the average citizen. Accordingly, and in anticipation of the election, discussion of economic policy is increasingly politicized. Issues such as the privatization of large enterprises and its possible effects on economic security have raised concerns among the population and have been used in the political debate not only by the opposition but also by some factions within the MPRP. To promote tourism, which is considered the most promising industry, the government declared 2003 "Visit Mongolia Year" and invested heavily in this project. However, the severe acute respiratory syndrome (SARS) epidemic in the region, which spread to Mongolia at the height of the tourist season, significantly reduced the projected number of visitors. The opposition is expected to attack this and other underperforming areas of the MPRP's economic policy.

Politics in Mongolia is marked by partisan accusations on issues ranging from parliamentary procedures to corruption. The major opposition parties represented in the Parliament—the Democratic Party (DP), the Civic Will-Republican Party (CWRP), and the Mongolian Democratic New Socialist Party (MDNSP)—are building a coalition to counterbalance the MPRP. Despite the preelection heat, the major parties maintain a basic consensus on foreign, defense, and security policy. In addition, both the ruling party and the opposition supported the coalition war efforts in Iraq. The only political objections to the government's decision came from the CWRP leadership and some individual DP members, but their objections were explained on procedural grounds. They argued that the Parliament as the organ vested by the constitution with the highest deliberative and legislative functions should make the final decision in matters of war and peace, and that the cabinet should not have made a unilateral decision on Iraq. This indicates that politicians generally perceived electoral advantage with the voting public in the substance of this decision and its display of independence from the policies of Mongolia's two powerful neighbors.

EXTERNAL   As stated in the nation's basic foreign policy concept adopted in the 1990s, and based on historical, geographical, and economic factors, Mongolia gives priority to its relations with its two immediate, giant neighbors. In 2003, visits by Mongolian Prime Minister Nambar Enkhbayar to Russia and by newly elected Chinese President Hu Jintao to Mongolia, as well as other mutual exchanges at various levels, provided impetus to both these bilateral relationships.

Mongolia's relations with Russia, and Russia's attitude toward Mongolia, are generally favorable. The issue of Mongolia's debt to the former USSR (and by succession to Russia) has dominated the headlines. A breakthrough was achieved during Enkhbayar's visit to Russia in June–July, which produced agreement at the political level on resolution of the debt issue, although the details remained to be worked out. The Russians offered what they termed a "favorable" solution that "would not bring about a heavy burden on Mongolia's economy." (The Russian attitude contrasted sharply with that during the 2002 visit of Russian Prime Minister Mikhail Kasyanov to Mongolia, when the Russian media published such comments as "Russia is not that rich to forgive the debts and Mongolia is not that poor to be exempt [from debt].") Since then, the Russian economy has continued to be buoyed by high oil prices, but Mongolia is still struggling. Some Mongolian opposition leaders and economists were pessimistic about the "deal," doubting whether the conditions were actually favorable to Mongolia. In their view, even if, as anticipated, Mongolia were to pay only 5 percent of the total debt, this would be an enormous burden for such a small and poorly performing economy. Opponents also called for revision of the underlying calculations. But the opponents' most serious argument related to economic security; in their view, the deal reflected Russia's desire to obtain, and the Mongolian government's willingness to offer, access to some of the strategic industries of Mongolia. Nevertheless, the government was consistently optimistic about the results of the negotiations—and on January 9, 2004, it was announced that the debt had been settled through a full payment of US$250 million.

Another factor that in the view of some analysts impedes Mongolian-Russian bilateral relations is that the "pure bilateralism" of the state-to-state relations between Ulaanbaatar and Moscow is increasingly giving way to a form of "quasi-multilateralism" involving Mongolia and the adjacent regions of Russian Siberia and the Far East. Some argue that this is the most pragmatic pattern for future economic relations, but others believe it is a result of a Russian policy to draw Mongolia into dependence on its frontier regions.

Meanwhile, Mongolia's relations with China have progressed to a new level. The warm welcome offered by Mongolian believers to their spiritual leader the Dalai Lama on his visit in late 2002 had triggered a sharp reaction from China—including official protests, unofficial expressions of discontent by various societal elements, and the temporary closure of the vital railroad gateway by the Chinese side, ostensibly for "technical reasons." The atmosphere changed significantly during 2003, however, when Hu made his first foreign visit to Russia, France, Kazakhstan, and Mongolia, which appeared to reflect the foreign policy objectives adopted at the Chinese Communist Party Congress to enhance the good-neighborly partnerships with neighboring countries.

Besides expressing political good will, the visit of the Chinese president marked increased interest in the success of Mongolian economic reforms. China promised US$300 million worth of loans, a huge amount compared to the level of assistance received by Mongolia since 1990. The visit also prompted increased Chinese investment in the Mongolian economy. Unlike much of the previous funds invested or lent to Mongolia by China, which used to be directed mainly to the "softer" sectors of the economy such as services and trade, investment into the strategically important infrastructure sector is now increasing significantly. But again this development raises some controversy in Mongolia as to whether it will promote the economic development by fostering close regional integration, or jeopardize the economic security of the otherwise unprotected, small, and weak market by increasing dependency on China.

As a small country with powerful neighbors, Mongolia seeks to reinforce its international position through its relations with "third neighbors"—a collective community of democracies supporting Mongolia's transformation—as well as its participation in international organizations. The government cultivates its relationships with the United States and European nations, and has particularly active bilateral relations with the other Northeast Asian states, including North Korea.

Mongolia, however, remains an outsider in the Northeast Asian multilateral process, most importantly the Six-Party Talks (among China, Japan, North and South Korea, Russia, and the United States) on the North Korean nuclear issue. In the view of some analysts, this "left out" condition could have unfavorable longer-term implications for Mongolia's national security interests. These analysts see the Six-Party Talks as potentially evolving into a solid regional security and developmental institution after the immediate crisis. Nonparticipation in such forums, they argue, risks isolating the country from regional collective security mechanisms, and then economic and infrastructure integration. Others, however, believe that ongoing Mongolian involvement in regional transportation, communication, and banking is a more important factor for the longer term and argue that the current "low profile" on the North Korean nuclear issue is not a serious disadvantage.

DEFENSE POLICIES AND ISSUES

Mongolia's defense policy has been one of the most stable components of national policy in the period following democratization. Defense policy derives from the nation's foreign policy, which is independent, neutral, and peaceful. The constitution and the laws of Mongolia define the mission of the Mongolian Armed Forces as exclusively that of self-defense. Being a small landlocked country with two gigantic neighbors, Mongolia's security concern is that its neighbors recognize its international boundary, primarily a diplomatic task. In other words, possessing no significant leverage/vital interest outside its borders, Mongolia can maintain only a small military, which is gradually being transformed into a more professional force. The mission of the armed forces stresses border defense and disaster relief. In addition, the increasing orientation of the armed forces toward international peacekeeping has received generally positive feedback from the Mongolian public.

Another key factor in Mongolia's defense policy is the persistent perception among the general public that military matters belong exclusively to the state. One result is the relative absence of major public and political debates on defense policy, and an absence of partisan involvement and political polarization in the military. A corollary benefit is that the armed forces have emerged as the most successfully apoliticized branch of the civil service. The negative aspect of this factor is its potential impact on civilian control of the military, especially when the political leadership lacks substantial expertise on defense matters.

Mongolia's defense spending of US$25 million in 2002 remained about 6 percent of the total government budget and just over 2 percent of gross domestic product. This represented a slight decline in spending in real terms from the previous year but only a third of the level of spending under the pre-1989 relationship with the Soviet Union.

CONTRIBUTIONS TO REGIONAL AND GLOBAL SECURITY

The Mongolian government's decision in March 2003 to join the U.S.-led "coalition of the willing" in Iraq was the first time since World War II that Mongolia had joined an international coalition in a military campaign. The government took this decision despite the difference between this position and the views of its two neighbors. Although the action was generally supported in Mongolia, and many viewed it as "bold," some considered it dangerous "adventurism." In September, Mongolian servicemen were dispatched to assist in the Iraqi reconstruction, as part of the multinational command. Mongolian military instructors are also involved in the training of the Afghan National Army units.

Within the limits of its capabilities Mongolia contributes to other global peacekeeping activities. For example, Mongolian officers completed peacekeeping duties in the Democratic Republic of the Congo during 2003, and Mongolian troops participated in a six-country UN peacekeeping exercise in Bangladesh in September. Mongolia is also actively engaged in promoting nontraditional aspects of security. In September 2003, Mongolia hosted the Fifth International Conference of New and Restored Democracies, which it regarded as a contribution to worldwide democratization and to global security, reflecting the concept of comprehensive human security.

At the regional level, the North Korean nuclear issue is the most significant current concern. Although it is not included in the Six-Party Talks, the Mongolian government attaches great importance to the resolution of this issue and supports the negotiations. It views its relationships with all six participants in the talks, including North Korea, as a potential asset in this regard. Mongolia's relations with North Korea are handicapped by the persistent issue of refugee flows from the North, but in the interest of preserving its diplomatic dialogue with North Korea, Ulaanbaatar maintains a low profile on the refugee issue while also showing concern for the safety of the individuals involved. In practice, Mongolia's approach on the Korean peninsula can be described as "developing with the South and revitalizing with the North."

Mongolia's limited participation in the regional multilateral dialogue generally is a subject of some concern within the country. In addition to its exclusion from the Six-Party Talks, Mongolia's participation in the ASEAN Regional Forum (ARF) is minimal. Nor has Mongolia made any significant progress in its effort to gain membership in the Asia-Pacific Economic Cooperation (APEC) forum. Thus, the future of Mongolia's regional identification is uncertain.

14 New Zealand

THE SECURITY ENVIRONMENT

Entering 2004 New Zealand's security concerns are dominated by Islamist terrorism, small-scale disturbances in the South Pacific, and the war in Iraq. However, there is little sense of immediate danger to the country or its citizens. The Iraq war, the major security topic of 2003, occasioned debates on public radio and television and to a lesser extent in the print media, but the issue aroused little passion.

Minister of Foreign Affairs and Trade Philip Goff probably reflected a national consensus when he said that terrorism is the main direct threat to the security of New Zealanders abroad. The death of three New Zealanders in the 2002 Bali bombings, the injury of many more in those blasts, and the lucky escapes of New Zealanders in the attack on the UN Headquarters in Baghdad and the bombing of the JW Marriott Hotel Jakarta in August 2003 underlined the foreign minister's assessment. Nevertheless, the threat of external terrorism has had little detectable impact on New Zealanders' longstanding tradition of frequent overseas travel.

Comments on the Iraq war by Prime Minister Helen Clark triggered an open breech in the New Zealand-United States bilateral relationship. Tensions in the Australia-New Zealand bilateral relationship also emerged in 2003. These tensions and differences could well deepen. They are a natural further evolution of New Zealand's opposition to visits by nuclear-powered or -armed warships in the mid-1980s that led to the suspension by Washington of New Zealand's membership in ANZUS, the Australia-New Zealand-United States defense alliance.

New Zealand's low level of investment in defense has further distinguished New Zealand's security approach from those of its traditional defense allies, offset by contributions to international peacekeeping and humanitarian missions including participation in Operation Enduring Freedom in Afghanistan.

INTERNAL   New Zealand's internal threat perceptions are, and are likely to remain, focused on terrorism and border security. Tighter domestic security has been introduced for passengers traveling by air (on aircraft with more than 90 seats), and new measures are now in place to ensure compliance with American security standards for passengers flying to the United States. New Zealand hosted a combined New Zealand-Australian counterterrorism exercise in 2003.

New Zealand concurred with the UN Security Council decision to ban groups and individuals listed as terrorist entities pursuant of the Terrorism Suppression Act. Terrorist groups banned by this measure include the regional groups Ansar Al-Islam, Lashkar I Jhangri, and Gulbuddin Hekmatyar. One person, an Algerian named Ahmed Zaoui, is detained in New Zealand under new counterterrorism measures. Zaoui arrived in New Zealand using forged travel documents, was arrested, and is now in solitary confinement. According to media reports, Zaoui has links with Islamist terrorist groups and is sentenced to death in Algeria. The New Zealand Security Intelligence Service's Security Risk Certificate for Zaoui classifies him as a security risk. (At the same time, consistent with New Zealand's civil libertarian traditions, various groups are defending Zaoui's rights and demanding his release.)

The Clark administration also emphasizes border security. New biosecurity legislation bans "eco terrorism," including the unauthorized release of bio-organisms into New Zealand that could damage agriculture and the environment.

EXTERNAL   Other than the generalized concern over terrorism, New Zealanders do not see serious external threats to the country's security. Political and opinion leaders tend to believe that international prosperity and security will prevail as long as the large powers exercise restraint. This translates into general support for New Zealand's pursuit of free trade and an independent approach to international political-security issues. Perhaps reflecting New Zealand's small absolute size there is little serious debate on these questions even though polling shows that around 60 percent of the public distrusts free markets and prefers strong defense relationships with traditional allies.

The problem of insecurity in the South Pacific is a subject of more immediate and continuing concern in New Zealand, and engagement in this region enjoys broad and enduring bipartisan support. New Zealand policy emphasizes a broad approach to countering insecurity and the balancing of political, economic, social, and military responses. The New Zealand government supported the Australian-led intervention in 2003 to restore order in the Solomon Islands. Clark, who chaired the Pacific Islands Forum summit meeting in 2003, openly lobbied in favor of Australian initiatives to bolster the institutional capacity of the forum. In addition, the prime minister backed Canberra's lobbying for an experienced Australian diplomat to head the forum secretariat.

While New Zealand's more than two years of political, military, and humanitarian support for the U.S.-led Operation Enduring Freedom in Afghanistan continues to enjoy broad bipartisan support, the war on Iraq has proved a more divisive issue. The minority Labour government, supported by the left—the small Alliance Party, whose votes give Labour its parliamentary majority, and the Green Party of Aotearoa New Zealand—opposed the war and for a short time openly criticized U.S., U.K., and Australian policy. The small new right ACT Party was the only political party to consistently support enforcement of the October UN Security Council resolution threatening forcible action if Iraq did not comply with UN demands. The principal conservative opposition party, the National Party, offered lukewarm support for the U.S., Australian, and U.K. positions on the eve of the onset of the war and then adopted a low profile on the issue.

The Iraq war stimulated generally tempered debate primarily among academic and media commentators, with the majority tending to oppose the war. A few anti-war protest marches and demonstrations were organized, but the numbers of participants were comparatively small, varying from a handful to several thousand. Polling showed about 80 percent support for intervention if sanctioned by the UN Security Council but as little as 8 percent support for intervention without the sanction of the council. These levels of support mirrored Australian public opinion polls taken at around the same time.

The Clark government's very public opposition to the war included an open critique of Australian, U.K., and U.S. policy. The prime minister told Parliament on March 18, 2003, that the government "did not believe" that the authorization of force "would be justified at [this] time," explaining that this stance was based on strong support for "multilateralism and the rule of law, and for upholding the authority of the Security Council." In an indirect reference to the United States, Australia, and the United Kingdom, Clark said that "it is a matter of profound regret to us that some of our closest friends have chosen to stand outside the Security Council at this point," adding that this established a "new and dangerous precedent" that other nations might use in the future.

A further public remark by Clark, that the war in Iraq would not have happened if Democrat Al Gore had won the U.S. presidential election in 2000, triggered rare open criticism from the United States. In the first statement of its kind directed toward New Zealand since the mid-1980s, a Department of State official said that these words were a "matter of regret." The prime minister subsequently apologized for the comments.

There may be more tangible consequences for New Zealand of the clash with the United States over Iraq. Shortly after Clark's March 18 statement to Parliament, a U.S. government spokesman dashed New Zealand's hopes for a free trade agreement (FTA) with the United States. (An FTA could have significant advantages for New Zealand; Goff puts the value of an FTA with the United States at NZ$1 billion [US$650 million at NZ$1 = US$0.65] a year.) New Zealand had pushed hard to open FTA talks with the United States. The U.S. reaction caused some political embarrassment for Clark, who had emphasized that a deal with the United States would be in the pipeline after New Zealand committed troops to Afghanistan and would follow the completion of U.S.-Australia FTA negotiations.

Defense Policies and Issues

POLICY   The Labour government's approach to defense policy, which caused considerable domestic controversy from 1999 to 2002 (see editions of *Asia Pacific Security Outlook* from 1999 to 2003), attracted little public attention in 2003. The exception was brief attention to remarks by the just-retired chief of defense force that "defense policy was being made on the run" by the Clark administration. There is a broad consensus among politicians, media, and academics that New

Zealand need not maintain a broadly balanced defense capability. Paradoxically, polling from a variety of sources shows that around 60 percent of New Zealanders support increased defense spending on conventional forces, including the reinstatement of the Air Combat Force that was disbanded in December 2001.

A review and restatement of the Closer Defense Relationship with Australia in 2003 suggested a further divergence in this relationship. Over the decade of the 1990s, New Zealand had agreed to commit combat forces to the defense of Australia, and both states agreed that they constituted a single strategic entity. This approach was ended under the Clark government. The 2003 review emphasized that both countries need to "understand" each other's approach to defense better. Practical cooperation is now largely confined to training opportunities and cooperation on border security, peacekeeping, and humanitarian assistance.

There has long been a general consensus that the ban on nuclear-powered or -armed ships is a fixed, accepted element of New Zealand policy. (The most natural moment for a change would have been when the conservative National Party won the government back from Labour in the 1990s, but the National under Prime Minister Jim Bolger chose not to challenge popular support of the non-nuclear policy.) However, there are indications of at least some questioning of the policy.

- Although a clear majority of New Zealanders continues to back the policy, a significant minority (33 percent–44 percent, according to polls in 2002–2003) favors revoking the banning of nuclear-powered or -armed ships, which is the key to restoring cooperation with the United States. And these readings were taken in the absence of a serious national debate on the issue.
- In August 2003, Michael Bassett, a respected member of Labour Prime Minister David Lange's government that adopted the anti-nuclear policy, publicly called on Clark to reexamine the policy. While the speech did not trigger an extended discussion, it did demonstrate a lack of unanimity within Labour on the subject.
- U.S. Ambassador to New Zealand Charles Swindells in a speech on October 8, 2003, directly linked the anti-nuclear policy to the George W. Bush administration's irritation over New Zealand's position on Iraq. Asserting that, "contrary to the views of some, the United States is not going to just 'get over it,'" Swindells stressed that the "nuclear issue inevitably . . . limits the scope for further deepening of cooperation in key areas." He urged that, "Twenty

years on, a reexamination of this issue could benefit us all." Such blunt talk from the American ambassador might be counterproductive with some segments of opinion, but the message about the potential benefits of rethinking the anti-nuclear policy was clear.

- Finally, the position of the conservative National Party on defense policy may be shifting. In 2003, the party commissioned a task force headed by a former deputy prime minister to review defense issues, including the anti-nuclear law, the relationships with the United States and Australia, and defense spending. A change in the party's leadership in late 2003 provides additional impetus for rethinking National's positions. National's prospects for returning to government remain highly uncertain, but a change in party policy would stimulate renewed debate.

As 2004 began, these developments were only straws in the wind. However, they suggested that the 20-year-old anti-nuclear position might not be totally immutable.

FORCE STRUCTURE   As indicated in previous editions of the *Asia Pacific Security Outlook*, New Zealand's conventional defense capabilities have experienced serious reductions under the Clark government. The major force structure and capability changes to the New Zealand Defense Force, designed to refocus the military on peacekeeping, humanitarian assistance, and border control, were reviewed in *Asia Pacific Security Outlook 2003*. The operational-level changes required to implement this restructuring are now occurring in the New Zealand army. These involve the phasing in of the new Light Armored Vehicles and the merging of light infantry, armored reconnaissance, and protected mobility roles for peacekeeping.

In the air force, two second-hand Boeing 757 passenger/cargo jets have now been purchased for the strategic air lift role, replacing aging Boeing 727s. This purchase cost approximately NZ$200 million (US$130 million).

BUDGET   The appropriation for defense for 2003–2004 is NZ$1,913 billion (US$1,243.45 billion) including goods and services tax. Thirty-seven percent of the total is allocated to personnel (NZ$534 million [US$347.1 million]), 30 percent to operations (NZ$430 million [US$279.5 million]), 15 percent (NZ$219 million [US$142.35 million]) to depreciation—which funds future capital purchases—and 18 percent (NZ$262 million [US$170.3 million]) to fund the capital charge, which is an internal levy on all government spending to cover the cost of capital. Overall defense spending is about 1 percent of gross domestic product and is unlikely to change.

Contributions to Regional and Global Security

The Clark government has strongly supported a range of non-alliance peacekeeping, counterterrorism, and humanitarian assistance contributions led by New Zealand's traditional allies (thus accommodating the public's continuing attachment to the traditional American and Australian alliance). New Zealand's contributions to Asia Pacific regional security are 222 personnel (an infantry company and a utility helicopter flight) assisting the Australian-led Regional Assistance Mission to the Solomon Islands and two officers with the Cambodian Mine Action Centre. New Zealand also participated in the Five Power Defense Arrangements exercises hosted by Malaysia and Singapore (and also including Australia and the United Kingdom).

New Zealand's contributions to international peacekeeping operations in 2003–2004 are 53 non-combat engineers under British command in Iraq, 15 personnel with the UN de-mining effort in Iraq, seven staff officers attached to Operation Enduring Freedom command headquarters in the United States and Afghanistan, 100 reconstruction personnel and a three-month deployment of a C-130 Hercules transport aircraft in Afghanistan (a P3K Orion surveillance aircraft and a frigate completed six-month tours supporting Afghanistan operations during 2002–2003), 26 personnel with the NATO stabilization force in Bosnia, an observer to the UN mission in Pristine, 27 personnel for the multinational force in the Sinai, seven observers with the UN Truce Supervision Organization in Israel/Syria, and two de-mining advisors with the UN team in Mozambique.

15 Papua New Guinea

THE SECURITY ENVIRONMENT

INTERNAL   While economic difficulties and problems of rural and urban lawlessness continue to plague Papua New Guinea (PNG), the coalition government led by Sir Michael Somare came through its first 18 months in office without serious challenge. In the Southern Highlands, where local unrest resulted in the declaration of "failed elections" for six of the nine seats in the province in the 2002 national election, new elections were held successfully in 2003, and a degree of peace was restored. Despite the passage in 2001 of an Organic Law on the Integrity of Political Parties and Candidates, designed to give greater stability to the political system, there was recurring talk of a prospective motion of no confidence against Prime Minister Somare. In November 2003, the government failed in an attempt to amend the constitution to extend the period during which a new government cannot be challenged. Within several parties, voting on the amendment was split; this will test the provisions of the organic law, which were intended to ensure that in parliamentary votes all party members vote the same way. Nevertheless, it still seems likely that the Somare government will be the first since independence to remain in office for a full parliamentary term.

Peace and reconstruction on Bougainville has continued to make slow but steady progress. Hard-line rebel leader Francis Ona has remained outside the peace talks and his Me'ekamui Defense Force (MDF) has maintained a "No Go Zone" around his headquarters in Central Bougainville, but Ona has not opposed the peace process and in early 2003 elements of the MDF announced their support for it. In April

2003, the remaining Papua New Guinea Defense Force (PNGDF) soldiers in Bougainville withdrew, and at the end of June the regional Peace Monitoring Group, comprising unarmed military and civilian personnel from Australia, Fiji, New Zealand, and Vanuatu, pulled out, though it was agreed to maintain a small Bougainville Transitional Team of monitors as a confidence-building measure.

When the UN Observer Mission on Bougainville verified that stage two of the weapons disposal program had been satisfactorily completed, with some 1,800 firearms (an estimated 85 percent–90 percent of the weapons in circulation prior to 1998) surrendered and placed in double-locked containers, the implementation of the legislative provisions setting up the Bougainville autonomous government became possible. The autonomous government was formally launched in August. Meanwhile, a Bougainville constitutional development commission had completed and submitted to the national government a second draft of the constitution for the autonomous province, but delays in the national government's response, which did not come until November, and negative comments on the draft by the attorney general, created tensions in what was described in Port Moresby as a "delicate and fragile" process. The situation has been made even more difficult by an increasing incidence of serious crime in Bougainville, due in part to inadequate policing and judicial services.

Amid criticisms from Australia that development assistance had not been well used, and the announcement that the Australian bilateral aid program was to be reviewed, PNG-Australian relations were at times tense during 2003. Somare took offense at a comment by the Australian prime minister, John Howard, that Papua New Guinea faced the prospect of becoming a "collapsed state" and suggested that Papua New Guinea would seek its aid elsewhere. Papua New Guineans' feelings on the bilateral relationship were aired during a visit by an Australian Senate Standing Committee on Foreign Affairs, Defense and Trade. The issue flared up again later in the year when the Australian government, following the Solomon Islands intervention, proposed to insert Australian public servants in key inline positions in the PNG bureaucracy and send some 200–300 police personnel to serve with the Royal Papua New Guinea Constabulary. Somare accused Australia of "neo-colonialism," but many in Papua New Guinea welcomed the proposal, and the terms of an "enhanced cooperation package" were agreed between the two governments in December 2003. Subsequently

Malaysian Prime Minister Mahathir bin Mohammed visited, bringing a delegation that included six cabinet ministers and more than 30 business people. The visit produced promises of increased Malaysian investment in the minerals and petroleum sector and provision of advice and expertise through Malaysia's technical cooperation program. There was also talk of Malaysia replacing Australia as Papua New Guinea's major trading partner. A joint Malaysia-PNG ministerial commission will hold its inaugural meeting in 2004.

In recent years, Papua New Guinea has also received increased development assistance from China, including funding and training support for the PNGDF. In the first half of 2003 trade between the two countries increased by some 60 percent. Subsequently, a Chinese delegation visited Papua New Guinea to look at investment opportunities in petroleum and mining. Papua New Guinea has also sought increased aid from Japan.

EXTERNAL   While Papua New Guinea continues to enjoy a relatively benign external security environment, developments on its western and eastern borders again raised some concern during 2003, and there has been discussion of Papua New Guinea's vulnerability to terrorism and international crime.

In late 2002, there were reports of an influx of border crossers from the Indonesian province of Papua (formerly Irian Jaya) into Papua New Guinea; this followed an attack by Organisasi Papua Merdeka (OPM, or Free Papua Movement) rebels on an Indonesian military border post at Wutung and Indonesian military action against Papuan activists who were attempting to raise the West Papuan Morning Star flag. It was also confirmed that the wife of the director of the Indonesian Institute for Human Rights Study and Advocacy (ELSHAM) had been shot while attempting to cross the border into Papua New Guinea to visit relatives. At the time, the local Indonesian head of police referred to the lack of PNG police and military along the border as "dangerous and inefficient."

In January 2003, PNGDF and police personnel met with members of the OPM and ordered them to remove camps on the Papua New Guinea side of the border, but Papua New Guinea maintained its long-standing policy against joint border operations with Indonesia. Subsequently, some 400 people who crossed over into Papua New Guinea in 2000 were ordered to return to Indonesia or face deportation. In mid-2003, Indonesia's foreign minister visited Papua New Guinea, where he thanked the government for its support of Indonesian sovereignty in West Papua and supported the idea of talks within the framework of the South West Pacific Dialogue. Concerns over the possibility of illegal migration across the border were evident at a joint border conference held in Madang, at which Papua New Guinea's minister for inter-governmental relations urged Indonesian authorities to speed up the passage of an extradition treaty and an agreement on the movement of third-country nationals.

To the east, the effective breakdown of government in the neighboring country of Solomon Islands in 2003 resulted in the intervention, at the Solomon Islands government's invitation, of a Regional Assistance Mission to the Solomon Islands (RAMSI). Papua New Guinea participated in this mission. Ahead of the RAMSI intervention there were reports of weapons moving between Solomon Islands and Bougainville, and reports that notorious Guadalcanal warlord Harold Keke had sought assistance from Bougainville—which, had it been the case, would have been a major embarrassment to the PNG government. The reports were denied in Bougainville, and ex-combatants of the Bougainville Revolutionary Army and the Bougainville Resistance Forces offered to provide border security operations to minimize cross-border movements; the commander of the PNGDF declined the offer. Local efforts were also initiated in 2003 to hold reconciliation meetings between Bougainvilleans and inhabitants of the Western and Choiseul provinces in the Solomon Islands, though these efforts are moving very slowly.

Against a background of growing concerns about international crime and people smuggling in the region, and the possible vulnerability of the region to terrorism, there has been a crackdown on illegal migrants to Papua New Guinea, in part in collaboration with Australia. Papua New Guinea's minister for internal security has estimated the number of illegal migrants at around 10,000. While most of these are from China, a number of illegal migrants from Lebanon, Afghanistan, and Pakistan were processed during 2003, and two Turkish nationals were apprehended for people smuggling. Following a break-in at the Migration Office in Port Moresby in late 2003, in which passports were stolen, investigations also uncovered fraudulent operations within the office, which resulted in charges against several migration officers and a number of foreigners. The PNG government is now taking steps (assisted by Australia under the "enhanced cooperation package") to tighten control over the issuance of passports and visas.

DEFENSE POLICIES AND ISSUES

After several years of unrest in the PNGDF, reflected in minor mutinies and political infighting, the force appears to have achieved a degree of stability. However, the disclosure that outside contractors have received substantial unauthorized payments and the disappearance of a small number of weapons from a warehouse at Murray Barracks suggest that serious management problems remain. The planned downsizing of the PNGDF to a force of 2,000 is proceeding, with some 700 soldiers retrenched and limited new recruitment commencing in 2003. PNGDF personnel assisted police in security operations during the Southern Highlands elections in mid-2003, PNGDF patrol boats took part in a naval exercise with the Australian navy, and the troops deployed to Solomon Islands as part of RAMSI are reported to have performed effectively.

CONTRIBUTIONS TO REGIONAL AND GLOBAL SECURITY

Despite funding limitations, Papua New Guinea continues to play an active role in regional and global forums and to support regional peacekeeping initiatives. During 2003, Papua New Guinea ratified two protocols and seven conventions related to counterterrorism and was represented at several regional and international conferences on terrorism. (There has been renewed interest within the government in the possibility of the PNGDF taking part in UN peacekeeping operations, but this option has to date been ruled out on the basis of insufficient resources.)

In January 2003, Somare called on the Australian government to consider carefully its support for a U.S.-led intervention in Iraq. "We do not accept the choice made by Australia to support the option of a war," he said. In March, Papua New Guinea supported a resolution of the Non-Aligned Movement in reference to the Iraq situation endorsing the role of the United Nations in maintaining international peace and security.

Somare emphasizes the need for regional cooperation to guard against the possibility that terrorism and transnational crime will penetrate the region, especially given that individual island states lack the capacity to provide security. Consistent with earlier support for Pacific Islands Forum initiatives on regional security, Papua New Guinea in

July 2003 backed the RAMSI intervention to restore law, order, and effective governance in Solomon Islands. The government initially proposed to contribute police and military personnel, but ultimately its contribution consisted of some 90 PNGDF personnel, including a rifle company (which served with Australian and Tongan troops) and about 35 army engineers. The RAMSI intervention is a major development in the island Pacific region, and the initial success of the operation has strengthened calls for a permanent regional security force. At a meeting of the Melanesian Spearhead Group in Gizo, Solomon Islands, in August, Papua New Guinea joined the Solomon Islands and Vanuatu in endorsing the idea of a regional rapid-response force.

In 2003, Papua New Guinea ratified the Pacific Island Countries Trade Agreement (PICTA) intended to establish a free trade area among the 16 Pacific Island Forum countries, as well as the Pacific Agreement on Closer Economic Relations (PACER), which allows the PICTA countries to negotiate free trade agreements with Australia and New Zealand. Former Prime Minister Sir Julius Chan was appointed to an Eminent Persons Group to review the role of the forum and its secretariat.

An agreement with Australia to maintain a refugee processing facility on Manus Island, as part of the Australian government's "Pacific solution" to the problems of "boat people" seeking asylum in Australia, expired toward the end of 2003—with one asylum seeker remaining in limbo.

Though itself a recipient of technical assistance, Papua New Guinea has signed technical cooperation agreements with both Solomon Islands and East Timor to assist their judicial services. Although these represent small initiatives, they are an indication of a growing commitment in Papua New Guinea to closer regional engagement.

16 The Philippines

Internal security will continue to preoccupy the Philippines in 2004 even as the country prepares for national elections in May that include choosing a president to lead the nation in the next six years. Whoever wins the presidential elections, whether President Gloria Macapagal Arroyo or another candidate, he or she may be expected to push for a final peace settlement with the Moro Islamic Liberation Front (MILF). At the same time, the Philippine government can be expected to sustain its campaign against the Abu Sayyaf Group (ASG) and other terrorist groups in the country. The United States is likely to continue providing military assistance to the Philippines as part of their close security alliance in the fight against international terrorism.

The Philippines faces a number of internal and external security challenges. Internal security threats basically stem from a few discontented junior officers in the Armed Forces of the Philippines (AFP) as well as from the secessionist Islamist groups led by the MILF. Large income disparities, rampant corruption, and weak economic growth contribute to the conditions conducive to internal unrest. In the external realm, the government's support for the American-led war in Iraq has had undoubted benefits, particularly increased military assistance from the United States, but closer military cooperation has created domestic tensions within the AFP, including new allegations of corruption.

INTERNAL The major internal concern of President Arroyo in 2003 was threats from soldiers led by a few junior officers possibly manipulated by opposition politicians. A failed mutiny (centered on a shopping mall in Manila) on July 27 underlined the precarious state of civil-military relations in the country. A government-convened commission concluded that the mutiny was part of a larger plot to oust the Arroyo government, but it also acknowledged the root causes of the rebellion —corruption and politicization of the Philippine military.

The country also faced a potential constitutional crisis in October when the House of Representatives of the national Congress impeached highly respected Supreme Court Chief Justice Hilario Davide Jr. The high court declared that the impeachment process violated a constitutional provision limiting impeachment charges against the same official to only one in the same year, but a Congress-Court confrontation was averted when the majority of the members of the House of Representatives voted against transmitting the articles of impeachment to the Senate.

Both negotiations and fighting with the Mindanao separatists will continue in 2004. The Arroyo government and the MILF have agreed to resume peace talks, stalled since May 2003, in January. Both parties are relying on mediation by Malaysia, which agreed to monitor the ceasefire agreement between Manila and the MILF on July 18, 2003. Prior to her departure for a visit to Washington, D.C., in May 2003, Arroyo ordered selective military strikes against "embedded terrorist cells" in Mindanao that were considered MILF strongholds. This action was evidently intended to show the United States her government's political will in dealing with the threat posed by terrorist groups in the Philippines. The AFP's military offensives against the MILF intensified following Arroyo's U.S. visit, leading to a 10-day unilateral MILF ceasefire beginning June 2 and the eventual ceasefire agreement in July.

Increased U.S.-Philippine cooperation has provided a much-needed moral boost for the AFP in the fight against the domestic Islamist rebel groups. It has also increased the political leverage of the Philippine government vis-à-vis the MILF in pushing for a negotiated settlement. The ability of the Philippine government to sustain the momentum in dealing with the threat of terrorism at home may be constrained by domestic politics as the country comes closer to the national and local elections in mid-2004. However, Arroyo appears steadfast in her determination to deal with domestic terrorism and the secessionist problem in Mindanao.

There is more to the revitalized Philippine-U.S. security relationship than closer military cooperation in the fight against terrorism. The United States has expressed its willingness to play a mediating role in the search for a political settlement to secessionism in Mindanao. It is also pouring in social and economic assistance to the predominantly Muslim areas of Mindanao, including socioeconomic projects such as road construction in Basilan during joint military exercises in 2003. During his brief visit to Manila in October, U.S. President George W. Bush declared before the Philippine Congress the willingness of the United States to provide additional socioeconomic support for Mindanao once a peace agreement with the MILF has been signed (on top of a US$30 million education initiative for Mindanao, which is tied to the achievement of a peace agreement with the MILF).

With the death of MILF chair Hashim Salamat in July, more moderate and pragmatic leaders of the rebel group have taken over. This has led some government officials to become more optimistic about the prospects for negotiations. Nevertheless, while the Philippine and Malaysian governments have been working on the terms of reference for monitoring the ceasefire, the Philippine military and the MILF rebels have been trading accusations about violating the ceasefire agreement. This situation is exacerbated by the AFP's continuing military operations against suspected terrorist groups and kidnap-for-ransom gangs that allegedly operate within MILF-controlled areas of Mindanao. Finally, government negotiators worry that unresolved issues of land or ancestral domains and control of local governments in Mindanao could delay or derail the talks.

Apart from the MILF problem, the Arroyo government is intensely focused on foreign terrorists linked to the Jemaah Islamiah (JI) network operating in the Philippines. There have been a number of recent positive developments in this campaign. The escape, with inside help, of convicted Indonesian terrorist Fathur Rahman Al-Ghozi in July 2003, on the heels of the failed mutiny, was initially thought to be part of a bigger plot designed to embarrass and destabilize the Arroyo administration. Al-Ghozi was gunned down in mid-October following an encounter with special police agents in Mindanao and just prior to the arrival of Bush for a brief state visit en route to the Asia-Pacific Economic Cooperation (APEC) leaders meeting in Bangkok. Subsequently, Arroyo announced on October 23 the capture of suspected Indonesian terrorist Taufik Rifqi, allegedly the No. 2 man in the JI network operating in Cotabato City in Mindanao and an understudy of Al-Ghozi. A raid in Cotabato that led to the capture of Rifqi also yielded documents reportedly indicating that the JI is producing biological weapons. Finally, on December 7, major ASG leader Ghalib Andang, alias

"Commander Robot," was captured by the Philippine military in Jolo, Sulu, following a brief encounter with the rebels. Andang had led a major ASG raid on the island of Sipadan, Malaysia, in April 2000, taking 21 Europeans, Malaysians, and Filipinos hostage.

EXTERNAL   The American-led invasion of Iraq is the major feature in the Philippines' external security concerns as 2004 opened. The Philippine government strongly supported the U.S.-led invasion of Iraq, despite substantial public opposition that led to a plunge in Arroyo's already low popularity. In a public opinion survey conducted nationwide in November 2002, some 45 percent of Filipinos polled had said they did not want the Philippines to be involved in the war. Twenty-eight percent supported multilateral action on Iraq within the UN framework, but half of this group did not support the use of military force. Sixteen percent agreed that the United States should oust Saddam Hussein, but again without the use of armed force. Only 10 percent of those polled said that the Philippine government should give the United States full support, and of those who favored supporting the Americans, 19 percent were from Mindanao—suggesting a more direct interest in U.S. support against the insurgency than U.S. action in Iraq per se.

Six months prior to the invasion of Iraq, Arroyo had categorically stated that her government would not support a U.S. attack, and would not allow the use of Philippine airspace, without a UN resolution. If at all, she said, the United States would only be allowed to use Philippine airspace for "humanitarian purposes." Apparently after her decision at the end of 2002 not to run for another term in 2004 she became more willing to go against popular opinion on this subject, saying publicly at one point that she was glad that she was not a candidate for president because she could make difficult political decisions. Nevertheless, on October 4, 2003, she announced that she would after all run for president again in 2004.

The Philippines has reaped a number of immediate benefits from supporting the Bush administration's war against Iraq. These include increased military assistance from Washington; designation of the Philippines as a major non–North Atlantic Treaty Organisation (NATO) military ally of the United States; and sustained American support for joint bilateral training with the AFP through the Balikatan exercises to stamp out the ASG. All these were announced during Arroyo's visit to the United States in May 2003.

Another external security issue of continuing concern is the possibility of military conflict across the Taiwan Strait, which would seriously destabilize the region and could directly affect the Philippines. Most recently, foreign affairs officials are worried by Taiwan President Chen Shui-bian's announcement of a referendum on the island's political status in March 2004. The Chinese ambassador warned directly that the Philippines' security could be affected if Taiwan's drive for independence triggers a war with China.

DEFENSE POLICIES AND ISSUES

The defense budget of the Philippines for fiscal year 2003 was P42.5 billion (US$765.63 million at US$1 = P55.51). The Philippine army's share was P18.89 billion (US$340.3 million), while the navy and air forces were allotted P7.34 billion (US$132.23 million) and P6.39 billion (US$115.11 million), respectively.

The "patron" role of the United States has become an object of criticism by some Filipino nationalist legislators as well as some military officers who see the AFP's growing dependence on the Americans in dealing with what is essentially a homegrown terrorist threat as dangerous. American military assistance has also contributed to an apparent "rift" within the AFP, particularly among junior officers, which partly led to the failed July 27 mutiny. Specifically, the rebel soldiers accused top military officials of the AFP of corruption and of staging bombings in Mindanao in order to get more military assistance from the Americans. Public opinion was sympathetic to the grievances of the rebel soldiers, although it did not support the unconstitutional means employed. Some government officials expressed sympathy for the rebel soldiers, including Vice President Teofisto Guingona, who called on the Arroyo administration to address the soldiers' legitimate complaints. The commission that investigated the July mutiny also recognized that the incident was rooted in corruption and politicization of the military.

The patron role of the United States has created domestic tensions not only within the military but also in civil-military relations. Bush recognized this problem during his address to the Philippine national Congress on October 18, in which he supported the legitimacy of the Arroyo government while underscoring the need to modernize and reform the AFP in order for it to be more effective in dealing with terrorism.

CONTRIBUTIONS TO REGIONAL AND GLOBAL SECURITY

The Philippines continues to rely on its revitalized security alliance with the United States as part of its overall strategy to deal with international and regional terrorism. Nonetheless, it also gives importance to regional efforts, particularly through bilateral and regional cooperation with other members of the Association of Southeast Asian Nations (ASEAN).

As part of its commitment to combating international terrorism, the Philippine Senate in October 2003 ratified six international agreements: on terrorist financing, acts of violence at airports, bombings, detection of plastic explosives, attacks on platforms at sea, and the safety of maritime navigation.

The Philippines also worked hard to win a non-permanent seat in the UN Security Council starting in 2004; the effort succeeded with the support of the 52-nation Asian bloc. President Arroyo has stressed that during its term on the council the Philippines will continue working with other countries to advance international consensus, multilateral peacekeeping, and the rule of law.

17 Russia

THE SECURITY ENVIRONMENT

INTERNAL   In terms of implications for 2004, the most significant political event of 2003 in Russia was the election for the Duma (the lower
chamber of Parliament) in December. The election clarified the political
power alignment and ensured well ahead of the presidential election
scheduled for March that Vladimir Putin will continue as president of
the Russian Federation. Terrorism in the Caucasus and Moscow is the
other major feature of the domestic scene.

In the December election, only four political parties were able to
overcome the 5 percent threshold to participate in the Duma for the
next four years. Due to Putin's popular support and active use of the so-
called administrative resource (the government apparatus), the United
Russia Party (URP) secured more than 300 seats in the 450-seat Duma.
This gives the party the votes—and a strong temptation—to change
the constitution. There is a strong probability that after the presidential elections the new prime minister would be chosen by the URP, thus
giving the party a chance to share with the president control over, and
responsibility for, the socioeconomic course of Russia.

The other Duma election winners were two nationalist parties: The
old Liberal Democratic Party led by the charismatic Vladimir Zhirinov-
sky, which increased its vote total and won 36 seats, and the brand-
new (Kremlin-created) Motherland Party led by leftwing economist
Sergey Glaziev and populist Dmitry Rogozin, which also won 36 seats.

The election dealt a devastating blow to the Communists, because
through the Motherland Party the Kremlin divided the leftwing vote.
As a result, and also due to Communist leader Gennady Zyuganov's

rigid stance, Zyuganov's faction won only 13 percent of votes (half of that in the previous election) and 52 seats in the Duma, thus transforming the faction's role from chief opposition force to bit player.

Another surprise was the fact that liberal reform-oriented parties, such as the Union of Right Forces (URF) and Yabloko, failed to win seats in the new Duma. This was partly due to a grave confrontation between the two during the campaign. In addition, most Russians remain unhappy with the results of privatization policies of the early 1990s, and so support by URF and Yabloko for Mikhail Khodorkovsky, the recently arrested president of Yukos, Russia's largest oil company, who had channeled huge financial resources to both parties, further eroded their political standing. Khodorkovsky is widely seen in Russia as having exploited privatization to unfairly enrich himself.

The fact that the Duma has lost the liberal, so-called right wing and that the left wing has been marginalized may create a systemic problem during Putin's second term. The president can easily win approval for legislation, but in the absence of independent sources of reform-oriented proposals and criticism from the left, Putin may actually have less room for political maneuvering on further reforms.

A related but potentially more significant change in the Russian political landscape was signaled by the resignation in October 2003 of presidential administration chief Alexander Voloshin, allegedly in protest over the selective application and misuse of laws by the government apparatus in the Yukos case. This resignation demonstrates a serious weakening of the two once-mighty Kremlin factions: the "new oligarchs" and the old Yeltsin "family." Two other factions—mostly from St. Petersburg—of active and retired military and security officers (so-called *siloviki*) and of liberal economic and political reformers could become the strongest forces in the Kremlin in the coming years, balancing each other in their influence on Putin.

The Russian economy is growing at the very decent rate of 7 percent, and inflation has been running at a reasonable 12 percent. Due to high oil prices, in 2003 the Russian government was able to pay off a record US$17 billion in foreign debt and also add US$20 billion to Russia's currency reserve, moving it to a record US$75 billion. This means that Russia can sustain the stability of the ruble and is protected from a repeat of the 1998 currency default.

By the end of 2004, the government plans to hold inflation at the 10 percent level and to form a stabilization fund of US$10 billion. Fiscal year 2004 will be the fourth consecutive year that Russia's federal budget is projected to be in surplus (the surplus should reach US$2.9 billion). The target for annual gross domestic product in 2004 is US$528 billion, allowing the federal government to spend the equivalent of US$91.7 billion.

However, the solid current economic growth rate is mostly the result of favorable oil prices rather than of the long-awaited economic structural reforms aimed at overcoming Russia's overdependence on extracting and exporting raw materials. In order to double Russia's GDP by 2010 (the objective announced by Putin in May 2003), the Russian economy needs to grow at least 8 percent annually. With unfavorable world oil prices that rate would be impossible to achieve. Besides, even such an annual rate is not enough for Russia to compete adequately in the global economic environment and to radically improve Russian standards of living (more than 31 million people in the Russian Federation live below the official poverty level of US$70 per month.) In other words, for the near-to-medium term the most critical threat for Russia is lagging behind in economic development.

Chechnya continues to be Russia's most formidable internal security challenge. Though a new legitimate president, Akhmad Kadyrov, has been elected in the Chechen Republic, fighting continues between the rebels and Russian regular forces and Chechen militia. Terrorist acts have occurred both in the Caucasus and Moscow. In 2003, Chechen female suicide bombers carried out the two dramatic actions in the capital, in July at the Tushino stadium when people were gathering for a rock concert and in December outside the National Hotel in the heart of the city. Public sentiment in Russia mostly supports a hard line against the rebels, whose terrorist tactics are also causing them to lose international sympathy. With lack of a serious challenge to Putin, the Chechen problem will not likely be a significant issue in the 2004 presidential election campaign.

EXTERNAL   Russia's position in world affairs today is determined not only by geopolitical factors, but mostly by domestic policy aimed at transformation into an economically, administratively, and militarily effective state. This is why Moscow is now primarily focused on increasing Russia's influence in its more immediate region of the Commonwealth of Independent States (CIS). In 2004, the key strategic goal is to form a real joint economic zone with Ukraine, Belarus, and Kazakhstan in accordance with an agreement signed in 2003.

Another major goal for 2004 is to further deepen military and political integration between Russia and five other CIS countries in the framework of the Collective Security Treaty Organization (CSTO). At an April 2003 summit, Armenia, Belarus, Kazakhstan, the Kyrgyz Republic, Russia, and Tajikistan formally created the CSTO, which will attempt to provide a more efficient response to strategic problems confronting member states, specifically terrorism and drug trafficking. Its Joint Staff became operational in January 2004 with the principal task of forming the organization's military structure and controlling its rapid deployment force to be stationed at a Russian military facility at Kant, Kyrgyz.

Moscow has only limited ability to influence conflicts such as those in Iraq and Afghanistan or that with North Korea. On the other hand, even in the more or less unilateral world the United States cannot solve all the problems itself. Thus, through constructive politics at the United Nations Russia has been able to help the United States overcome the post–Iraq war crisis. Moscow has also been instrumental in alleviating tensions in Washington's relationship with Iran. In keeping with its commitment to control weapons of mass destruction, in 2004 Russia will continue trying to avert nuclear crises with Iran or North Korea, but will oppose the use of force against those two countries.

In spite of disagreements during 2003 over Russia's accession to the World Trade Organization (WTO), Russia's opposition to further enlargement of the North Atlantic Treaty Organisation (NATO) and the European Union, and serious disagreements over Iraq, Russia is consolidating its mostly economics-oriented relationships with Washington and the European Union. Russia is trying to orchestrate a long-term, pragmatic "asymmetrical partnership" with Washington, not rivalry. The asymmetry means that, for example, while preferring a peaceful solution for the Iraq problem, being interested in getting a share of the international reconstruction contracts in Iraq, Moscow did not actively oppose the use of force against Baghdad. Another example is the Russian reaction to American plans to deploy a missile defense (MD) system in the Pacific. In view of Washington's hard attitude on MD, Moscow ended its earlier harsh criticism of MD and started considering how to reach an informal understanding with the United States. Similarly, although unhappy with the European Union's very tough stand on terms for Russia's WTO accession, Moscow nevertheless has continued negotiations aimed at joining this organization sometime in 2004 or perhaps later. Moscow does not like the upcoming NATO enlargement, but continued productive work in the Russia-NATO Council. At the same time, Russia will be insisting that anti-Russian politics and rhetoric be avoided within and by NATO.

In contrast to Russia's stable relationships with its American and European partners, Moscow's Asia policy is undergoing significant transformations, especially its approach toward Korean peninsula security issues and relations with Tokyo.

For security and economic reasons, Russia's policy in Asia still gives priority to its partnership with China. In 2000–2005, the overall value of Russian arms exports to China is projected to be US$5 billion–US$6 billion. To some extent China depends on Russian military technology, while the Russian Federation depends on Chinese purchases of arms to sustain its military-industrial enterprises in East Siberia and the Far East. Moscow and Beijing have become partners in strengthening stability in adjacent regions, such as Central Asia (through the Shanghai Cooperation Organization) and the Korean peninsula (through the Six-Party Talks).

However, China's recent leadership change has coincided with two phenomena that are having a chilling effect on the Russian-Chinese relationship. These are (1) the final disappearance from Moscow's rhetoric of the anti-American themes that cemented the Russian-Chinese relationship in the 1990s, and (2) the new primacy of economic factors in Russia's relations in Asia.

Beijing was unhappy with Putin's strong interest in cooperation with NATO and with his apparent willingness to coordinate his policies with Washington but not Beijing, Moscow's official strategic partner. Presumably in reaction to Russia's hesitant position concerning the timing and even the necessity of constructing an oil pipeline route going directly from Angarsk (Eastern Siberia) to Daqing (Northern China), Beijing has toughened its stance on Russian WTO accession terms and introduced antidumping measures against Russian steel exports to China. It is clear that in the near term Russian-Chinese relations will lack the previous geopolitical romanticism about an alliance relationship and will be characterized by more pragmatic economic considerations.

Partly related to these developments in Russia-China relations has been a very positive trend in Russia's bilateral relationship with Japan, as manifested in a Japan-Russia Action Plan signed by Putin and Japanese Prime Minister Koizumi Jun'ichirō in January 2003. Koizumi has lobbied for a change in the main route of the oil pipeline from the Irkutsk area to Primorsky krai, where Tokyo can get more reliable access to the Russian energy resources. In the defense area, the two countries have exchanged visits by high-level officials as well as naval vessels, and in August 2003 the Japanese Maritime Self-Defense Force took part in a strategic exercise held in Russian Far East waters. This new trend is expected to continue, as Russia launches several major projects to develop its regional infrastructure in which Japanese capital and technology could play an important role, while Japan seeks political support from Russia on issues such as North Korea's nuclear programs as well as diversification of its energy resources.

Russia's Korea policy over the last couple of years has been aimed at maintaining balanced relationships with both Koreas, and Moscow will continue that course, trying to secure full participation for itself in dealing with problems on the peninsula. In the meantime, there has been little progress in economic relations between Russia and South Korea.

Military-technical cooperation remains the central component of Russia's ties with India. However, the two countries also cooperate in science and technology. Economic ties are not so strong, though recent Indian investments in Sakhalin Island energy projects might signal a new trend.

DEFENSE POLICIES AND ISSUES

DEFENSE POLICY AND BUDGET   In October 2003, the Russian Federation defense ministry for the first time in the post-Soviet era adopted a concept for the development of the Russian Armed Forces and released a public version of the Modernization Doctrine. Key points of the doctrine stand out:
- The armed forces should be prepared to counter external, internal, and so-called transborder threats, including international terrorism;
- When critical state interests are threatened Russia may resort to the preventive use of force;
- Russia remains committed to nuclear arms reductions; Moscow is obligated under a treaty with the United States to cut its nuclear arsenal to 1,700–2,200 weapons by the end of 2012;
- Despite the absence of immediate direct threats, Afghanistan and the adjacent Central Asia region are potentially dangerous to Russia's southern borders; and

- Without resorting to further mobilization, the armed forces should be able to handle two simultaneous military conflicts and take part in peacekeeping operations, either unilaterally or in a multinational framework.

Military and law enforcement (including paramilitary) development is one of the priorities of the Russian federal budget for 2004. The planned allocation for defense is the equivalent of US$14.2 billion (2.7 percent of the GDP), while spending on law enforcement will be around US$10.7 billion. These figures represent increases of 19 percent and 27 percent, respectively, over the previous year.

Military procurement approved for 2004 totals US$11.8 billion (a 20 percent increase from the previous year), and approval came unexpectedly early, in December 2003, enabling the military industrial enterprises to start production on the orders in January. In the meantime, the armament procurement system has undergone positive changes. The lion's share of the government debt to military industrial enterprises was finally paid off in 2003. In March 2003 a new State Committee on Military Procurement was formed within the Ministry of Defense to centralize all defense procurement orders by the ministry and other state law enforcement agencies.

FORCE STRUCTURE   Several years of reforms have resulted in a military structure of three services (army, air force, navy) and three arms (strategic missile force [SMF], airborne troops, space troops).

By the year 2008, the SMF will consist of no more than ten divisions equipped with ground-based strategic missiles that should be operational until 2030. Development of the SMF air component is based on modernization of Tu-160 strategic bombers. The SMF naval component will be strengthened by parallel development of a new "Bulava" nuclear missile and construction of the new generation of nuclear submarines capable of handling that missile.

During the last several years, the Union of Right Forces and Yabloko had vocally advocated a much more open military budget as well as military reform aimed at terminating conscription and introducing the principle of an all-volunteer force (AVF). Although they had only moderate success in achieving budgetary transparency (much of the budget is still closed), they succeeded in persuading Putin to take a compromise stand on military reform. As a result, a plan has been adopted to gradually transform the military to an AVF. The plan is contained in a program called "Transformation to recruitment for the number of military formations and units by volunteer servicemen," issued in September 2003 and covering the years 2004–2007.

According to the new program, by the year 2008 those 80 formations and units considered most critical for sustaining the combat readiness of the armed forces will be staffed by volunteers only. Besides, by that time conscripts will not exceed 50 percent of the total armed forces (and the term of conscript service will decrease from two years to one). An indication that the AVF reform has really started is the fact that, by the end of 2003, the airborne division based in Pskov had become the first in modern Russian history to be 100 percent staffed by volunteers.

By the end of 2003, the overall strength of the Russian Armed Forces had decreased to 1,132,000 personnel, and by 2005 it should not exceed one million. No further cuts are currently planned, although independent experts argue that such a number is still too many (and thus too expensive) if the armed forces are to be transformed to an AVF system.

Contributions to Regional and Global Security

Being an inseparable part of the Asia Pacific region, Russia is very interested in sustaining peace and stability in the region. Russia pursues these goals by improving bilateral relationships with neighboring countries, as well as through active participation in the work of intergovernmental organizations such as the Shanghai Cooperation Organization, the Asia-Pacific Economic Cooperation (APEC) forum, and the ASEAN Regional Forum.

In October 2003 for the first time in its history, Russia took part in the annual session of the Organization of the Islamic Conference. Putin made an unexpected trip to Malaysia in an apparent move to start more active dialogue with the Muslim world and to gain mainstream Muslim countries' support in Russia's fight with religious fundamentalists in Chechnya.

However, the most striking recent development in Russia's regional and global cooperation is in energy policy. In October 2003, Russia became for the first time the world's largest oil producer (8.5 million barrels of oil per day), replacing Saudi Arabia. Addressing participants at the APEC Summit in Bangkok the same month, Putin announced that Russia was prepared to contribute to a new energy and transportation configuration in Asia Pacific. He urged foreign business to invest in the gas and oil industry in Siberia, and announced that one of the largest natural gas liquefying plants in the world would open in 2007 on Sakhalin Island. Russia's growing economic potential in the Asia Pacific region is also demonstrated by ongoing international debates on routes for the Eastern Siberia oil pipeline and alternative ways of connecting Trans-Siberian and Trans-Korean railroads. However, the North Korean nuclear crisis has inhibited several countries from moving actively into major infrastructure projects in the Russian Far East and Eastern Siberia.

This consideration is a major reason why Russia seeks to improve the security situation on the Korean peninsula. After a decade of being largely excluded from the negotiation process, recent Russia-North Korea summits have been helpful in reestablishing Moscow as one of the principal players on the Korean issue. Russian policy is aimed at securing nuclear-free status for the peninsula. Moscow is ready to provide North Korea with multilateral security and noninterference guarantees if its nuclear program is placed under control of the International Atomic Energy Agency. However, the Six-Party Talks process could extend for a considerable period of time, leading to a serious aggravation of North Korea's energy problem. In such circumstances, Russian participation in supplying energy to North Korea would be one of the practical options.

At the same time, however, recent strategic exercises in the Russian Far East—including a scenario in which Pacific Fleet ships stopped a hypothetical North Korean vessel carrying a nuclear weapon and a scenario in which a hypothetical flow of 100 thousand North Korean refugees was stemmed at the Russian borders—have signaled to Pyongyang that persisting in nuclear weapons programs will undermine its relationship with Moscow.

Elsewhere, Russian units have completed their commitment in the peacekeeping operations in Kosovo and Bosnia. Moscow is participating in the formation of a Central Asia rapid deployment force, and a Russian air force base has been formed at Kant (the Kyrgyz Republic) in support of this regional force.

18 Singapore

The Security Environment

External and internal factors have colluded in a way that has sapped confidence in Singapore's economy and its ability to manage change, and produced overall pessimism about Singapore's future. Thus the outlook for 2004 for Singapore remains uncertain.

The year 2003 was an *annus horribilis* for Singapore. There were the Iraq war, the outbreak of severe acute respiratory syndrome (SARS), and continued acrimonious debates with Malaysia. Beyond these high-profile, externally driven events, over which Singapore had relatively little influence, were a spate of domestic issues. On the economic front, the double whammy of the Iraq war and the SARS outbreak halted the already slow recovery of the Singaporean economy. Unemployment was at a 17-year high, reaching 5.9 percent at one point. Further, underlying structural weaknesses in Singapore's economy impede the response to these external challenges.

An almost yearlong series of accidents and mishaps, policy flip-flops, and public relations fiascos raised questions in the minds of some Singaporeans about the political and economic models so long successfully followed by the People's Action Party (PAP) government. Events such as a collision between a navy patrol boat and an Indonesian oil tanker resulting in the deaths of four navy personnel, the death of a National Service soldier due to "unorthodox" training, and the case of a research student who caught the SARS virus while working in a lab run by the Environmental Health Institute, plus a string of policy about-turns, could erode the confidence and trust that are seen as so important to social stability and orderly growth.

EXTERNAL   The post–September 11 world with the new geopolitical realities of increasing uncertainties coupled with the general economic slowdown poses great challenges to Singapore. The global war on terrorism and the preoccupation with security and safety in the wake of the Iraq war and the SARS outbreak may come at the expense of the openness in the global political and economic order that is so vital for Singapore's continued prosperity and survival. Any retreat from globalization and any measures to restrict the movement of goods and people as experienced at the peak of the SARS outbreak hurt small nations like Singapore much more than big countries.

In general, Singapore's external security environment remains difficult. The threat of terrorism continues to loom large, with increasing concerns over possible attacks on shipping in the Strait of Malacca. While there is clear acknowledgement in the region of the need to weed out terrorism, resources limit the capacity to do so. The fact that 2004 is an election year for several key countries in the region—Indonesia, Malaysia, and the Philippines—may also divert attention and lessen the political resolve of some governments in confronting these issues.

Economic challenges posed by a highly competitive regional environment, with head-on competition from Malaysia and Thailand, the continued ascendance of China, and a rising India add to the sense of vulnerability felt by the leadership of Singapore. Many of these international and regional dynamics are beyond the control of Singapore, but the difficulties are compounded by internal factors discussed below.

The war in Iraq and the government's agreement to participate in the U.S.-organized coalition raised the eyebrows of the public. While public response was muted, more than half of Singaporeans, cutting across religions and races, were against the war in Iraq for pragmatic and/or humanitarian reasons. Letters from readers to local newspapers reflected doubts about the wisdom of U.S. policy and Singapore's close alignment with the United States. In addition to principled objections, there were also pragmatic fears that support of the United States in this war would invite retaliation from Muslim fundamentalists in the region or undermine relations with Singapore's closest Muslim neighbors, Malaysia and Indonesia.

As the repercussions of the war and the situation in Iraq are being played out, Singaporeans remain concerned about the wider implications of the global war on terrorism. The bombing of the JW Marriott Hotel Jakarta in early August 2003 further fueled concerns about the spread of terrorism in the region. However, there were also positive developments such as the capture of Riduan Isamuddin, alias Hambali, and the death of Fathur Rahman al-Ghozi, and seemingly greater cooperation within the region against terrorist networks. Still, the fight against terrorism in Southeast Asia is hampered by issues of governance and corruption.

The spread of the SARS epidemic to Singapore in 2003, while not seen as a security threat per se, impacted the economy and the people directly and vividly. During the three-month SARS outbreak, Singapore's gross domestic product contracted 11.8 percent. Tourism-related industries were most severely hit, with visitor arrivals falling by 60 percent–80 percent and hotel occupancy rates dropping to 20 percent–30 percent. This was a reminder to Singapore of the vulnerabilities of a small, open economy. Had the SARS outbreak been longer or more widespread, Singapore's economy would have been much worse off, which could have impacted the socioeconomic fabric of the country. The region is now braced for further outbreaks. It seems that lessons have been learned from the SARS outbreak, but how well prepared the region is, especially for a mutated and more virulent disease, is very uncertain. The SARS episode also raised the issues of vulnerability to biological or bio-chemical weapons and bio-terrorism.

The silver lining in the SARS episode has been stepped-up regional cooperation in East Asia as the realities of interdependencies hit home. China's apologies and commitment indicated that China is becoming more keenly aware of its regional image and responsibilities. China is slowly discarding its earlier reserve toward multilateralism and is beginning to play a more active role in promoting East Asian regionalism. Though a full Sino-Japanese reconciliation is still not in sight, and the response of the United States to an increasingly integrated East Asian region is still not clear, there is increasing optimism that East Asians will work toward a more closely knit community in the future.

At the subregional level of the Association of Southeast Asian Nations, there is a renewed push for greater ASEAN cooperation after years of the grouping being seen as losing its relevance and usefulness in the aftermath of the Asian financial crisis. The October 2003 Bali Summit meeting endorsed the idea of an ASEAN Economic Community, yet at the same time was pragmatic enough to agree on the ASEAN "2 + x" principle allowing member states to push ahead with faster integration and cooperation in areas where at least two partners are in agreement. While putting on a brave front of unity, however, the reality is that ASEAN members continue to be plagued by their own domestic and internal problems that divert attention and energy from serious region building. Without closer regional cooperation, many of the security and development problems cannot be successfully resolved.

Singapore's survival is very much tied to its continued prosperity and economic and strategic relevance in the global arena, so the external economic environment is another critical part of its security outlook. Singapore's economy is under tremendous pressure from competition not only from China, but also India and, closer to home, Malaysia and Thailand. Indeed, the number of competitors will only increase in the coming years. At the same time, Singapore's natural hinterland, the Southeast Asian region as a whole, has not recovered fully from the Asian financial crisis. The region is not generating enough growth in demand for Singapore-based services to maintain the critical mass so vital to Singapore's role and competitiveness as a regional hub. And the added political risk of terrorism and political transitions in the region make it more difficult to attract new investment.

INTERNAL   Internally, cracks are showing in the economic and political model so successfully applied for almost 40 years. The PAP's effective and efficient management of the whole society and its pervasive influence have resulted in widespread political apathy and a certain dependency. Singaporeans have come to rely on the government to solve most of their problems. The exercise of extensive controls over so many important public and social institutions by the PAP government has retarded the development of a citizenry willing to take greater responsibility for their own actions.

The formula of control and co-option is beginning to show signs of dysfunctionality, as the need to move into a knowledge-based economy requires individuals who are nonconformist, more creative, and more willing to take risks. The government's rather paternalistic approach has stifled the much-needed creative and questioning processes critical for a knowledge-based economy, and with the current decline in economic performance there is an urgent need to restructure the economy to ensure the continued economic vitality of Singapore. Singapore's problems in the economic arena are made worse by its inability to respond quickly enough to these changes.

It remains extremely unlikely that the PAP government will be thrown out of power in the short to medium term, but the governing party is also beginning to show signs of frailty. The "we know best" attitude is undergoing a severe test, following a spate of unfortunate accidents, policy flips-flops, public relations fiascos, misreading of public sentiments and reactions, and the admission of mistakes. The need to apply "bitter medicine" in the form of cuts in wages and retirement benefits (through the government-run Central Provident Fund) in the name of saving jobs and restructuring of the economy also aroused mixed feelings at the grass-roots level. Resentment seems to be growing and trust of the government is being diluted. While these sentiments are unlikely to be translated into mass unrest, the implications for social cohesion over the longer term could be serious.

The impending political transition from Prime Minister Goh Chok Tong to Lee Hsien Loong (son of Singapore's first prime minister and long-time guiding force Lee Kuan Yew) is expected to be smooth. However, the general perception of the younger Lee as aloof and not in tune with the concerns of the man in the street might exacerbate discontent should the economy remain in the doldrums and unemployment not improve. The fact that the younger Lee's wife, Ho Ching, is chief executive officer and executive director of Temasek Holdings, the economic arm of the Singapore government, has also added to the unease over economic policy.

Another source of disquiet is the decision by Senior Minister Lee Kuan Yew to remain in the cabinet even after his son becomes the prime minister. There is a feeling in some quarters that the senior minister's decision to stay on will impede Lee Hsien Loong's stature as his own man. Finally, there is concern about how the younger Lee will handle foreign relations in general and prickly relations with Malaysia in particular. On a more positive note, the transition from Mahathir bin Mohammed to Abdullah Ahmad Badawi, and the latter's less confrontational style plus his open expression of desire to reopen talks with Singapore on the various difficult issues between the two neighbors, opens a window of opportunity for the relationship to improve.

DEFENSE POLICIES AND ISSUES

The heightened awareness of unconventional threats posed by terrorism, piracy along the sea lines of communication (SLOC), and the spread of infectious diseases demonstrated by the SARS outbreak have stimulated the push toward a more comprehensive approach combining defense and security, and toward greater coordination among the various civilian agencies. Because of the SARS outbreak, the multi-agency approach is aimed at managing risks to national interest, not just responding to security threats.

Tony Tan, deputy prime minister, was named coordinating minister for security and defense in a cabinet reshuffle in mid-2003 designed to emphasize the importance of greater coordination of responses to nonconventional threats. The National Security Secretariat has been further strengthened to coordinate this effort. The Singapore Armed Forces' (SAF's) capability in chemical and biological defense has also been boosted with the formation of a new integrated group comprising the Explosive Ordnance Disposal Unit, the Chemical, Biological, Radiological and Explosive Defense Group, and the Medical Response Force.

Maritime security has been stepped up amidst intelligence reports that the al Qaeda terrorist network is planning attacks from the sea. Police coast guards and maritime security measures in the Singapore Strait have been stepped up considerably. Related to this effort is tightened border control; Singapore was the first port in Asia to sign on to the U.S. Container Security Initiative.

Several new laws have been enacted in the name of defense against terrorist attacks, including a law to regulate the trading and transshipment of munitions, chemicals, biological products, and certain types of technology. A new Computer Misuse Act allows the government to empower any person or organization to take preemptive action against computer terrorism. The possibility of abuse of this act was vigorously debated, however, amid concerns about intrusion into the privacy of individuals.

DEFENSE SPENDING   The defense budget for the 2003–2004 fiscal year has increased from S\$8.2 billion (US\$4.84 billion at S\$1 = US\$0.59) in the previous year to S\$8.25 billion (US\$4.87 billion). The security budget for the Ministry of Home Affairs also increased, to S\$2.31 billion (US\$1.36 billion). Together they constitute 36 percent of the 2003–2004 budget.

A major priority in the next few years for the defense ministry is to replace the large number of weapons systems in current use that are fast becoming obsolete. These include armored personnel carriers, tanks, and fighter-bombers. First in the list for replacement are the aging A-4 U.S. Super Skyhawk fighter jets. Three models have been shortlisted for replacement: the 232 Eurofighter Typhoon manufactured by BAE

Systems, the French-built Dassault Rafale, and Boeing's F-18. The SAF in 2003 took delivery of eight Apache Longbow Attack helicopters, and a search is under way for ship-borne helicopters to improve the maritime defense capability.

The Singapore navy in early 2003 unveiled its first locally built stealth frigate, the second in a series of six stealth frigates which, carrying the latest weapons and sensors, will form the core of the navy. Another new locally designed and produced weapon is a self-propelled, lightweight and highly mobile howitzer, Primus. It is significant that Singapore is becoming more and more involved in the design and production of its own weaponry.

CONTRIBUTIONS TO REGIONAL AND GLOBAL SECURITY

At the multilateral level, Singapore contributes to regional defense and security cooperation in the region by seeking to strengthen multilateral arrangements such as the Five Power Defense Arrangements (FPDA, with Australia, Malaysia, New Zealand, and the United Kingdom) and the ASEAN Regional Forum (ARF). Bilateral and regional cooperation to address the threats of terrorism have been stepped up considerably. The SAF also participates in regular exercises with U.S. forces in Thailand and Australia.

Increased cooperation with Malaysia and Indonesia is focused on ensuring the safety of the SLOC. There are fears that terrorists may link up with pirates to hijack fuel-laden ships and crash them into ports. The fact that more than half of the world's oil passes through the Strait of Malacca and the waters around the Indonesian archipelago means that if terrorists and pirates should succeed in such an attack, world trade would suffer and insurance rates in the shipping industry would skyrocket.

Singapore is already participating in a regional antipiracy program initiated by Japan, which involves a total of 16 nations in the region. Singapore has also offered to host and fund part of the cost of running an information-sharing center.

In recent years, Singapore has begun to participate more actively in peacekeeping missions such as the international force in Timor Leste. In response to a request from the United States, Singapore has deployed 30 police officers to Iraq to help train their Iraqi counterparts.

Singapore has also committed a Landing Ship Tank, one C-130, and 192 SAF personnel to help in the reconstruction of Iraq.

Singapore's contributions to regional and global security can be further enhanced by working closely with ASEAN and other partners such as the European Union, not just the United States, to build capacity to deal with terrorist threats. One consideration in this regard is the need to address the development aspects and not just the military aspect of tackling terrorism, and there is little doubt that Singapore has much to contribute in the development area especially if it works closely with external partners such as Japan and the European Union.

19 Thailand

THE SECURITY ENVIRONMENT

It is ironic that in the democratic era, Thailand's politics and foreign policy are now more dominated by the driving ambition of one individual, Prime Minister Thaksin Shinawatra, than ever during previous periods of military governance. The former policeman and hugely successful telecommunications entrepreneur has also proved enormously successful (as well as lucky) in political life, proudly proclaiming that his ruling Thai Rak Thai (TRT) Party will remain in power for 20 more years. Not content with the national stage, he is also attempting to assume a mantel of regional leadership through new initiatives such as the Asian Cooperation Dialogue (ACD). Some Thais, obviously including many voters, believe that strong political leadership is just what Thailand needs to overcome the deficiencies of the political fragmentation of earlier years. Others worry that Thaksin's powerful position is subverting the normal checks and balances of a healthy democratic system and discouraging real institutional development of the Thai polity, and thus that the Thaksin period may be a setback for Thailand's greatest security need, which is to consolidate and institutionalize its still-new democracy.

INTERNAL   Thaksin's TRT and its political allies constitute an overwhelming base of 338 seats in the 500-seat House of Representatives of the National Assembly, and the prime minister continues to set the political agenda. The former ruling and now main opposition party, the Democrat Party, provides only a weak, nondirectional challenge. It has a new leader, Banyat Bantadtan, but this has not improved its position. Former party leader and prime minister Chuan Leekpai is openly skeptical of Banyat's abilities. For the moment, there seems no serious challenge to the prime minister. A solid victory by Thaksin seems virtually assured in the elections due to be held at the end of 2004 or in early 2005.

The government position has been strengthened by Thailand's economic performance. Although "Thaksinomics" had been widely scorned by professional economists, the economy has been steadily improving. Economic growth in 2003 was about 6 percent, and estimates for 2004 are between 6.5 and 8.5 percent. The improved credit rating from Moody's and Standard & Poor's during the past year and Thailand's declaration in August 2003 of freedom from assistance by the International Monetary Fund piqued Thai pride.

Two important internal challenges are the drug wars and terrorism in the Muslim-dominated provinces in the extreme south. In a country with high and escalating use of methamphetamines, the government's determination to control illegal drug trafficking and reduce substance abuse was widely appreciated. But the situation nevertheless has seemed to spin out of control, with hundreds of deaths. When the king himself asked for an investigation, the authorities argued that many of the deaths were caused by drug traffickers killing each other to ensure that informants did not reach the police, or by police in self-defense. Critics both at home, including the Thai Human Rights Commissioner, and abroad believe that police have frequently acted arbitrarily. The Thai Third Army, which patrols the border with Myanmar and was tasked to destroy poppy fields, claims to have cut opium production by 80 percent.

The government has tried to play down violence in the south, and there is considerable controversy over its significance. The one-time separatist insurgency in the region has been in disarray for years, but assorted acts of banditry and violence continue. Thailand's neighbors and outside powers have been concerned that the region could be an ideal hideaway for al Qaeda and Jemaah Islamiah (JI) terrorists, but the Thai government initially discounted this, arguing that Thailand's terrorists are homegrown. More recently, the government has acknowledged that local groups have contacts with outside networks. Bangkok recognizes the danger that a terrorist incident on Thai soil or launched from Thailand could harm the country's image and its economy. The Thai government reportedly established a counterterrorism intelligence center in 2001, which has been working closely with U.S. and other officials. This group was responsible for the capture of Indonesian JI terrorist Riduuan Isamuddin, alias Hambili, in Ayuttaya in August 2003.

EXTERNAL Thaksin is pressing for a leading role in regional affairs through his proposal for an ACD. The stated objective of the ACD is to provide a link between Asia's subregions. The grouping is somewhat eclectic, and includes three Northeast Asian countries (China, Japan, and South Korea), nine members of the Association of Southeast Asian Nations (ASEAN, without Myanmar), three South Asian countries (India, Pakistan, and Bangladesh), and two oil-rich Persian Gulf states (Bahrain and Qatar). Four other countries—Kazhakstan, Oman, Kuwait, and Sri Lanka—have expressed interest in participating. The initiative emphasizes informal and noninstitutionalized discussions, as well as strategic partnerships with other parts of the world. The importance attached by Thaksin to the proposal was indicated by the convening of ACD ministerial meetings in Thailand in June 2002 and 2003. Critics, however, argue that the ACD was merely launched to give Thaksin a regional leadership role.

Bilateral Thai-Cambodian relations have become increasingly acrimonious, prompted by violent anti-Thai protests in Phnom Penh at the end of January 2003. The protests led to the burning of the Thai embassy and Thai business properties. Responsibility is still being debated in Cambodia, but the immediate consequence was suspension of diplomatic ties and cancellation of an official visit to Phnom Penh by the Royal Thai Crown Princess. The Thai government also suspended technical and economic assistance, closed border checkpoints, and demanded financial compensation for the property damage. Less than two months after the onset of the crisis the Cambodian government agreed to pay B250 million (US$6.3 million at US$1 = B39.62) in compensation. A joint cabinet meeting and resumption of economic assistance are planned, but at the level of public opinion the relationship remains very volatile and its future uncertain.

Bilateral relations with most of the other ASEAN member states are smoother. Agreements are planned with Laos to promote cooperation in intelligence sharing, a crackdown on drug trafficking, cultural and student exchanges, and border demarcation. The two governments have also agreed to commission a further study of the impact of blasting rapids and reefs in the Mekong River. On the negative side, the Thai criminal court in 2003 once again turned down the Laotian government's request to extradite 16 Laotian suspects in an attack on a Laotian customs office in 2000.

The Thaksin administration agrees with the Singapore government's proposal that the concept of an ASEAN Economic Community (AEC) should be accelerated, to provide a mechanism for fostering economic cooperation and integration among the more economically developed member states. The Thai government is working with the Malaysian government to promote a more active business relationship, and the Thai navy has welcomed Malaysian proposals for more naval exercises between the two navies. And relations with Vietnam are progressing; a Thaksin government initiative led to the scheduling of the first joint cabinet meeting.

Thai relations with Myanmar, where a new prime minister, Khin Nyunt, assumed office in August 2003, have not improved. Although fewer armed clashes occurred along the border in 2003, the Thai government has still not secured full cooperation from the regime in Rangoon in cracking down on drug flows and trafficking along the border. The ethnicity problem in Myanmar, violations of human rights, the gloomy outlook for democratic reforms, and the lucrative business of drug trafficking contribute to a deadlock in dealing with Myanmar's military regime. A roadmap proposed by the Thai government to solve the political crisis and promote democracy in Myanmar met a cool reception in Rangoon, despite support from both the Chinese and Japanese governments.

Close U.S.-Thai relations will be presented as the Thaksin government's major success in foreign policy during the 2004 general election campaign. Thaksin can claim three major successes with Washington in 2003. These are agreement to negotiate a free trade agreement (FTA), cooperation on counterterrorism during the Asia-Pacific Economic Cooperation (APEC) summit in Bangkok, and Thailand's designation as a "major non-NATO ally." It is widely speculated that for its part the Thai government granted permission for covert U.S. military use of the U-Tapao military base located to the east of Bangkok during the Iraq campaign.

Increased cooperation with the United States has produced some criticism of the Thaksin government. The former foreign minister and leading scholars argue that this unusually close alliance endangers the country's security. But the Bush administration initially appeared dissatisfied with such "quiet" support from Thailand. During an "unofficial" visit to Washington in June 2003, Thaksin reportedly secured an opportunity to explain his position to President George W. Bush, although Thaksin himself denies this. The Thaksin-Bush meeting produced assurances that Thailand will grant the United States forward positioning rights for its antiterrorism campaign in Southeast Asia and that Thai authorities will not bring American citizens before the International Criminal Court. Arrests of three JI suspects in Thailand, while Thaksin was still in Washington, provided a demonstration of Thai seriousness in fighting terrorism, although the actual links of these suspects with the JI remain unsubstantiated.

DEFENSE POLICIES AND ISSUES

BUDGET   The Thaksin government approved a defense budget of B78 billion (US$1.97 billion) for 2004. This represented a slight decrease in bhat terms from B80 billion (US$2.02 billion) in 2003, significantly less than the B114 billion (US$2.88 billion) requested by the Ministry of Defense. (The defense budget is 7.58 percent of the total national budget for 2004.) However, Thaksin has pledged to increase the budget to a total of B200 billion (US$5.05 billion) over the next nine years in order to upgrade the Defense Ministry's information and computer technology.

ARMS PROCUREMENT   Within the constraints of the budget allocation for defense, Thailand is pursuing a multiyear program of modernizing its military equipment. It has weaponry procurement contracts with many of the major arms-exporting countries, often on favorable terms. The Indian government has agreed that the Thai navy and air force may purchase Indian weapons at concessionary prices. The Russian government also agrees to provide weapons for the Thai armed forces in exchange for the purchase of Thai rice worth more than US$40 million. The Chinese government will supply US$600 million worth of weapons and spare parts under a long-term agreement. The Thai navy has ordered two frigates costing a total US$100 million from BAE Systems in a barter trade arrangement with Britain.

Debates over arms procurement are rife. The army and its chief of staff support acquiring 160 second-hand Swiss-made PZ-68/88 tanks, for US$49 million, on the grounds that they have better defensive and fire control systems than U.S. M41-A3 tanks. However, the defense minister has reservations over the purchase. The supplier of four medium-sized conventional submarines for the navy is still undetermined, this delay presumably also reflecting internal disagreements. Signs of disagreement have also emerged between the Defense Ministry and the military leadership over a purchase of 33 Black Hawk helicopters for the anti-drug Task Force 399. The ministry proposed, ostensibly due to budget constraints, that the task force be scaled down, reducing the purchase to eight helicopters. The prime minister, however, approved the purchase of 33 helicopters by the year 2009.

EXERCISES   Thailand's major training activity with foreign militaries is the annual joint Thai-U.S. Cobra Gold exercise, involving multiple countries and, in recent years, some 10,000–20,000 troops. As in 2002, the 2003 exercise was focused on nontraditional security issues, but with more emphasis on antiterrorism and counterterrorism operations, together with peacekeeping missions. Malaysia did not participate in 2003, but British forces participated for the first time and there is speculation that the Philippines and Japan will participate in 2004. Bilateral exercises in 2003 included a joint exercise with the Indonesian navy aimed at curtailing clandestine arms smuggling to rebel groups in Aceh, and an exercise with the Indian navy to curb the illegal arms flow to the separatist group in Sri Lanka.

CONTRIBUTIONS TO REGIONAL AND GLOBAL SECURITY

Along with other U.S. allies Thailand is participating in U.S.-led reconstruction and rehabilitation programs in Iraq. A total of 443 officers, comprising 250 engineers, 70 doctors, 26 frontline command officers, 50 security personnel, and a bomb disposal team will provide humanitarian assistance in southern Iraq. The decision to send Thai military personnel caused public outcry and a barrage of criticism based on concern for the safety of the personnel, and with continuing attacks on foreign personnel even in Baghdad itself, pressure is mounting on the Thai authorities to withdraw the Thai military personnel from Iraq. But the Thaksin government is determined to carry on with its commitment.

Thailand continues to play a role in East Timor's nation building. At the request of the United Nations, Thailand extended the assignment of 40 military doctors until June 2004. In addition, Thailand and East Timor have concluded a memorandum of understanding under which the Thai government will assist East Timor in nine areas of national development such as agriculture, public health, fishery, and tourism.

The United Nations has also requested the participation of about 400–500 Thai army engineers in the reconstruction effort in Liberia. Similarly, the Indonesian government asked for Thai involvement in monitoring the ceasefire negotiated for Aceh province in late 2002 (which did not last). As Thailand is regarded as a devout Buddhist country, the government of Afghanistan has requested Thai assistance in reconstructing the historic site of the Bamiyan Buddhas, which were demolished by the Taliban regime in March 2001.

As part of its contribution to regional and global security, Thailand has hosted an increasing number of international conferences and meetings in recent years. The most significant of these in 2003 to the Thaksin government was the APEC summit in Bangkok, which showed the Thai government's willingness and ability to host such a major international event despite the threats of terrorism in the region.

Other meetings in 2003 concerned regional issues. In January 2003, the Thai government provided "good offices" for the fourth round of negotiations between the Sri Lankan government and the Liberation Tigers of Tamil Eelam (LTTE), brokered by the Norwegian deputy foreign minister. (Thailand is also providing Sri Lanka assistance in defusing land mines.) After the outbreak of the severe acute respiratory syndrome (SARS) epidemic in the region early in 2003, the Thai government hosted a summit of ASEAN leaders with China, Japan, and Hong Kong to agree on a series of precautionary measures, and set up the Special Fund for SARS Prevention.

On the global level, in September 2003 the Thai government hosted an international conference on the Mine Ban Treaty. Chinese delegates attend this conference as observers for the first time. At the conference, delegates representing 136 countries called on the United States, Russia, China, and India to join the treaty.

20 The United States

At the start of 2004, the ongoing occupation and conflict in Iraq—and the associated steady drip of American casualties—dominates the international security landscape and outlook in the United States. The threat of terrorism, both international and domestic, is palpable to the public and even more so to the administration of George W. Bush. A national opinion poll on the second anniversary of the September 11 attacks found that fully three-quarters of the American people expect another terrorist attack and 60 percent worry about a terrorist attack on the United States with nuclear weapons. Events in 2003 in the Asia Pacific region, including the bombing at the JW Marriott Hotel Jakarta on August 5 and trials and further arrests of terrorists in Southeast Asia, sustained American attention on the terrorism threat in this region.

The frustrating pace of post-Taliban reconstruction in Afghanistan is an element of the larger security picture, though it is a secondary focus to Iraq, as is the Israeli-Palestinian relationship and the "Road Map" for Middle East peace launched with great fanfare by Bush in May–June 2003 but quickly stalemated due to actions by both sides. Bush administration policies in Iraq, along with the state of the U.S. economy, are also the major issues in U.S. domestic politics, and together will likely determine the outcome of the 2004 presidential and congressional elections. If the situation in Iraq appears under control and the domestic economy is growing at a healthy pace in November 2004, the Bush administration will most probably be returned for a second term; if both are going badly, the administration will be in serious electoral trouble, and if there is a split the outcome will be a tossup. As always in an election year, other issues are likely to arise in the course of the campaign, such as human rights or economic/trade policy, and could lead to pledges by the administration or its Democrat opponents that may be unrealistic or disruptive if implemented.

The set of issues surrounding North Korean nuclear weapons development is the second major security concern for the United States in the Asia Pacific region (and the world) at the start of 2004. These issues include the North's claims of nuclear capability and threat to use its weapons, perceptions of the North's willingness to provide weapons and technology to other states and to non-state actors such as terrorists, efforts to persuade the North to abandon its nuclear program, and the impact of these factors on U.S. relations with South Korea and other regional governments. The public profile of the North Korean nuclear crisis has been partially obscured by the prominence of Iraq, but it is still a very serious concern. The Bush administration approach to the issue has settled into essentially a holding action, emphasizing multilateral negotiations with the North and abjuring interest in a military solution. But the sheer opaqueness and unpredictability of the North Korean government means that this will remain a tense and volatile situation for the foreseeable future.

The Iraq conflict, and more broadly the war on terrorism, are also major elements in official U.S. relations with other governments, including in the Asia Pacific region. The Bush administration is clearly rewarding governments, such as Australia and Singapore, that are strongly supporting U.S counterterrorism actions, while conspicuously not catering to governments, such as New Zealand, that are not, and engaging in tough bargaining with governments, such as Thailand or Indonesia, in the middle. The results of this differentiation have been felt in areas ranging from trade negotiations to assistance issues and the U.S. military presence. In the Asia Pacific region, examples include acceleration (at Bush's personal direction) of negotiations for a U.S.-Australian free trade agreement, increases in security assistance to the Philippines, and insistence that the Indonesian government resolve the murders of two Americans in Papua as a precondition for improving military-to-military ties.

Bush's whirlwind trip to Asia in October for the Asia-Pacific Economic Cooperation (APEC) heads of government meeting in Thailand, bracketed by visits to Japan, the Philippines, Singapore, Indonesia, and Australia, and a meeting with Pacific Island leaders in Hawaii on the homebound leg, was almost totally focused on rallying cooperation in the war on terrorism and on the North Korean nuclear issue.

In the same context, U.S. relations with China have probably reached a post–cold war peak, with active cooperation on counterterrorism and with the Bush administration looking to China to play a key role in restraining North Korea and in persuading the North Korean regime to dismantle its nuclear weapons program. Differences between the United States and China remain, including over human rights issues and—potentially most critical in terms of security—Taiwan, but the Bush administration's priority on stable relations with China seems likely to prevail. The most explicit evidence to this effect was Bush's reaction to Taiwanese President Chen Shui-bian's proposal in late 2003 to hold a referendum on Taiwan-China relations. In his first year in office, Bush had declared (more explicitly than previous U.S. statements) that the United States would oppose any effort by China to incorporate Taiwan by force. In response to Chen's referendum talk, Bush pointedly and publicly stated that he would "oppose" a declaration of independence by Taiwan. Bush's statement did not constitute a change of policy, but coming in the context of a meeting with Chinese Premier Wen Jiabao it constituted a sharp warning to the Taiwanese not to jeopardize Washington's rapprochement with Beijing.

Similarly, U.S. relations with lynchpin ally Japan have been consolidated, with longstanding frictions over such topics as force relocations put to one side as both countries concentrate on stepped-up cooperation across the board including an unprecedented Japanese military contribution to the Iraq coalition. In the Philippines, domestic political criticism of cooperation with the United States has not kept President Gloria Macapagal Arroyo from pursuing joint antiterrorism efforts, including against Abu Sayyaf and other armed groups in the southern Philippines.

However, as acknowledged by Bush to the press toward the end of his Asian trip, there remains a serious issue of negative public perceptions and elite criticism of the United States and Bush administration policy, especially with respect to Iraq, Israel, and Islam. Bush attributed the persistent problem to a lack of time to fully explain administration objectives and policies, and repeated his consistent insistence that the war on terrorism is not a war against Islam. The report of a Congressionally chartered commission headed by former diplomat Edward Djerejian echoed the same themes and called for increased spending and a new high-level coordinator for American public diplomacy, but also acknowledged the difficulty of identifying short-term fixes. In the meantime, further developments on the ground in Iraq (and, for Muslim communities, in the Israeli-Palestinian conflict) seem more likely to be the major determinant of attitudes toward the United States and its security contribution.

DEFENSE POLICIES AND ISSUES

TRIAL OF THE BUSH DOCTRINE   The U.S. invasion of Iraq in March 2003 was the first explicit exercise of the Bush administration's doctrine of preemptive defense, formally announced in the *National Security Strategy of the United States of America* (NSS) released in September 2002. Although the NSS covers a broad range of issues and reiterates longstanding U.S. support for greater international security cooperation including in such areas as intelligence sharing, the principal focus and major new emphasis in the NSS relates to terrorism and weapons of mass destruction (WMD). The assessment postulates that the most serious near-term hazards to American national security stem from terrorism, "rogue states," and the spread of WMD, and it argues that these types of threats are not likely to be deterred by traditional means. In its most controversial element, the NSS states that the United States explicitly reserves the right of unilateral, preemptive attack on adversaries if necessary to meet threats of terrorist attack or the use of WMD.

While the right to engage in preemptive war—striking first against an imminent, specific attack—is enshrined in Article 51 of the Charter of the United Nations, the Bush administration policy appears to go beyond Article 51 in positing a unilateral right to take anticipatory action to address the "capabilities and objectives of today's adversaries" —in other words, to mount preventive war rather than to preempt an imminent attack. Much of the lingering debate over the validity of the invasion of Iraq relates to whether the threat was sufficiently imminent to justify the essentially unilateral American action. More generally, critics (including various U.S. allies, most acerbically France and Germany) argue that U.S. unilateral behavior of the sort envisioned in the NSS will undermine the foundations of international institutions and laws. They see the Bush Doctrine as essentially a declaration of U.S. hegemony based on military might.

The Democratic Party in Congress—a minority in the House of

Representatives but until January 2003 the majority party in the Senate—mounted relatively little concerted opposition to the administration's request for authority to attack Iraq during debates on the issue in the fall of 2002. This was probably due in large part to a sense that the public strongly supported a continuing muscular response to September 11 and terrorism. However, the decision remains controversial in Congressional circles including among Republicans as well as in the media and the foreign policy elite.

The Bush administration itself was clearly divided on the approach if not on the ultimate objective of deposing Saddam Hussein. On one side was a group of so-called neo-conservatives, primarily in the Pentagon and the vice president's office, who advocated prompt unilateral action. These Iraq hawks believed strongly that years of unenforced UN resolutions had only emboldened Saddam, and that the overthrow of his regime would contribute to global stability. On the other side was a group of more cautious multinationalists centered around Secretary of State Colin Powell who advocated obtaining UN endorsement for any military action. (There are numerous more nuanced differences among administration policy makers, including between Asianists and non-Asian specialists, but these tended to be overshadowed in the debate over strategy on Iraq.) Powell won the president's agreement to go to the United Nations, and against expectations succeeded in obtaining a unanimous Security Council resolution in November 2002 threatening "serious consequences" if Iraq refused to comply with the long list of previous resolutions and to disarm. But the unusual gains for the Republican Party in the midterm Congressional elections, in which the president's personal campaigning was seen as a critical element, increased the confidence of the neo-conservatives that the American public would support forceful action in Iraq. Then in early 2003 a surprise turnabout by the French government, backed by Germany and Russia, scuttled any possibility of a second UN resolution authorizing the use of force, cutting the ground from under Secretary Powell's international strategy. Thus the Bush administration was left with a choice between implementing its preemption option or embarrassing public backdown.

Another element of the Iraq policy conundrum was the specific case for action. When initially asking for UN authorization to use force against Iraq, the Bush administration focused on disarmament as the primary objective and stressed the imminence of a threat of use of WMD. This argument was central to the case laid out by Powell before the Security Council in February 2003. However, starting just before the March invasion, and progressively becoming stronger as the coalition was unable to find WMD in Iraq, the public rationale shifted toward the desirability of regime change and the creation of a more stable, secure Middle East with a democratic, secular Iraq as a keystone.

As the fighting dragged out and the Bush administration began feeling the burdens of peacekeeping and state building in Iraq, emphasis shifted toward expanding the coalition force in Iraq, reducing the American profile and target, and ultimately to announcement of an accelerated return of sovereignty to an Iraqi government by July 2004. This shift assisted in gaining in October 2003 a UN Security Council resolution supporting members' participation in the U.S./coalition effort. The action in Iraq made both less feasible and less likely an American military response to other near-term international crises. Most immediately, the administration began downplaying the likelihood of resorting to preemption in dealing with the North Korean nuclear issue, despite the fact that North Korea, unlike Iraq, openly declared that it had a nuclear weapons program. While the administration insisted on its determination to stay the course in building stability and democracy in Iraq, the outlook was for further deemphasis of the preemption option and a much more cautious and consultative approach in practice in 2004.

One example of the increased emphasis on multilateralism in counterterrorism and counterproliferation policy was the Proliferation Security Initiative, launched in May 2003. Most immediately directed at North Korea, this proposal aims at creating a network of international agreements to intercept ships and aircraft suspected of carrying WMD-related material once they enter member countries' territories. North Korea unsurprisingly labeled the initiative "terrorism in the sea and a gross violation of international law," and stated that any attempted interdiction by the coalition would be considered an act of war. Some international law experts argue that the initiative is inconsistent with the accepted international law of the sea. Nevertheless, in July 2003, 11 countries (including China and Russia) agreed to share intelligence on arms trafficking and to hold a series of air and sea training interception exercises.

"TRANSFORMATION," RESTRUCTURING, AND REALIGNMENT   Bush administration defense policy before September 11 was most noteworthy (and controversial) for its emphasis on transforming America's military into a more flexible, high-technology force including such capabilities as missile defense. After September 11 this thrust has continued, despite having been rendered both publicly less conspicuous and financially less controversial by the overriding priorities of the war on terrorism. However, it is intersecting with the more topical issues of counterterrorism and WMD in complicated ways.

The planned realignment of U.S. bases in South Korea—to move the 2nd Infantry Division away from its 50-year-old positions on the Demilitarized Zone to a more efficient configuration south of Seoul—is the most visible of these issues in the Asia Pacific region, having overtaken the question of missile defense development and U.S.-Japanese cooperation in this area. The realignment question gained public attention in early 2003 shortly after the election of President Roh Moo Hyun on a wave of anti-American popular sentiment and simultaneous with moves toward talks with North Korea over the nuclear weapons issue. A further complication was introduced by press reports in October of a possible reduction of U.S. troop strength in Korea by up to 20 percent from the current level of 37,000. Despite ample reason (based on new technologies and mobility considerations) for a change in the configuration of American forces, and the lengthy (at least five years) time line for implementing any significant relocations, the publicity led to questions being raised in both North and South as to the underlying American motivation. Some in the South expressed a concern over lessened U.S. commitment in the event of war, while the Kim Jong Il government in the North charged that the move was in fact a preparation for a U.S. attack.

Other changes that will affect the American forward presence in the region in the future include the assignment of additional submarines to bases in Guam, possible drawdowns over time in the Marine Corps presence in Okinawa, and the probable need to relocate the navy's 7th fleet from Japan when the current (last and aging) non-nuclear carrier flagship is inevitably replaced with a nuclear carrier within the decade. All these steps are examples of longer-term adjustments that almost inevitably will have immediate political reverberations.

A further note in this context is the absence in Bush administration policy documents and statements of reference to the Bill Clinton administration's iconic pledge to keep 100,000 troops forward deployed in the region. This number was essentially a political and rhetorical device intended to reassure allies and never had a firm relationship to power-projection capabilities or strategic necessity, so its passing is a step toward a more practical and realistic understanding of the American regional presence. But the importance once attached to it in U.S. policy again demonstrates the continuing general sensitivity of the American presence and the difficulties associated with even justified change— which will almost always be incremental and politically visible rather than gradual and steady.

DEFENSE BUDGET   The post–September 11 rise in the U.S. defense budget continues—though the rate of growth is less than in the first two years after September 11—with an additional spike due to the Iraq war and occupation costs. The Congress approved US$375.3 billion in the regular defense appropriations bill for fiscal year 2004, plus a US$66 billion supplemental for the Iraq and Afghanistan operations (and US$20 billion more for Iraqi reconstruction). U.S. defense spending represents an investment of more than US$1,500 per capita for the roughly 290 million people of the United States, a number that exceeds the average per capita gross domestic product of the entire world minus the member countries of the Organisation for Economic Co-operation and Development and helps explain the absolute magnitude of U.S. military power. This level of spending in part reflects historical circumstances (the legacy of the cold war) as well as high U.S. personnel costs, but still might become a domestic political issue particularly if current huge budget deficits continue or if in response to Iraq a consensus develops that military might had led to reckless decisionmaking.

CONTRIBUTIONS TO REGIONAL AND GLOBAL SECURITY

U.S. UNILATERALISM VS. MULTILATERALISM   The Iraq experience demonstrated the desirability of having maximum international support and participation before embarking on a risky international intervention. The achievement of a united front among the five powers meeting with North Korea in the Six-Party Talks in August 2003 further reinforced this in the sense that it showed the possibility of gaining consensus. A renewed intensive effort succeeded in obtaining the UN Security Council resolution endorsing the leading U.S. role in Iraq in mid-October. And Bush's series of meetings on his Asian trip later in the month produced a string of statements of support for counterterrorism cooperation and announcements of contributions to the Iraq peacekeeping and reconstruction operation.

As if to confirm the new sensitivity toward internationalism, Bush administration spokesmen place the greatest emphasis on the multilateral and cooperative nature of the U.S. approach on both Iraq and the Korean peninsula. Nevertheless, the demonstration in Iraq of increased U.S. willingness to take unilateral action in the face of perceived threats is deeply embedded in the international consciousness and can be expected to remain so for some time to come.

ASIAN REGIONAL COOPERATION   At the same time, several developments in 2003 suggest a trend toward regional cooperation in Asia Pacific without U.S. involvement that could have significance for future U.S. relations with the region. These include such disparate events as the establishment of the Southeast Asia Regional Centre for Counter-Terrorism (SEARCCT), a Malaysian counterterrorism training school (originally proposed by the United States) from which the Malaysian government spoke of barring U.S. participation; agreements by Association of Southeast Asian Nations on trade negotiations with China, South Korea, and Japan; and moves by India to deepen its collaboration with the Southeast Asian nations. While a deepening of Asian-to-Asian ties is supported by and consistent with declared American policy, to the degree that these new arrangements reflect a desire to bypass U.S.-connected arrangements or to hedge against American influence there is a message for the United States about the cost of being perceived to be a self-seeking or insensitive hegemon.

INTERNATIONAL SECURITY   The Bush administration perceives its intervention in Iraq as being a significant contribution to international security. It removed an undesirable regime, ended Iraq's flouting of UN Security Council resolutions and inspections, and, in the eyes of some, may have a transforming effect on the entire Middle East. Critics argue otherwise: that the Iraq action may have increased rather than decreased the impetus toward terrorism. It is too soon to know which of these views will be more borne out in practice, but the action in Iraq clearly has at minimum committed the United States to a major and long-term new involvement in the Middle East.

21 Vietnam

THE SECURITY ENVIRONMENT

Vietnam continues to enjoy a stable internal and external environment, which enables the country to concentrate on economic development. Despite numerous threats and challenges including regional economic stagnation, regional terrorist acts, and the outbreak of the severe acute respiratory syndrome (SARS), in 2003 Vietnam recorded the second highest economic growth rate in the Asia Pacific region. Vietnam continues to pursue an outward-looking foreign policy aimed at making friends with as many countries in the world as possible. By the end of 2003, Vietnam had established diplomatic relations with 168 countries and territories in the world and had ties with most of world's major political, economic, and financial organizations and institutions. It has active trade ties with more than 100 countries. Vietnam is now placing highest emphasis on deepening these relationships, in order to reap maximum benefits from globalization and the country's integration into the outside world.

INTERNAL In contrast to many other Southeast Asian countries, Vietnam is not faced with direct threats from Islamic extremism and terrorism. This is due to the tiny size of the Muslim community living in Vietnam (currently less than 1 percent of the population) and the lack of linkages with regional or international terrorist networks like Jemaah Islamiah or al Qaeda. However, Vietnam feels the indirect impact of terrorism in Southeast Asia. Most basically, terrorism is a global phenomenon and terrorist acts affect all nations worldwide. Second, due to its geographical proximity to some member countries of the

Association of Southeast Asian Nations (ASEAN) with large Islamic populations, Vietnam considers it important to fully participate with other countries in the Southeast Asian region to counter terrorism. Third, there is always the possibility that terrorists or terrorist organizations might seek to enter Vietnam, laundering money from there and then transferring the newly laundered money to assist terrorist activities in Southeast Asia or the world at large.

Vietnam is joining forces with other countries, especially the United States and the ASEAN countries, in the effort to curb the spread of terrorism in Southeast Asia and worldwide. Bilaterally, Vietnam's Interpol bureau works closely with U.S. law enforcement agencies, notably the Federal Bureau of Investigation, in locating terrorists who might be in Vietnam and in checking suspicious bank accounts. At the regional level, Vietnam and the other ASEAN countries have signed a number of antiterrorist declarations and agreements aimed at countering terrorist activities in Southeast Asia. Vietnam is a member of the Southeast Asia Regional Centre for Counter-Terrorism (SEARCCT) in Malaysia, and shares intelligence relating to terrorist acts with the other ASEAN countries. Vietnam has also adopted measures to further tighten the security of its airports and harbors to stop terrorists from entering the country. The Vietnamese government has placed highest priority on antiterrorist measures in connection with hosting the 22nd Southeast Asian Games (SEA Games) in December 2003 and the upcoming 5th Asia-Europe Meeting in Hanoi in October 2004.

Vietnam has maintained both political stability and a high economic growth rate despite instability and economic stagnation in some neighboring Southeast Asian countries. According to a recent World Bank report, in 2003 Vietnam achieved an economic growth rate of 7.2 percent, the second highest rate in East Asia after China. This high growth rate is the result of a number of cumulative factors, including economic reform measures, restructuring of the state-owned enterprises, and a boom in the private sector. Another important factor has been the rapid increase in exports, especially to U.S. markets since the signing of the Vietnam-U.S. Bilateral Trade Agreement in 2000. In 2003, Vietnam exported more than 17 million tons of crude oil and 4 million tons of rice, making the country the second largest rice exporter in the world.

In an acknowledgement by the international community of Vietnam reform efforts, at the Consultative Group Meeting in Hanoi in December 2003, international donors pledged nearly US$2.9 billion in loans and grants for the 2004 fiscal year, the highest figure ever. This assistance will be particularly useful in view of decreasing levels of foreign direct investment (FDI).

In 2004, the government of Vietnam is aiming at an economic growth rate of 8.2 percent, considered achievable based on the economic dynamism of recent years. However, to achieve that objective, Vietnam must continue to improve its investment environment, to attract more Official Development Assistance (ODA) and FDI as well as more investment from domestic sources. Vietnam also needs to explore new export markets.

Vietnam is negotiating with various members of the World Trade Organization (WTO), laying the necessary groundwork for the country's admission into the world's largest trading organization in 2005. WTO membership will, in turn, help speed up economic reforms in Vietnam and its integration into the regional and world economies.

EXTERNAL   Since initiating its economic reforms in 1986, Vietnam has made adjustments in its foreign policy aimed at furthering Vietnam's integration into the Southeast Asian region and the international community. This process is expected to continue in 2004 and beyond.

China occupies a very important place in Vietnam's diplomacy both as a major world power and as Vietnam's giant neighbor. A visit to China by General Secretary Nong Duc Manh of the Communist Party of Vietnam in early 2003 helped to consolidate Sino-Vietnamese relations under the principles of "neighborly friendship, comprehensive cooperation, long-lasting stability and forward looking." Since the signing of an agreement demarcating the two countries' land borders in December 1999, the two countries have been engaged in intensive negotiations for a protocol supplementing the Agreement on Fishery Cooperation intended to minimize disputes over fishing grounds off their coasts. Vietnam and China aim to boost two-way trade to US$5 billion in 2005.

Ties between Laos and Vietnam are multifaceted and are sustained by frequent high-level visits and exchanges. Vietnam allows Laos to use Danang Port in central Vietnam to facilitate Laotian exports to foreign markets.

The government of Vietnam has followed with great concern political developments in its other land neighbor, Cambodia, since general elections in that country in 2003. Cambodia's three political parties are engaged in an ongoing power struggle. These tensions have yet to lead to the outbreak of civil conflict, but if the current situation continues it could have a serious impact not only on the daily life of the Cambodian people, but also on the stability of the whole of Southeast Asia. However, generally speaking bilateral relations have been good between Vietnam and the successive governments of Cambodia since Cambodia's first free elections under UN supervision in 1993.

Japan is Vietnam's largest trading partner and has the highest number of FDI projects in Vietnam. Japan's ODA to Vietnam accounts for 40 percent of total ODA committed to Vietnam and plays an important role in assisting Vietnam to upgrade its infrastructure and train its human resources. Though over the past decade Japan has dramatically reduced its ODA, Vietnam still receives substantial ODA from Japan and Japan is still Vietnam's largest donor, with ¥91.7 billion (US$856 million at US$1 = ¥107.13) in 2003 and up to US$840 million pledged for 2004.

U.S.-Vietnamese relations have improved remarkably since Vietnam and the United States normalized their political and economic relations in 1995 and 2000, respectively. In 2003, Vietnam's Foreign Minister Nguyen Dy Nien, Deputy Prime Minister Vu Khoan, and Defense Minister Pham Van Tra all visited the United States. On the economic front, the United States has become Vietnam's leading economic partner and most rapidly expanding market. Vietnam exports to the United States mainly garments, shoes and sandals, and seafood. However, U.S.-Vietnamese economic relations have also experienced problems, such as a 46 percent tariff imposed on Vietnamese catfish exports to the United States in response to complaints by an association of U.S. catfish producers of dumping by Vietnam in the U.S. market. The catfish case was a "wake-up" lesson for Vietnam's enterprises doing business with the United States, and other countries in general, that they need not only to obey the laws and regulations of other countries but also to be prepared for unpredictability and uncertainty. The government of Vietnam also remains concerned over hostility toward rapprochement in U.S.-Vietnamese relations from some quarters in the United States and whom the government considers are intervening in Vietnam's internal affairs on issues of democracy and human rights.

DEFENSE POLICY

Since the withdrawal of Russia's remaining forces from the Cam Ranh Bay in mid-2002, for the first time in Vietnam's contemporary history there has been no foreign military installation on Vietnam's territory. In the rapidly changing regional and international environment, a foreign military presence in Vietnam is not seen as the best way to guarantee Vietnam's security and safeguard its territorial integrity. Therefore, the Vietnamese government has announced that it will not lease Cam Ranh Bay to any country for military use, but rather keep it open to visits by foreign military ships regardless of nationality.

The resolution on defense adopted at the 8th plenum of the Vietnamese Communist Party's Central Committee in July 2003 places priority on the maintenance of a stable and peaceful external environment conducive to Vietnam's economic development, social progress, and international integration. In the resolution, national defense is not purely confined to the strengthening of Vietnam's military force, but is seen as part of the country's grand strategy.

Vietnam is actively developing military ties with the major regional powers, namely, the United States, Japan, and China. The year 2003 saw visits paid by Vietnam's top-ranking defense officials to all three countries, including the first visit paid by a Vietnamese defense minister since the end of the Vietnam War in 1975. (Also, in November 2003 the first U.S. warship visited a Vietnamese port since 1975.)

CONTRIBUTIONS TO REGIONAL AND GLOBAL STABILITY

Vietnam participates actively in the principal regional and international cooperation forums, such as ASEAN, ASEAN + 3 (China, Japan, and South Korea), the ASEAN Regional Forum, the Asia-Pacific Economic Cooperation (APEC) forum, and the Asia-Europe Meeting (ASEM) in addition to the United Nations and related bodies. As a founding member and Asian coordinator in ASEM, Vietnam has been doing its best to promote mutual understanding and cooperation between Asia and Europe. In October 2004, Vietnam will host the ASEM-5 Summit meeting in Hanoi.

As one of the countries that vehemently opposed the use of force to change regimes in Afghanistan and Iraq, Vietnam quickly adjusted its attitudes toward both Afghanistan and Iraq after major wars ended there. This should not be seen as Vietnam's endorsement of the use of force to settle disputes in international relations or its approval of the right to intervene in the internal affairs of other countries. Instead, Vietnam desires to see the situation in Afghanistan and Iraq stabilized soon, so the peoples of these two countries can restore law and order and concentrate on economic development. Vietnam has participated in reconstruction conferences on Afghanistan and Iraq held in Tokyo and Madrid, respectively, and is sending 500,000 tons of rice to Iraq to help overcome economic difficulties.

As a Third World country that has experienced successful economic reforms, Vietnam is eager to share its experiences with other interested countries. For example, in May 2003 Vietnam hosted the first Vietnam-Africa conference in Hanoi. Vietnam has pledged to participate in some development projects in African countries, either on a bilateral basis or a "2 + 1" formula (Vietnam and one African country with financial assistance from another donor country or institution).

List of Abbreviations

AC   ASEAN Community
ACD   Asian Cooperation Dialogue
ADB   Asian Development Bank
ADF   Australian Defense Force
AEC   ASEAN Economic Community
AEW&C   airborne early warning and control
AFP   Armed Forces of the Philippines
AFP   Australian Federal Police
ANZUS   Australia-New Zealand-United States (defense alliance)
APEC   Asia-Pacific Economic Cooperation
ARF   ASEAN Regional Forum
ARNO   Arakan Rohingya National Organization (Myanmar and Bangladesh)
ASDF   Air Self-Defense Force (Japan)
ASEAN   Association of Southeast Asian Nations
ASEM   Asia-Europe Meeting
ASG   Abu Sayyaf Group (Phillipines)
AVF   all-volunteer force
BEDB   Brunei Economic Development Board
BIMST-EC   Bangladesh-India-Myanmar-Sri Lanka-Thailand Economic Cooperation
BJP   Bharatiya Janata Party (Indian People's Party)
BSE   Bovine Spongiform Encephalopathy
CCP   Chinese Communist Party
CFSP   Common Foreign and Security Policy
CIS   Commonwealth of Independent States
CoHA   Cessation of Hostilities Agreement (between Indonesian government and GAM)
CSTO   Collective Security Treaty Organization (CIS)
CWRP   Civic Will-Republican Party (Mongolia)
DAP   Democratic Action Party (Malaysia)
DMZ   Demilitarized Zone

DND   Department of National Defense (Canada)
DP   Democratic Party (Mongolia)
DPJ   Democratic Party of Japan
EEZ   Exclusive Economic Zone
ELSHAM   Indonesian Institute for Human Rights Study and Advocacy
ESDP   European Security and Defense Policy
ESS   European Security Strategy
EU   European Union
FDI   foreign direct investment
FPDA   Five Power Defense Arrangements (Australia, Malaysia, New Zealand, Singapore, and the United Kingdom)
FPI   Islamic Defenders Front (Indonesia)
FTA   free trade agreement
FTA   free trade area
GAM   Gerakan Aceh Merdeka (Free Aceh Movement, of Indonesia)
GMS   Greater Mekong Subregion
GNP   Grand National Party (South Korea)
GSDF   Ground Self-Defense Force (Japan)
IAEA   International Atomic Energy Agency
ISAF   International Security Assistance Force
IMET   International Military Education and Training
JCP   Japan Communist Party
JDA   Japan Defense Agency
JI   Jemaah Islamiah
JS   Jemmah Salafiyah (Thailand)
KEDO   Korean Peninsula Energy Development Organization
KMM   Kumpulan Militan Malaysia
LDP   Liberal Democratic Party (Japan)
LFO   Legal Framework Order (Pakistan)
LTTE   Liberation Tigers of Tamil Ealam
MAF   Malaysian Armed Forces
MBT   main battle tank
MD   missile defense
MDF   Me'ekamui Defense Force (PNG)
MDNSP   Mongolian Democratic New Socialist Party
MDP   Millenium Democratic Party (South Korea)
MILF   Moro Islamic Liberation Front (Philippines)
MONUC   United Nations Organization Mission in the Democratic Republic of the Congo
MPA   maritime patrol aircraft

MPRP   Mongolian People's Revolutionary Party
MRCA   multirole combat aircraft
MSDF   Maritime Self-Defense Force (Japan)
NAM   Non-Aligned Movement
NATO   North Atlantic Treaty Organisation
NDPO   National Defense Program Outline
NGO   nongovernmental organization
NGPV   New Generation Patrol Vessel
NORAD   North American Aerospace Defense Command
NPT   Nonproliferation Treaty
NSC   National Security Council (Pakistan)
NSS   *National Security Strategy of the United States of America*
ODA   Official Development Assistance
OECD   Organisation for Economic Cooperation and Development
OIC   Organization of the Islamic Conference
OPM   Organisasi Papua Merdeka (Free Papua Movement)
OSCE   Organization for Security and Co-operation in Europe
PACER   Pacific Agreement on Closer Economic Relations
PAP   People's Action Party (Singapore)
PAS   Parti Islam SeMalaysia (Islamic Party of Malaysia)
PECC   Pacific Economic Cooperation Council
PICTA   Pacific Island Countries Trade Agreement
PNG   Papua New Guinea
PNGDF   Papua New Guinea Defense Force
PSI   Proliferation Security Initiative
QMV   qualified majority voting
RAMSI   Regional Assistance Mission to the Solomon Islands
RMAF   Royal Malaysian Air Force
RMN   Royal Malaysian Navy
RSO   Rohingya Solidarity Organization (Bangladesh)
SAARC   South Asian Association for Regional Cooperation
SACO   Special Action Committee on Okinawa (Japan–United States)
SAF   Singapore Armed Forces
SARS   severe acute respiratory syndrome
SCO   Shanghai Cooperation Organization
SDF   Self-Defense Forces (Japan)
SDP   Social Democratic Party (Japan)
SEARCCT   Southeast Asia Regional Centre for Counter-Terrorism
SHIRBRIG   Multi-national Standby Force High Readiness Brigade for
    UN Operations

SLOC   sea lines of communication
SMF   strategic missile force
TAC   Treaty of Amity and Cooperation (in Southeast Asia, of ASEAN)
TCOG   Trilateral Coordination and Oversight Group (Japan-Korea-U.S.)
TFAP   Trade Facilitation Action Plan
TNI   Tentara Nasional Indonesia (Indonesian National Military)
TRT   Thai Rak Thai Party
ULD   United Liberal Democrats (South Korea)
UMNO   United Malays National Organization
UN   United Nations
UNDOF   UN Disengagement Observer Force
UNMISET   UN Mission of Support in East Timor
UNSC   UN Security Council
URF   Union of Right Forces (Russia)
URP   United Russia Party
USNORTHCOM   United States Northern Command
WHO   World Health Organization
WMD   weapons of mass destruction
WTO   World Trade Organization

The APSO Project Team

A distinctive feature of the *Asia Pacific Security Outlook* is that it is based on background papers developed by analysts from the region, many of them younger specialists. An annual workshop brings a group of analysts together to examine draft country papers and discuss the overall regional outlook. The project also circulates a questionnaire, which provides an indication of changing perceptions over time and is used in developing the regional overview. For 2004, additional theme papers were commissioned from senior subject matter experts as a supplement to the country papers and workshop discussion.

The following individuals were involved in the 2004 *Asia Pacific Security Outlook*. (Note: Paper writers participate in their personal capacities; their views do not necessarily represent those of the institutions with which they are affiliated. The chapters in this volume are based in large part on the background papers, but the project editors, not the authors, are responsible for the content and any errors in the final texts.)

COUNTRY ANALYSTS

AUSTRALIA   Ross Cottrill, Australian Institute of International Affairs, Canberra

BRUNEI DARUSSALAM   Pushpathavi Thambipillai, University of Brunei Darussalam

CANADA   Allen G. Sens and Brian L. Job, University of British Columbia, Vancouver

CHINA   Chu Shulong, Tsinghua University, Beijing

EUROPEAN UNION   Sebastian Harnisch, University of Trier, Germany

INDONESIA   Rizal Sukma, Centre for Strategic and International Studies, Jakarta

JAPAN   Katahara Eiichi, Kobe Gakuin University

REPUBLIC OF KOREA   Chung Oknim, Sunmoon University, Asan, South Korea

MALAYSIA   Elina Noor, Institute of Strategic and International Studies, Kuala Lumpur

MONGOLIA   Munkh-Ochir Dorjjugder, Institute for Strategic Studies, Ulaanbaatar

NEW ZEALAND   David Dickens, independent policy analyst

PAPUA NEW GUINEA   Ronald May, Australian National University, Canberra

PHILIPPINES   Noel Morada, Institute for Strategic and Development Studies, Quezon City

RUSSIA   Sergei Sevastyanov, Valadivostok State University of Economics

SINGAPORE   Yeo Lay Hwee, Singapore Institute of International Affairs

THAILAND   Chookiat Panaspornprasit, Institute of Security and International Studies, Bangkok

UNITED STATES   Richard W. Baker, East-West Center (with Sarabecka Mullen, Johns Hopkins University School of Advanced International Studies, Washington, D.C.)

VIETNAM   Hoang Anh Tuan, Research Institute for International Relations, Hanoi

THEME PAPERS

NORTHEAST ASIA   Ralph A. Cossa, Pacific Forum CSIS, Honolulu

SOUTHEAST ASIA   Rohan Gunaratna, Institute of Defense and Strategic Studies, Singapore

SOUTH ASIA   Dipankar Banerjee, Institute of Peace and Conflict Studies, New Delhi

OVERVIEW AND EDITORS

Richard W. Baker, Special Assistant to the President, East-West Center

Charles E. Morrison, President, East-West Center

PROJECT DIRECTORS

Charles E. Morrison, President, East-West Center, United States

Jusuf Wanandi, Chairman of the Supervisory Board, Centre for Strategic and International Studies, Indonesia

Yamamoto Tadashi, President, Japan Center for International Exchange, Japan

PROJECT COORDINATOR

Ito Hyōma, Japan Center for International Exchange

Index

Abdullah Ahmad Badawi, 125–126, 128, 172
Abu Sayyaf Group (ASG), 15, 36, 39, 153,
    155–156
  and al Qaeda, 36
Aceh, 101
  and al Qaeda, 37
  and Thailand, 182
Afghanistan
  governance in, 64
  illegal immigration from, 150
  and Pakistan, 50
  polio, 133
  reconstruction of, 18
    and Brunei, 69
    and Canada, 74, 77–78
    and European Union, 90, 95
    and India, 50
    International Security Assistance Force
      (ISAF). *See* International Security
      Assistance Force
    and Japan, 115–116
    and Malaysia, 133
    and Mongolia, 139
    and New Zealand, 140–141, 146
    and Thailand, 182
    and United States, 183
  and Russia, 164
  terrorist training in, 35
Agreed Framework, 24
Agreement on Information Exchange and
    Establishment of Communication
    Procedures, 70
AIDS, 10
Al Arqam, 67
al Qaeda, 35–42, 58, 61
  and Malaysia, 127–128
  and North Korea, 23
  and Pakistan, 47
  and Singapore, 173
  and Southeast Asia, 34–42
  and Thailand, 177
Anwar Ibrahim, 126
Armenia, 161–162
Arroyo, Gloria Macapagal, 153, 156, 185

arms exports
  to China from Russia, 163
  to India from Israel, 53
  to India from Russia, 53
  to India from United Kingdom, 53
  to India from United States, 53
  to Indonesia from Netherlands, 106
  to Indonesia from Russia, 106
  to Indonesia from South Korea, 106
  from Japan, 115
  to Malaysia from France, 131
  to Malaysia from Pakistan, 129
  to Malaysia from Poland, 129–130
  to Malaysia from Russia, 129
  to Malaysia from Ukraine, 131
  to Pakistan from United States, 50
  Proliferation Security Initiative, 91, 97
  to Singapore from France, 174
  to Singapore from United Kingdom, 173
  to Singapore from United States, 174
  to Thailand from China, 180
  to Thailand from India, 180
  to Thailand from Russia, 180
  to Thailand from Switzerland, 180
  to Thailand from United Kingdom, 180
  to Thailand from United States, 181
ASEAN (Association of Southeast Asian
    Nations), 13, 86, 170
  and Brunei, 70
  and China, 86
  and European Union, 91
  and Indonesia, 107
  and Japan, 106, 112
  regionalism, 170
  terrorism, 70
  and United States, 183, 191
  and Vietnam, 196
ASEAN Regional Forum (ARF)
  and Canada, 75
  and European Union, 96
  and Mongolia, 139
  and Russia, 166
  and Singapore, 174
  and Vietnam, 196

Asia-Europe Meeting (ASEM)
and European Union, 91, 96
and Vietnam, 196
Asian Cooperation Dialogue (ACD), 176, 178
Asia-Pacific Economic Cooperation
(APEC), 11, 25
and Canada, 75, 78
and Mongolia, 139
and Russia, 166
and Thailand, 182
and United States, 184
and Vietnam, 196
Aung San Suu Kyi, 132
Australia
and Afghanistan, 61, 64
Bali bombings, 58, 64
and Bougainville, 65
and Cambodia, 64
and China, 58–59
trade with, 58
defense, 59
budget, 62–63
expenditure, 61
procurement, 60–63
regional, 59–60
risks, 61
strategy, 60
and East Timor, 62, 65
economy, 59
and Fiji, 64
and India, 64
and Indonesia, 58, 60, 64
and Iraq war, 58, 61–63
costs, 64
and Malaysia, 64
and Muslims, 57
and New Zealand, 60
and North Korea, 59
and Papua New Guinea, 65, 148, 152
peacekeeping operations, 60
and Philippines, 64
regional partners of, 59–60, 64
security
global, 57, 63
regional, 57, 61
and Solomon Islands, 59, 62, 64
and Southwest Pacific, 59, 64
terrorism, 57
external, 58–59, 61, 64
internal, 57
and Thailand, 64
trade
with China, 58
with United States, 58

and United States, 57–58, 61
North Korean policy, 59
weapons of mass destruction, 64
See also Howard, John
avian flu, 10

Bali bombings
and Australia, 58, 64
and Indonesia, 100, 106
and Jemaah Islamiah, 35
and Malaysia, 128
Bangladesh, 44
and China, 51
and Congo, 54
defense budget, 53
democracy, 47
economy, 48, 50
and India, 48, 50, 52
investment, 48
Islam, 48
and Mongolia, 139
and Myanmar, 50
peacekeeping operations, 54
terrorism, 36, 39, 52
and Thailand, 50
and United States, 50
Belarus, 161–162
Belgium
and European Union security policy, 93
Bhutan
defense, 52
economy
and India, 49
insurgencies, 45
and Nepal, 51
security, internal, 44, 49
terrorism, 45
bin Laden, Osama, 36–37, 47
Blair, Tony, 69
Bosnia, 146, 167
Bougainville
and Australia, 65
and Papua New Guinea, 147
and Solomon Islands, 150
Bovine Spongiform Encephalopathy (BSE),
74
Brunei Darussalam
and ASEAN members, 69–70
and Australia, 69
and China, 69
defense and military
armed forces, 68
military contacts, 69
diplomacy, 70

and France, 69
and India, 69
insurgencies, 69
Islam, 66–67
  Jemaah Islamiah, 68
and Japan, 69
and Malaysia, 68
oil, 66–69
and Palestine, 69
security
  external, 68
  internal, 66–68
  nonconventional threats, 70
  regional, 70
territorial disputes, 68
terrorism, 70
trade, 69
and United Kingdom, 69
and United States, 69
See also Sultan Haji Hassanal Bolkiah of
  Brunei
Bush, George W.
and Asia Pacific, 184–185
and Australia, 184
and Canada, 71, 74
and China, 14, 59
domestic concerns, 183
and Indonesia, 106
and North Korea, 25–26, 184
and Pakistan, 50
and Philippines, 155–156
preemptive defense, 186–188
Proliferation Security Initative, 64, 91, 97,
  111, 121, 188
and Taiwan, 14, 185
and Thailand, 180
unilateralism, 186–188, 190–191

Cambodia
and Australia, 64
and Canada, 78
and China, 86–87
and European Union, 91
and Thailand, 178
and Vietnam, 194
Canada
and Afghanistan, 74, 77–78
and Asia Pacific, 71
  security of, 74–75, 78
and Bosnia, 79
and Cambodia, 78
and China, 78
defense
  armed forces, 76

budget, 75–76
cooperation with United States, 76–77
deployment, 77
policy, 75, 77, 79
procurement, 75
and East Timor, 78
foreign affairs, 71, 73
  multilateralism, 73–75
and India, 78
and Iraq war, 71, 74, 77
mad cow disease, 74
and NATO, 75, 79
and North Korea, 77–78
SARS, 73
security, 75, 78
  external, 73
  global, 78
  internal, 71–72
  and United States, 76–77
and Sri Lanka, 78
terrorism, 72, 76–77
trade, 71, 78
and United Nations, 73–75, 79
and United States, 71, 73, 77
  and terrorism, 72, 77
Central Asia
and India, 50
and Russia, 164, 167
Chechnya, 161, 166
and Muslims, 36
Chen Shui-bian, 14, 31, 157, 185
China
and ASEAN, 82, 86–87
  trade with, 81, 86
and Bangladesh, 51
and Congo, 87
defense
  expenditure, 83
  personnel, 84
  procurement, 83–84
economy, 80, 82
and Hong Kong, 84–85
and India, 82–83
and Iran, 87
and Iraq war, 87
and Japan, 81–83, 111
and Mongolia, 136–137
and Nepal, 51
and North Korea, 30–31
  Six-Party Talks, 23
  and United States, 30–31
and Pakistan, 85
and Papua New Guinea, 149
peacekeeping operations, 87

China (*continued*)
and Russia, 83, 163
SARS, 80, 82, 86
security, 84–86
dialogue, 82
nontraditional, 80, 84
regional, 85–86
subregional, 86
and South Korea, 81–82
and Taiwan, 31, 81
terrorism, 84
trade, 81–82, 86
and United States, 13–14, 82
Chrétien, Jean, 71, 73–74, 78
Clark, Helen, 140, 143
Collective Security Treaty Organization
(CSTO), 162
Commonwealth of Independent States
(CIS), 161–162
Congo
and Bangladesh, 54
and China, 87
and European Union, 93
and Mongolia, 139

Dalai Lama, 136

East Timor
and Australia, 62, 65
and Canada, 78
and Japan, 116
and Malaysia, 132
and Papua New Guinea, 152
and South Korea, 124
and Thailand, 181
Egypt
and Malaysia, 133
Enkhbayar, Nambar, 135
European Union (EU)
and Afghanistan, 90, 95
and ASEAN members, 91
and Asia Pacific, 90–91
economic involvement with, 91
humanitarian aid to, 98
security of, 95–96
and China, 91, 95
and Congo, 89, 93
defense, 92–93
budget 94
policy, 93
and India, 95
and Indonesia, 91
and Iraq war, 90, 93, 95

and Japan, 91, 95–96
and Korean Peninsula Energy Development Organization, 96
and Macedonia, 89
military operations, 93
and Moldava, 89
multilateralism, 90, 96
Official Development Assistance (ODA),
97
peacekeeping operations, 95
and Russia, 162
security, 89–91
global, 95–96
policy, 90, 93
and Singapore, 91
and Taiwan, 91
terrorism, 91, 93
trade, 91
and United Nations, 93, 96
and United States, 89
and Yugoslavia (former), 91

Fiji
and Australia, 64
Five Power Defense Arrangements (FPDA),
132, 146, 174
France
and Asia Pacific, 95
and Brunei, 69
and China, 137
and Congo, 93
defense expenditure, 94
and European Union security policy, 93
and Iran nuclear progam, 93
and Iraq stabilization, 90
and Proliferation Security Initiative, 97
security, 94
and United States, 186
free trade agreements (FTAs)
ASEAN and China, 86
Australia and United States, 184
India and ASEAN, 50
of Japan, 112
New Zealand and United States, 143
Pacific Agreement on Closer Economic
Relations (PACER), 152
Pacific Island Countries Trade Agreement
(PICTA), 152
South Asia, 45
Thailand and United States, 179

Georgia
and South Korea, 124

Germany
  and Afghanistan, 90
  defense expenditure, 94
  and European Union security policy, 93
  and Iran nuclear program, 93
  and Iraq stabilization, 90
  and Proliferation Security Initiative, 97
  security, 94
  and United States, 186
Goh Chok Tong, 128, 172
Golan Heights, 116
Greater Mekong Subregion (GMS) Economic Cooperation Program, 87

Hambali, 37, 42, 127, 170, 178
Howard, John, 57, 128, 148
  and Malaysia, 128
  and Papua New Guinea, 148
Hu Jintao, 58, 81, 135
  and Australia, 58
  and Mongolia, 135, 137
Hussein, Saddam, 156, 187

India
  and Afghanistan, 50
  and ASEAN, 50, 191
  and Australia, 64
  and Bangladesh, 50, 52
  and Central Asia, 50
  and China, 49, 82
  defense
    budget, 52
    policy, 51
    procurement, 53
  economy, 17, 44, 46, 50
  insurgencies, 46, 50–51
    and Nepal, 51
  investment, 49
  and Iran, 50
  and Israel, 53
  and Jammu and Kashmir, 46, 51
  and Myanmar, 46, 50
  and Nepal, 51
  nuclear capacity, 51
  and Pakistan, 44–45, 51
  peacekeeping operations, 53
  politics, 46
  and Russia, 53, 164
  security
    global, 53
    internal, 44
  and South Korea, 124
  and Tajikistan, 50

  terrorism, 46, 51
  and Thailand, 50, 180
  trade
    with ASEAN, 50
    with China, 49, 82
    and United States, 49
    and Vietnam, 50
  See also Vajpayee, Atal Bihari
Indonesia
  and ASEAN, 107
  and Australia, 64, 100, 106
  and Brunei, 106
  communal violence, 103
  defense
    procurement, 105
    strategy, 105
  economy, 99
  investment, 99
  and Islam, 100–101, 104
  and Japan, 106
  and Jemaah Islamiah, 39, 57, 58, 101,
    103
  military, 103–104, 106
  political situation, 100
  secessionist movements, 101–103
  security, 99, 101–103
    regional, 107
  and Singapore, 104
  terrorism, 36, 39, 58, 99, 101, 103–104,
    107
    Bali bombings, 100
    threat of, 39, 101
  and United States, 104, 184
    military-to-military relations, 104, 106
    and terrorism, 99, 104, 184
insurgency movements
  Bhutan, 45
  Brunei, 69
  India, 46, 50–51
    and Nepal, 51
  Nepal, 17, 46, 49–52
    and India, 46, 50–51
    and United Kingdom, 51
    and United States, 51
  and Philippines, 154
  South Asia, 44
  Sri Lanka, 17, 52
  Thailand, 127
  Vietnam, 50
International Atomic Energy Agency
    (IAEA)
  and China, 87
  and North Korea, 24, 32, 96

International Monetary Fund (IMF)
and Indonesia, 99
and Pakistan, 47
and Thailand, 177
International Security Assistance Force
(ISAF)
and Canada, 74, 77
and European Union, 90
Iran, 93
and India, 50
and Russia, 162
Iraq reconstruction
and Canada, 74, 77
and Japan, 110
and Mongolia, 139
and New Zealand, 146
and South Korea, 9, 123
and Thailand, 181
Iraq war
and Australia, 58, 63
and Brunei, 69
and Canada, 71, 74
and China, 87
and European Union, 89
and Japan, 109
and Mongolia, 134–135, 138
and New Zealand, 140, 143
and Philippines, 156
and Russia, 162
and Singapore, 169, 174
and Thailand, 179
and United States, 9, 184–186
and Vietnam, 196
Irian Jaya. *See* Papua
Islam, 9
and Bangladesh, 47
and Brunei, 66–67
and Malaysia, 129, 133
Organization of Islamic Conference, 133
and Russia, 166
and Vietnam, 192
and Yemen, 127
Islamic terrorism, 9, 58
and Brunei, 68
and Canada, 72
and Chechnya, 36
and Indonesia, 100–101, 104
and Malaysia, 126–127, 129
and Pakistan, 47, 127
and Philippines, 127, 153
and Russia, 36
and Singapore, 169
and Southeast Asia, 34–36, 38
and Thailand, 177

and United States, 36, 185–186
Israel, 146, 183, 186
and India, 53
Italy
defense expenditure, 94
and Proliferation Security Initiative, 97

Jammu and Kashmir, 45–46, 51
Japan
and Afghanistan, 115–116
and ASEAN, 112
and China, 111
defense
expenditure, 114–115
planning, 113
procurement, 113, 115
and East Timor, 116
and Golan Heights, 116
humanitarian assistance, 110
and Iraq
reconstruction, 110
war, 109
and Malaysia, 112
missile defense system, 113, 115
multilateralism, 109
nongovernmental organizations, 117
and North Korea, 109, 111, 113–114
abductions by, 29
Six-Party Talks, 23, 26, 111
Trilateral Coordination and Oversight
Group (TCOG), 25, 111
and United States, 29, 109
Official Development Assistance, 108,
115
peacekeeping operations, 116
and Philippines, 112
politics, 108
and Russia, 112, 163
security, 113, 115
external, 109, 111, 113–114
Self-Defense Forces (SDF), 110, 116
and South Korea, 111
and Sri Lanka, 115
terrorism, 114, 116
and Thailand, 112
trade, 112
free tree agreements, 112
and United States, 109
See also Koizumi Jun'ichirō
Jemaah Islamiah (JI), 58
and al Qaeda, 34–42
and Bali bombings, 35
and Brunei, 68
and Indonesia, 41, 100, 103

and Malaysia, 40, 126–128
and Moro Islamic Liberation Front, 16,
    35–40
and Philippines, 155
and Singapore, 36, 40
and Southeast Asia, 34–42
and Thailand, 41, 177, 180
Joint Agreement on the Denuclearization of
    the Korean Peninsula, 24
JW Marriott Hotel Jakarta, 101, 107, 128
and al Qaeda, 36
and Singapore, 169
and United States, 183

Kazakhstan, 161–162
and China, 137
Kim Dae Jung, 118
and North Korea, 25, 28, 120
Kim Jong Il, 14–15, 28, 31–32, 189
and United States, 189
Koizumi Jun'ichirō, 108, 163
and ASEAN, 112
and China, 111
and North Korea, 25–26
    and United States, 29
and Russia, 163
and South Korea, 111
Korea, Republic of. See South Korea
Korean Peninsula Energy Development Or-
    ganization (KEDO)
and European Union, 96
Korean peninsula nuclear crisis. See North
    Korean nuclear crisis
Kosovo, 167
Kyrgyz Republic, 161–162, 167

Laos
and China, 86–87
and Thailand, 178
and Vietnam, 194
Lebanon, 150
Lee Hsien Loong, 172
Lee Kuan Yew, 172
Liberia
and South Korea, 124
and Thailand, 182
Luxembourg
and European Union security policy, 93

Macedonia
and European Union, 89
mad cow disease, 74
Mahathir bin Mohammed, 125–126, 129,
    149

Malaysia
and ASEAN, 131
and Australia, 64, 128, 132
and Brunei, 128
defense
    forces, 129
    policy, 129
    procurement, 129–130
and East Timor, 132
and Indonesia, 128
Islam, 126, 129, 133
Jemaah Islamiah, 126
and Myanmar, 132
and New Zealand, 132
and Papua New Guinea, 149
and Philipppines, 127, 154–155
SARS, 131
security
    global, 132
    internal, 125
    regional, 131–132
and Singapore, 128, 132
terrorism, 36, 58, 126, 128, 132
and Thailand, 127, 179
and United Kingdom, 132
and United States, 129
Maldives, 44
Marriott Hotel Jakarta bombing. See JW
    Marriott Hotel Jakarta bombing
Martin, Paul, 71
Megawati Sukarnoputri, 100
and Bali bombings, 100
military-to-military relations
Brunei
    and China, 69
    and India, 69
    and Indonesia, 69
    and Japan, 69
    and Malaysia, 69
    and Philippines, 69
    and Singapore, 69
    and United States, 69
China and Pakistan, 85
Indonesia
    and Brunei, 106
    and Japan, 106
    and United States, 104, 106
Malaysia and Thailand, 127, 179
Mongolia and Afghanistan, 139
Philippines and United States, 156
Russia and Japan, 164
Singapore and United States, 174
Thailand and India, 181
Thailand and Indonesia, 181

military-to-military relations (*continued*)
Thailand and Japan, 181
Thailand and Philippines, 181
Thailand and United Kingdom, 181
Thailand and United States, 181
See also Five Power Defense Arrangements
Mindanao
and Jemaah Islamiah, 39, 42
terrorist camp in, 16, 39
See also Moro Islamic Liberation Front
missile defense system
and Canada, 73, 77
and Japan, 29, 113, 115
and Russia, 162
Mongolia
and Bangladesh, 139
and China, 134, 136–137
and Congo, 139
defense
expenditure, 138
policy, 138
economy, 134, 137
and China, 137
and Russia, 136
and European Union, 137
foreign policy, 134–135, 138
and Iraq, 138
globalization, 134
and Iraq war, 134–135, 138–139, 142–143
and North Korea, 137, 139
peacekeeping operations, 139
and Russia, 134, 136
SARS, 135
security
economic, 134, 137
global, 139
regional, 139
Six-Party Talks, 137, 139
and United States, 134, 137
Moro Islamic Liberation Front (MILF), 127, 153, 155
and al Qaeda, 35–40
and Jemaah Islamiah, 16, 39
and Philippines, 154
and United States, 154
Mozambique, 146
multilateralism
and Canada, 73–75, 78
and China, 170
and European Union, 90, 96
and Japan, 109

and Korean peninsula, 24–26, 188
and New Zealand, 142
and Philippines, 156
and United States, 186–188, 190–191
Musharraf, Pervez, 17, 45–47, 50
Muslims. *See* Islam; Islamic terrorism
Myanmar, 46
and Bangladesh, 50
and China, 86–87
economic cooperation, 50
terrorism, 36, 39, 46
and Thailand, 50, 179

NATO (North Atlantic Treaty Organisation)
and Canada, 75, 79
and European Union, 89–90
and Philippines, 156
and Russia, 162–163
and Thailand, 179
Nepal
and Bhutan, 51
and China, 51
defense, 52–53
economy, 49
and India, 51
insurgencies, 46, 49–53
peacekeeping operations, 54
security, internal, 44, 49
Netherlands
and Afghanistan, 90
defense expenditure, 94
and Proliferation Security Initiative, 97
New Zealand
and Afghanistan, 140–141, 146
anti-nuclear policy, 145
ANZUS, 140
and Australia, 141–142, 144, 146
and Bosnia, 146
and Cambodia, 146
defense, 140–141, 143
budget, 144–145
forces, 145
procurement, 145
Five Power Defense Arrangements, 146
Iraq war, 140, 142, 144
and Israel, 146
and Malaysia, 146
and Mozambique, 146
multilateralism, 142
peacekeeping operations, 140–141, 144–146
and Pristine, 146

security, 140–141
  external, 141
  internal, 141
  regional, 142, 146
  and Sinai, 146
  and Singapore, 146
  and Solomon Islands, 142, 146
  and Syria, 146
  terrorism, 140–141
  trade, 141, 143
  and United Kingdom, 146
  and United Nations, 141–142
  and United States, 140, 143, 146
    and anti-nuclear policy, 144
  See also Clark, Helen
Niger
  and Malaysia, 133
Nigeria
  and Malaysia, 133
Non-Aligned Movement (NAM)
  and Iraq war, 151
  and Malaysia, 129, 133
  and Papua New Guinea, 151
nongovernmental organizations (NGOs)
  in Indonesia, 102–103
  and Japan, 116–117
Nonproliferation Treaty (NPT)
  and Canada, 78
  and China, 87
  and European Union, 97
  and North Korea, 24, 78, 96
North American Aerospace Defense Command (NORAD), 77
Northeast Asia
  and North Korea, 23
  security, 23, 31–32
North Korean nuclear crisis, 23–24, 32
  and Canada, 78
  and China, 30, 85–86
  and European Union, 96
  and Japan, 29, 111
  and Mongolia, 137, 139
  multilateral approach to, 24–26
  Proliferation Security Initiative, 97, 188
  and Russia, 30–31, 162, 164, 167
  and South Korea, 27–29, 120
  and Taiwan, 31
  terrorism, implications for, 23
  United States, 24, 26
  See also Six-Party Talks
nuclear nonproliferation
  China, 82

global regime, 23
North Korea, 23, 32

Official Development Assistance (ODA)
  European Union, 97
  Japan, 108, 115
  Vietnam, 195
Organization of the Islamic Conference
    (OIC), 50, 129, 133, 166
Organization for Security and Co-operation
    in Europe (OSCE), 89

Pakistan, 44
  and Afghanistan, 50–51
  and al Qaeda, 47
  and Bangladesh, 50
  and China, 50, 85
  defense
    budget, 52
    forces, 51
  economy, 47
  and foreign relations, 50
  and India, 44–45, 51
  and International Monetary Fund, 47
  and Islam, 47
  and Malaysia, 133
  peacekeeping operations, 53
  and Papua New Guinea, 150
  security
    global, 53
    internal, 46–47
  and South Korea, 124
  terrorism, 47, 127
  and United States, 47, 50
  and World Bank, 47
  See also Musharraf, Pervez
Palestine
  and Brunei, 69
  terrorist camp in, 39
  and United States, 183, 186
Papua (Irian Jaya), 101–102
  and Papua New Guinea, 149
  and United States, 184
Papua New Guinea (PNG)
  and Afghanistan, 150
  and Australia, 65, 148, 150, 152
    and Iraq, 151
    trade with, 152
  and Bougainville, 147–148
  and China, 149–150
  and East Timor, 152
  illegal migration, 150, 152
  and Indonesia, 149

Papua New Guinea (PNG) (*continued*)
  and Iraq, 151
  and Japan, 149
  and Lebanon, 150
  and Malaysia, 149
  and New Zealand, 152
  and Pakistan, 150
  and Papua, 149
  Papua New Guinea Defense Forces
      (PNGDF), 147, 149, 151
  peacekeeping operations, 151
  security
    external, 151
    internal, 147
  and Solomon Islands, 150–152
  terrorism, 149–150
  trade, 152
peacekeeping operations
  and Australia, 60
  and Bangladesh, 53–54, 139
  and China, 187
  and India, 53
  and Japan, 116
  and Mongolia, 139
  and Nepal, 54
  and New Zealand, 146
  and Pakistan, 53
  and Papua New Guinea, 151
  and Russia, 167
  and Singapore, 174
  and South Korea, 124
Philippines
  Abu Sayyaf Group, 153, 155–156
  armed forces, 153–155, 157
  and ASEAN members, 158
  and Australia, 64
  and China, 157
  defense
    budget, 157
    policy, 156–157
  insurgencies, 154
  and Iraq war, 153, 156
  Jemaah Islamiah, 40, 155. *See also* Je-
      maah Islamiah
  and Malaysia, 127, 154–155
  military-to-military relations, 156
  Moro Islamic Liberation Front, 40, 153–
      154, 156–157
  and NATO, 156
  security
    global, 158
    internal, 153, 157–158
    regional, 158

separatist movements. *See* Moro Islamic
    Liberation Front
  and Taiwan, 157
  terrorist groups, 36, 39–40, 155, 157–158
  and United Nations, 158
  and United States, 153–154, 156–158
    military assistance, 156–157
Poland
  and Iraq, 90
  and Proliferation Security Initiative, 97
polio, 133
Portugal
  and Proliferation Security Initiative, 97
Powell, Colin
  and Bangladesh, 50
  and Iraq, 187
preemptive defense, policy of, 186–188
Pristine, 146
Proliferation Security Initiative (PSI), 91, 97
  and Australia, 64
  and China, 188
  and European Union, 91, 97
  and Japan, 111
  and North Korea, 97, 121, 188
  and Russia, 188
  and South Korea, 121, 189
  and United States, 121, 188
Putin, Vladimir, 159–160, 163
  and Chechnya, 166

Regional Assistance Mission to the Solo-
    mon Islands (RAMSI)
  and Australia, 64
  and Papua New Guinea, 150–151
Riduan Isamuddin. *See* Hambali
Roh Moo Hyun, 118–119
  and United States, 26, 28, 120, 189
Russia
  and Afghanistan, 162, 164
  and Asia Pacific, 166
  Central Asia, 164, 167
  Chechnya, 161, 166
  and China, 83, 163
  and Commonwealth of Independent
      States (CIS), 161–162
  defense
    armed forces, 165–166
    budget, 165
    policy, 164
    procurement, 165
  drug trafficking, 161–162
  economy, 160
  energy policy, 166

and European Union, 162
and India, 164
and Iran, 162
and Iraq, 162
and Islam, 166
and Japan, 112, 163
and Kyrgyz Republic, 161–162, 167
military-to-military relations, 164
missile defense, 162
and Mongolia, 134, 136
and NATO, 162–163
and North Korea, 30–31, 162, 164, 167
    Six-Party Talks, 23, 31
peacekeeping operations, 167
security
    external, 161–162
    internal, 159, 161
    regional, 166
and South Korea, 164
terrorism, 159, 161–162
and United States, 162–163
and World Trade Organization, 162
See also Putin, Vladimir

SARS (severe acute respiratory syndrome),
    10
and ASEAN members, 82
and Canada, 73
and China, 80, 82, 86
and Malaysia, 131
and Mongolia, 135
and Singapore, 168, 170, 172
and Thailand, 182
and Vietnam, 192
secessionist movements
Indonesia, 101–103
Shanghai Cooperation Organization (SCO),
    85, 163, 166
Singapore
and ASEAN, 170, 175
and Australia, 174
and China, 169–171
defense
    armed forces, 173
    budget, 173
    policy, 172
    procurement, 173
economy, 168–169, 171
and European Union, 91, 175
globalization, 169
and India, 169, 171
and Indonesia, 169, 174
investment in, 171

and Iraq, 168–169, 174
and Islam, 169
and Japan, 174–175
and Malaysia, 168–169, 171–172, 174
military-to-military relations, 174
and New Zealand, 174
SARS, 168, 170, 172
sea piracy, 169, 172, 174
security, 169, 171
    global, 175
    internal, 171
    regional, 174–175
terrorism, 36, 169–171, 173, 175
and Thailand, 169, 171, 179
and United Kingdom, 174
and United States, 169, 174–175
Six-Party Talks, 26–27, 32–33
and China, 86, 163
and Japan, 111
and Mongolia, 137
and North Korea, 23
and South Korea, 120–121
and Russia, 163, 167
and United States, 190
Solana, Javier, 92, 97
Solomon Islands, 59, 64
and Australia, 142
and Bougainville, 150
and New Zealand, 142
and Papua New Guinea, 150
Regional Assistance Mission to the
    Solomon Islands (RAMSI), 64–65,
    146, 150–152
Somalia
    and Malaysia, 133
Somare, Sir Michael, 147–148, 151
South Asia
    Bangladesh-India-Myanmar-Sri Lanka-
        Thailand Economic Cooperation
        (BIMST-EC), 50
    defense budget, 52
    economy, 44–45
    free trade agreement, 45
    India-Pakistan relations, 44–45
    insurgencies, 44
    security
        global, 53
        regional, 45
        terrorism, 44–45
    See also Bangladesh, Bhutan, India,
        Nepal, Pakistan, Sri Lanka
South Asian Association for Regional Co-
    operation (SAARC), 45

Southeast Asia, 15, 40
  and al Qaeda, 34–39
    groups, 36
      and United States, 36–37, 183
    groups supported by, 36
    and United States, 37
  Islam, 34–35
    as opposed to Middle East, 35
    and United States, 36
  and Jemaah Islamiah, 34–35, 58
  terrorism, 15, 34–42, 58, 64
    and Indonesia, 34
    and Malaysia, 34
    response to, 40–42
    and Singapore, 34
    tactics, 16, 42
    and Thailand, 34
  See also al Qaeda; Jemaah Islamiah;
      Moro Islamic Liberation Front
Southeast Asia Regional Centre for
    Counter-Terrorism (SEARCCT)
  and United States, 191
  and Vietnam, 193
South Korea
  and Afghanistan, 124
  and China, 120
  defense
    budget, 122
    issues, 121–123
  and East Timor, 124
  and Iraq, 120, 123
  and Japan, 111
  and North Korea, 32–33, 119–120
    Six-Party Talks, 23, 26–29, 121
    "Sunshine Policy," 28
    Trilateral Coordination and Oversight
        Group (TCOG), 25
    and United States, 25, 28, 119–120, 122
  peacekeeping operations, 124
  security, 28
    external, 119–123
    internal, 118
  terrorism, 124
  and United States, 28, 119, 121–123, 189
  See also Roh Moo Hyun
Southwest Pacific
  and Australia, 59, 61, 64
Spain
  defense expenditure, 94
  and Proliferation Security Initiative, 97
Sri Lanka, 44
  and Canada, 78
  defense, 52
  economy, 48, 50

insurgencies, 52
  and Japan, 115
  Liberation Tigers of Tamil Eelam (LTTE),
      48, 182
  and Thailand, 50, 182
Sultan Haji Hassanal Bolkiah of Brunei,
      66–67, 69
  and security, 69–70
Syria, 146

Taiwan
  and China, 81
  and European Union, 91
  and North Korea, 31
    Six-Party Talks, 23
  and Philippines, 157
  and United States, 185
  See also Chen Shui-bian
Tajikistan, 161–162
  and India, 50
Taliban, 38
territorial disputes
  between Brunei and Malaysia, 68, 128
  between Malaysia and Singapore, 128
terrorism, 10
  and ASEAN, 41, 70
  and Australia, 59, 64
  and Brunei, 70
  and Canada, 72
  and European Union, 90
  and India, 46
  and Indonesia, 100–101, 104, 107, 140,
      169
  and Japan, 116
  and Malaysia, 58, 126, 128, 132
  and North Korea, 24
  and Pakistan, 50, 127
  and Papua New Guinea, 149
  and Russia, 161–162
  and Singapore, 169–171, 173, 175
  and South Korea, 124
  and Thailand, 177, 179
  and Vietnam, 193
  and Yemen, 127
terrorist organizations, 58, 101, 127
  al Qaeda, 34–36
  and Indonesia, 100–101
  and Malaysia, 126–127
  and New Zealand, 141
  and North Korea, 23–24
  and Singapore, 170
  and Southeast Asia, 35–40
  and Vietnam, 193
Thailand

and Afghanistan, 182
and Australia, 64
and Bangladesh, 50
and Cambodia, 178
and China, 86–87, 180
defense
  budget, 180
  procurement, 180
drugs, 177
and East Timor, 181
economy, 44, 177
and India, 50, 180
and Indonesia, 182
insurgencies, 127
International Monetary Fund, 177
and Iraq war, 179, 181
and Jemaah Islamiah, 39, 177
and Laos, 178
and Liberia, 182
and Malaysia, 127, 179
military-to-military relations, 179
and Myanmar, 50, 179
and NATO, 179
and Russia, 180
SARS, 182
security
  global, 181
  internal, 176
  regional, 176, 178, 181
and Singapore, 179
and Sri Lanka, 50, 182
and Switzerland, 180
terrorism, 36, 58, 127, 177, 179–180
trade, 179
and United Kingdom, 180
and United Nations, 181
and United States, 179, 181, 184
and Vietnam, 179
See also Thaksin Shinawatra
Thaksin Shinawatra, 176–182
trade
  ASEAN and China, 191
  ASEAN and Japan, 191
  ASEAN and South Korea, 191
  Australia and United States, 184
  Brunei and China, 69
  Canada and Asia Pacific, 71
  China and ASEAN members, 81, 86
  China and India, 49, 82
  China and Japan, 81
  China and South Korea, 81
  East Asia Free Trade Area, 86
  European Union and ASEAN members,
    91

European Union and China, 91
  India and ASEAN, 50
  Japan and China, 112
  Japan and United States, 112
  New Zealand and United States, 143
  Papua New Guinea and Australia, 152
  Papua New Guinea and New Zealand,
    152
  South Asia, 45
  Thailand and United States, 179
  Vietnam and China, 194
  Vietnam and Japan, 195
  Vietnam and United States, 193
  See also free trade agreements
Trilateral Coordination and Oversight
    Group (TCOG), 25, 28–29, 111
  and Japan, 111
Tung Chee Hwa, 85

Ukraine
  and Malaysia, 131
  and Russia, 161
United Kingdom
  and Asia Pacific, 95
  and Brunei, 69
  defense expenditure, 94
  and Iran nuclear program, 93
  and Proliferation Security Initiative, 97
United Nations
  authorization for Iraq war
    and Canada, 74
    and European Union, 90
    and France, 187
    and Germany, 187
    and Japan, 109
    and New Zealand, 142
    and Non-Aligned Movement, 129, 133,
      151
    and Papua New Guinea, 151
    and Philippines, 156
    and Russia, 187
    and South Korea, 123
    and United States, 186–187, 190
  and Brunei, 70
  and Cambodia, 195
  and Canada, 78
  and China, 87
  and European Union, 93, 96
  and Iraq, 187, 191
  and Malaysia, 132
  and New Zealand, 141, 146
  and North Korea, 24, 30
  and Pakistan, 50
  and Papua New Guinea, 148

United Nations (*continued*)
peacekeeping operations. *See under specific countries*
and Philippines, 158
and Russia, 162
and Solomon Islands, 65
and Taiwan, 14
and Thailand, 181–182
and United States, 186–188, 190–191
and North Korea, 30
and Russia, 162
and Vietnam, 196
United Nations Mission of Support in East Timor (UNMISET)
and Australia, 65
and Japan, 116
and Malaysia, 132
and South Korea, 124
and Thailand, 181
United States
and Afghanistan, 183
and Asia Pacific, 183, 191
and Australia, 184
and China, 13–14, 82, 185
defense
Asia policy, 188–190
budget, 190
preemptive defense, 186–188
domestic politics, 183
economy, 183
foreign relations, 184
and France, 186
and Germany, 186
and Indonesia, 104, 184
and Islam, 185
and Israel, 183, 185
and Iraq war, 184, 186–187
and Japan, 185
and multilateralism, 188, 190–191
and New Zealand, 184
and North Korea, 24, 121, 184
and Japan, 29
and preemptive defense, 188
Six-Party Talks, 26–27, 190
and South Korea, 25, 27–29, 119–120, 184
and Taiwan, 31
Trilateral Coordination and Oversight Group (TCOG), 25
and Philippines, 184
and Russia, 162–163
security
international, 18, 74, 77, 90, 183–184, 191

and Singapore, 184
and Southeast Asia, 183
and South Korea, 121–123, 189
and terrorism, 183–184
and multilateralism, 188
preemptive defense, 186–188
and Thailand, 179, 181, 184
trade, 184
and Australia, 184
unilateralism, 186–188, 190–191
weapons of mass destruction, 186–187
See also Bush, George W.

Vajpayee, Atal Bihari, 17, 45–46, 49–50, 82–83
Vanuatu, 152
Vietnam
and Afghanistan, 196
and Africa, 197
and ASEAN members, 193
and Asia-Europe Meeting (ASEM), 196
and Cambodia, 194
and China, 86–87, 194, 196
defense, 50, 196
economy, 192–194
foreign relations, 192–194
globalization, 192
and India, 50
insurgencies, 50
investment, 194
and Iraq, 196
Islam, 192
and Japan, 195–196
and Laos, 194
Official Development Assistance, 194–195
SARS, 192
security, 193
external, 196
terrorism, 39, 192–193
trade, 192–195
and United States, 193, 195–196
and World Trade Organization, 194

weapons of mass destruction (WMD)
and Australia, 64
and Canada, 78
and China, Japan, and South Korea, 86
and European Union, 90–91, 93
and Iran, 87
and North Korea, 78
Proliferation Security Initiative, 97
and United States, 186–188

Wen Jiabao, 14, 86, 185
World Bank
  and Pakistan, 47
World Health Organization (WHO)
  polio, 133
  SARS, 73

World Trade Organization (WTO)
  and Malaysia, 129
  and Russia, 162
  and Vietnam, 194

Yemen, and terrorism, 127

Asia Pacific Agenda Project

The Asia Pacific Agenda Project (APAP) was established in November 1995 to enhance policy-oriented intellectual exchange at the nongovernmental level, with special emphasis on independent research institutions in the region. It consists of four interconnected components: (1) the Asia Pacific Agenda Forum, a gathering of leaders of Asia Pacific policy research institutes to explore the future agenda for collaborative research and dialogue activities related to the development of an Asia Pacific community; (2) an Asia Pacific policy research information network utilizing the Internet; (3) annual multilateral joint research projects on pertinent issues of regional and global importance undertaken in collaboration with major research institutions in the region; and (4) collaborative research activities designed to nurture a new generation of Asia Pacific leaders who can participate in international intellectual dialogues. APAP is managed by an international steering committee composed of nine major research institutions in the region. The Japan Center for International Exchange has served as secretariat since APAP's inception.

ASEAN Institutes for Strategic and International Studies

ASEAN-ISIS (Institutes for Strategic and International Studies) is an association of nongovernmental organizations registered with the Association of Southeast Asian Nations. Formed in 1988, its membership comprises the Centre for Strategic and International Studies (CSIS) of Indonesia, the Institute of Strategic and International Studies (ISIS) of Malaysia, the Institute for Strategic and Development Studies (ISDS) of the Philippines, the Singapore Institute of International Affairs (SIIA), and the Institute of Security and International Studies (ISIS) of Thailand. Its purpose is to encourage cooperation and coordination of activities among policy-oriented ASEAN scholars and analysts, and to promote policy-oriented studies of, and exchange of information and viewpoints on, various strategic and international issues affecting Southeast Asia's and ASEAN's peace, security, and well-being.

East-West Center

Established by the United States Congress in 1960 to promote mutual understanding and cooperation among the governments and peoples of the Asia Pacific region, including the United States, the East-West Center seeks to foster the development of an Asia Pacific community through cooperative study, training, and research. Center activities focus on the promotion of shared regional values and the building of regional institutions and arrangements; the promotion of economic growth with equity, stability, and sustainability; and the management and resolution of critical regional as well as common problems.

Japan Center for International Exchange

Founded in 1970, the Japan Center for International Exchange (JCIE) is an independent, nonprofit, and nonpartisan organization dedicated to strengthening Japan's role in international affairs. JCIE believes that Japan faces a major challenge in augmenting its positive contributions to the international community, in keeping with its position as one of the world's largest industrial democracies. Operating in a country where policy making has traditionally been dominated by the government bureaucracy, JCIE has played an important role in broadening debate on Japan's international responsibilities by conducting international and cross-sectional programs of exchange, research, and discussion.

JCIE creates opportunities for informed policy discussions; it does not take policy positions. JCIE programs are carried out with the collaboration and cosponsorship of many organizations. The contacts developed through these working relationships are crucial to JCIE's efforts to increase the number of Japanese from the private sector engaged in meaningful policy research and dialogue with overseas counterparts. JCIE receives no government subsidies; rather, funding comes from private foundation grants, corporate contributions, and contracts.